Microeconomic Essentials

Microeconomic Essentials
Understanding Economics in the News

Jay Prag

The MIT Press
Cambridge, Massachusetts
London, England

This book was set in Times LT Std and Helvetica LT Std by New Best-set Typesetters Ltd. Printed and bound in the United States of America.

Library of Congress Cataloging-in-Publication Data

Names: Prag, Jay, author.
Title: Microeconomic essentials : understanding economics in the news / Jay Prag.
Description: Cambridge, Massachusetts : MIT Press, [2020] | Includes index.
Identifiers: LCCN 2019051434 | ISBN 9780262539272 (paperback)
Subjects: LCSH: Microeconomics.
Classification: LCC HB172 .P693 2020 | DDC 338.5—dc23
LC record available at https://lccn.loc.gov/2019051434

10 9 8 7 6 5 4 3 2 1

Contents

Preface

This book was inspired by Peter Kennedy's (now Kennedy and Prag) wonderful macroeconomics text *Macroeconomic Essentials: Understanding Economics in the News*. That book took a practical, applied approach to macroeconomics, providing students in many disciplines a text that is approachable and relevant. Microeconomics, in many ways the more newsworthy half of the discipline right now, needed a similar book.

This text offers a nontechnical, intuitive exposition of the microeconomic concepts and principles that are on display in news stories every day. From labor markets and the dicey issue of minimum wages to the health care market; from trade theory to game theory; this book covers the issues that students need to understand in this ever-changing world.

I have kept the style of the book breezy and straightforward in the hope that students who think economics is too abstract and arcane will see its usefulness. I have minimized the use of heavy-duty mathematics, opting instead for intuition. I have tried, in effect, to return microeconomics to the people.

I would like to thank everyone at the MIT Press who supported me in this project and helped get the final product done. I would especially like to thank Emily Taber at MIT for her immeasurable contribution to my publishing career. And most of all, I would like to thank Amanda Ishak Prag, my wonderful wife, my sounding board, and my editor without whom this book would not exist. It is my fondest hope that our darling daughter, Julianna, will learn microeconomics from this text when she grows up.

1   Introduction

Economics is a social science. It uses the approaches of science to study the activities of people. The earliest economists focused on obvious economic activities—consumer behavior and the like—but modern economists use their tools to analyze human activity far outside this early view. In the two hundred-plus years since its formalization, economics has helped us develop some powerful tools and a lot of useful, sometimes unexpected insights.

But it is important to note that economics is not a pure science; it is a *social* science. Human behavior is not really waves and particles that can be modeled and understood the way physicists explain matter or the Universe. People are messy and unpredictable; they are complicated and hard to formalize. Therefore, the nature of the choices and decisions people make means economics is much harder—and much less precise—than the pure sciences. So we have to make some choices in teaching and using economics. Sometimes the most accurate model isn't very useful in the real world. Sometimes formulas aren't helpful in daily decision-making. And so sometimes economics as an exercise in mathematics needs to be balanced with economics as a social process. That is the task we undertake in this book.

1.1   Concepts versus Calculus

One microeconomic concept that I use in many different classes (which gets full coverage in chapter 4) is *utility theory*. Built from the observation that people don't usually consume large amounts of just one good all the time, utility theory is a model that employs a mathematical concept in which some things grow at a decreasing rate; that is, every step forward is smaller than the previous step. In math- or calculus-speak, this is represented by an equation that has a positive first derivative (every step is forward) and a negative second derivative (the steps get smaller with each iteration). This is the mathematical approach.

In chapter 4, I relegate this approach to an appendix in favor of a simple table showing levels of consumption and their associated levels of happiness (utility). When I do this in the classroom, occasionally someone who has had a previous class in microeconomics will say, "That's not correct! You can't do it that way! You have to use calculus and derivatives!" I will ask the student if she remembers how calculus works: specifically, how big is the change that we represent with a first derivative? The answer: infinitely small. Then I ask, "Do you buy in infinitely small increments of something in the real world?" The answer is probably not. The point is, neither approach, neither the table nor the calculus, is perfect and right.

The math, the calculus, is more formal and elegant, but it isn't right because people don't behave that way. You don't buy a miniscule piece of a candy bar; you buy a big, lumpy, not-very-derivative-sized candy bar (or sometimes the bulk pack). This is not a knock on calculus and math in economics. It is a reminder that formality is not the same thing as accuracy. What matters in most of our economic models is the concept, not the math. We want to understand why people do what they do by watching how they do it.

The math that we use in economics—graphs and equations—is the proverbial picture that's worth a thousand words. It summarizes the economic activity. But the math isn't what's "right." Sometimes we can communicate the concept without the math, and when we can, we might have a better understanding of the activity in question. This book does not focus on math. Instead, we focus on concepts. That said, there are situations in which math is the very best way to teach and learn a concept (the Bertrand model in chapter 8, for example). What I've tried to do is use the method for teaching a concept that gets the biggest bang for the buck. Sometimes that's a story, sometimes it's graphs, sometimes it's calculus.

1.2   Weeds

When you leave much of the math behind, you invariably run into things you cannot explain. Fortunately, the math is still there to help out. What we want to do is avoid getting too deep into the math—the weeds. That too is problematic. When are we using just the right amount of math? That will likely be a point of contention for anyone using this book. Of course, your instructor can always put in more math. My hope is that you will understand the concepts and see how the mathematical models can be used to explain economic activities without depending on them to understand economic realities.

To wit, math in economics always reminds me of my dear departed father and his tendency to constantly correct people's grammar. If I ever dared call him pedantic, he would paraphrase H. W. Fowler, the author of *Modern English Usage*, and say, "One man's pedantry is another man's irreducible minimum of education." In the same way, one instructor's weeds are another's irreducible minimum of mathematical modeling. Our goal is to find the happy medium. Just remember: the math, in economics, is never right. The human activity that we are trying to explain is the foundation of our discipline. It's what we're really studying, after all.

1.3   Microeconomics, Macroeconomics, and Pragmatic Economics

The prefixes in economics tell much of the story: *micro* means small and *macro* means big. Microeconomics applies the tools of economics to the study of individual markets and choices. It considers a consumer's decision to buy an apple (versus all other goods) and a producer's decision to grow that apple. Macroeconomics looks more at the forest (in the forest-versus-trees analogy) and analyzes the entire economy's level of production.

Many of the concepts and tools that we use and discuss in this book are applied to the study of both micro- and macroeconomics. I wish I could say that there is broad agreement and consistency across the two sides of economics, but that is not the case. Not wishing to exacerbate a discussion that has been raging since John Maynard Keynes formally divorced classroom microeconomics from macroeconomics, I will—true to my name—try to be pragmatic. When a microeconomic concept is at odds with macroeconomics, I will briefly outline the issue and leave it to students and instructors to arbitrate whether it is necessary to determine "which side of economics is right." But, as was the case with our discussion of math versus concepts, it's probably best for economics students to give up the notion that someone is right or wrong. Economists are all simply trying to explain human activity—and we all know that's messy.

1.4   Microeconomics in the Media

Macroeconomics would seem to have an advantage when it comes to media examples. Most of the problems that are discussed in macroeconomics are in every news source, at least in the business section, every day: unemployment, inflation, exchange rates, interest rates, government spending, deficits, and the list goes on.

Arguably, microeconomics is just as prevalent in the media, but it's not as obvious. Market outcomes are discussed all the time, but you have to know what you're looking for. Gas prices, wage increases, illegal drugs, the rising cost of health care, international trade, and, really, all advertisements are microeconomic topics. They simply need their economic context to be explained. By definition, everywhere and every day, microeconomics is part of our life. This microeconomics class will show you that. That said, many of the examples and exercises, especially in the early chapters, are generic, not literally drawn from media sources. This is done on purpose. We want the examples to feel "timeless."

1.5   An Overview of the Book

Let's take a brief look at each chapter and get a sense of what we will be covering in this book.

Chapter 2: The Market Model

Economics starts from observations of human behavior. We are social scientists. The most mathematical models ever derived by an economist try to prove something humanistic, real world, and describable. We will build the basic market model from that perspective. Simple examples of basic supply and demand are powerful teachers of the forces that bring forth most goods. This chapter derives, intuitively, both sides of the market and shows how our little powerhouse model can explain most of the price changes we see in the marketplace. Traditional graphs are introduced in this chapter, along with differences between shifts in lines versus moving along lines and short runs versus long runs (steeper lines for the former, flatter lines for the latter).

Frankly, the market model's graph is too familiar to ignore. It can be described verbally and shown traditionally in such a way that students can grasp the concepts behind it one way or another. So we will have a heavy dose of the supply and demand diagram in chapters 2 and 3.

Chapter 3: Applications of (and Interference with) the Market

While it might seem out of place (too early) to talk about government intervention in the market, I find it useful to challenge students to think about why it isn't as simple as saying "Let's legally set the price of a sixteen-inch pizza at $1 so that students can all get cheap pizza." I discuss price ceilings and price floors early on and try to get students to think about the difference between interfering in a market (legally setting a price) and using the market (trying to change supply or demand) to get a desired outcome. While much of the government-oriented material is covered in chapter 11, we begin to discuss the limits and problems of government intervention in the market in chapter 3. We discuss topical issues such as minimum wages and rent control while students have the market model, short and long run, fresh in their heads. Similarly, we discuss tax incidence in this chapter.

Chapter 4: Behind the Demand Line: Consumer Theory

To differentiate or not to differentiate: that is the question. Consumer theory and utility maximization is where math often loses more students than it convinces. The first step, the idea that we are buying things to fulfill needs and increase happiness, is never the biggest problem; it's those first derivatives that seem out of place (or perhaps too hard). Students are wrong about this. Calculus-based utility maximization is correct in the classroom only. No one ever buys an infinitely small additional amount of any good. But we can teach the ideas without the calculus. Nothing big is lost in consumer theory if we show it in a way that reminds people of how they really shop. In this chapter I use a more hands-on approach to consumer theory, and, while likely eliciting criticisms about cardinality, it should resonate with most students.

Having communicated the concepts of utility maximization, we can discuss real-world issues such as information problems and marketing, the units problems and how Costco makes utility maximization harder (this is a real-world problem that the calculus approach completely ignores), and even snob appeal (high price as a positive factor in utility).

Chapter 5: Behind Supply: Theory of the Firm

As in the previous chapter, in this chapter we de-mathematize marginal revenue, marginal cost, and all the familiar determinants of output and explain them instead with numbers and examples. Having introduced marginal analysis in chapter 4, we show how powerful and useful it can be for the decision-makers in a firm. We discuss marginal and average cost with simple examples, economies of scale and short-run versus long-run average cost, and other, subtler cost issues (e.g., average variable cost) that ultimately determine production. Theory of the firm and its cost curves are notoriously confusing, so we relegate the cluttered graphs to an appendix and get the important concepts across using charts and examples.

This chapter's appendixes also include an expanded, real-world discussion of economies of scale and economies of scope. These are important extensions of traditional microeconomic topics, especially for students in business schools.

Chapter 6: Perfect Competition

Perfectly competitive businesses, or what economists now call "price takers," are more of a metaphor than a reality. Still, in this chapter we show how the description that we apply to such firms gives us the zero-profit result and how the closer a firm is to this setup, the more likely it is to be a break-even business. Some useful, real-world discussion evolves as this chapter discusses the definitions of profit, short- versus long-run profits, entry, and resource cost.

Chapter 7: Monopoly

As in chapter 6, monopolies, or "price setters," as discussed in a microeconomics class are more of a metaphor than a reality, but a firm having the ability to control output and thus price is something we can see in in the real world. There are also important, often overlooked aspects of this "ability." We tend to teach the profit potential of monopolies by emphasizing their control over the market. So, when asked why a monopoly like Microsoft can't use its market power to sell five million units of Windows at $1,000,000 each, students often don't know. The monopoly's market power still depends on a market-determined demand line.

In working through the monopoly model, we will emphasize the concept of marginal revenue. This concept is interesting and intriguing when we look at it in the real world. It is also something that might well be changing as retail moves away from the traditional brick-and-mortar store.

Chapter 8: Imperfect Competition and Oligopoly Models

All the usual suspects show up in this chapter, but the emphasis is on observations and intuition. Monopolistic competition can be seen with restaurants on Main Street, cartels, and collusion (and cheating) with OPEC. The Cournot model (competition on quantity, by strategically managing production) can be used to explain why companies sometimes produce their own competitors. The Bertrand model (competition on price) can be applied to pricing differentiated goods (Coke and Pepsi or Dairy Queen and Baskin-Robbins). And price cooperation can be found in any store that offers to accept any competitor's advertised price. These models also allow us to discuss strategic-economic topics, such as market entry.

Chapter 9: Game Theory

Discussion of the skillset engaged in game theory fits neatly after oligopoly, but it becomes a more powerful tool when we show how strategic decision-making is all around us. While this chapter offers the models and concepts that instructors are familiar with (Nash equilibrium, dominant strategy, coordination games, prisoner's dilemma, and strategic moves), we want to show students that game theory is actually a state of mind more than anything else.

Our setups, payoff matrices, and strategies are never realistic. They are intended to model choices and activities that we encounter every day that are less precise, but no less solvable. We show how we need to think differently when our choice alone does not determine our outcome. We also discuss the deeper implications of these models, such as the self-interest that results in the inferior outcome of prisoner's dilemma models.

Chapter 10: Input Markets

Few things in economics change as quickly as input markets. Robotics, health insurance costs, high minimum wages, and so on are featured in this chapter. As in other microeconomics texts, labor and other input markets will be explicated and relationships (input cost = value of marginal product) will be described. As in the chapter describing the theory of the firm, this chapter attempts to stay out of the weeds. Important input-related concepts such as monopsony are included and the connection with minimum wages is made. Though we maintain our pragmatic approach in this chapter, eliminating the heavy math while leaving the important concepts, we also change the point of view a bit compared to that in most microeconomics texts. We usually think about capital, labor, and other input markets from the perspective of the firm. That perspective remains, but I add the perspective of an outside contractor trying to get work from the firm as well.

Chapter 11: Welfare and Public Economics

In this chapter I had to make some choices. There are, after all, entire courses on welfare and public economics, and this book covers only the essentials. Starting where chapter 2 (the market model) leaves off, the discussion focuses on markets and the government. Tax incidence is always fun and lets us use the basic market model again. Similarly, market failures part one—externalities—describes the limitations of the market and how the government can fix them. Market failures part two—public goods—describes this set of goods with copious examples and talks about some of the approaches that have been tried for providing these goods.

Welfare economics issues such as social welfare functions, deadweight loss, and cost-benefit analysis are also discussed. In this chapter we can apply the tools that we've discussed throughout the book thus far.

Chapter 12: International Economics

Few areas of applied microeconomics are more interesting and more contentious than trade theory. Having taught trade theory for many years, I have a good sense of how to show the powerful results of the simple models (models with and without production) and the limits of these models. Trade is now, and likely will be for many years, a hot topic. We have always known that (free) trade is good for countries and the world, but not necessarily for all citizens. As was the case with the previous chapter's topics, trade theory allows us to review and apply many important observations from earlier chapters.

2   The Market Model

Economists often use some version of this statement when teaching the market model: "Seventy-five percent of economics problems can be answered with a supply and demand diagram." While the truth of this blanket statement is impossible to verify, the rationale behind it is easy to see. Most things in life have to be produced and distributed, and the market model—supply and demand—gives a good explanation of this process.

But economics students need to remember that the market model springs from observed human activity. The concepts of supply and demand are not ideas that economists thought up and made the market do. Models are formalized ways of illustrating economic activity. They draw on observations of human activity (sometimes using equations or graphs) to help us quickly explain what a market has done or to predict what it will do in the foreseeable future. For reasons we discuss throughout the book, we avoid saying that the market model (or any model) is "right"; let's just say that this method of storytelling has a good track record. Over time, it has explained and predicted the production and distribution of goods very well.

The market model separates the market into consumers and producers. This sounds innocuous, but we are simplifying the process a lot when we do this. A number of market participants exist between, say, the apple orchard owner and the apple buyer (e.g., delivery truck drivers, warehouse operators, grocery stores) that we don't explicitly include in the story. We aren't ignoring their existence; they just aren't crucial to the basic story of production and consumption that we want to tell.

In this chapter, we start by describing consumers and intuitively deriving the demand line. We follow that with a discussion of producers and draw the supply line. Then we put them together and play with our model a bit. While our book avoids the more complex derivations of curve shifting, the market model is one case where a picture is worth a thousand words.

On completion of this chapter, you should

- understand the basics of supply and demand,
- see how underlying changes in a market—shifts in supply or demand—affect the market price and quantity, and
- be able to show how the impact of changes in the market differs in the short run and in the long run.

2.1   Demand

The consumer side of the market—*demand*—is the most easily understood. As a consumer, you act out this behavior every day. We observe that consumers buy less of any good as its price rises. Let's consider an easy example: as the price of apples rises, people buy fewer apples. If you ask consumers (or economists) why, they will likely give the same two explanations: the availability of substitutes and consumers' own budget constraints. First, if apples cost too much, people would buy other fruits (or, you know, ice cream). If we assume that apple prices are the only prices that rise, people will buy oranges or bananas or grapes instead of apples. The model assumes that consumers don't usually shop for apples specifically; they shop for fruit or, perhaps more generically, food. There are many available substitutes for apples, so shoppers can and will purchase something cheaper if they find apples to be too expensive. This is known as the *substitution effect*.

Consumers have another reason to buy fewer apples if their price is high: they simply can't afford as many. When you shop, you have a fixed amount of money available. Economists call this a budget constraint. Even if you put your grocery bill on your credit card, you have to pay your credit card bills eventually. Suppose you've budgeted $10 per week for apples and apple prices have risen from $1 per pound to $2 per pound. Your consumption of apples would fall from ten pounds to five pounds (your price doubled, so you have to cut your quantity in half). You want apples, but given your income and the new price, that's all you can afford. Economists call this the *income effect*. When we put the substitution and income effects together, we get a pretty good explanation for why we usually buy less of a good when its price rises. Economists observed this and made this observation formal by drawing the graph in figure 2.1.

We discuss more of the fundamentals behind the demand curve in chapter 4, but let's move on to the producer's side of the market for apples.

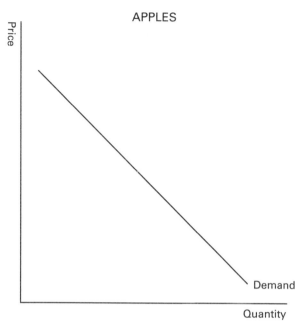

Figure 2.1 The Demand Curve for Apples

Curiosity 2.1
Opportunity Cost

If you ask someone to define "price," she will almost certainly define it in terms of money; in the United States, this means the dollars and cents that one must pay to buy a good. Economists often use a somewhat broader definition of price that relates one good to another. In this broader view, the dollars and cents that something costs are a proxy for the actual price of a good.

   If you pay $10 to eat lunch at the local diner downtown, you are making a choice to use your $10 at the diner versus anywhere else downtown (or anywhere else in the city). Specifically, if the local hardware store is near the diner, you could have used your $10 to buy a hammer. If the local clothing store is also nearby, you could have purchased two pairs of socks. When we think about price this way, we are defining price as an *opportunity cost:* the price of your lunch is everything else you could have purchased with the $10.

   Opportunity cost is a useful way to think about price because it allows us to include nonmonetary things. Your lunch, for example, also cost you an hour and a half of your time, which you could have used to read your economics book. It might also have put you in a bad mood because the waitress spilled coffee on your shirt. Opportunity cost is everything you give up when you make one particular purchase.

Curiosity 2.1 (continued)

We will continue to say "price" in our models and stories throughout this book, but we really mean opportunity cost. Everyone taking an economics class and using this book knows that the price of going to college is tuition and time plus many other things. For some purchases, the monetary part of the price is less important than, say, the time. Our modern world with home-delivered everything and streamed movies is testament to that reality.

Sample Exam Question 2.1
For a nonessential, repeat purchase such as a new package of underwear or socks, Amazon could charge the same price as the department store at the mall and still get your business. Why?

2.2 Supply

The producer's side of this market—*supply*—is frankly easier to understand if you are the apple orchard owner. There is a popular belief that owning a business automatically correlates with exorbitant wealth or high profits. Many business owners would tell a different story. About half of all businesses fail within the first five years of operation. The market forces behind what we call supply are a crucial part of business success.

We observe that apple growers produce more apples as the price of apples rises. To understand the forces at work here, let's focus on the last step in the apple production process: picking the apples from the tree. Suppose apples sell for $0.10 per pound and an apple picker can pick twenty pounds in an hour. The apples picked will sell for $2 ($0.10 per pound × 20 pounds). If all of that money was used to pay the picker, it would represent a wage of only $2 per hour. No one would pick apples at a wage of $2 per hour. If apple prices are too low, the apple grower won't be able to pay anyone to pick the apples. There are other, higher-paying jobs available. But, as the price of apples rises, the apple grower can pay higher wages, attract more labor, and get more apples off the trees and to market. And this doesn't just apply to wages. Moving backward in the apple production process, this logic applies to the cost of land, apple seeds, fertilizer, and everything it takes to grow apples. If the price of apples is very low (perhaps apples are unpopular at some point in time), then apple growers can't sell them for enough to pay all the costs of growing apples. As apple prices rise, more apples can be produced. Roughly speaking, the supply side of any market connects the sale price of the good with the cost of producing it.

But we also observe that the cost of producing apples generally rises as more are produced. To understand this, we need to focus on the beginning of the process. If you want

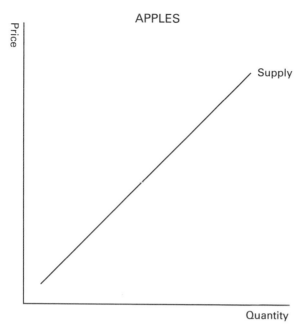

Figure 2.2 Supply Curve for Apples

to plant more apple trees, you'll need more land. You start by buying the cheapest land that's suitable for growing apples, but as you expand, you'll have to buy land that was already being used for other things. That land will cost more. Since your costs are higher, you'll need to charge higher prices to defray the higher cost of increasing your output.

If we turn this observation into a picture, we get the graph we call the supply curve, shown in figure 2.2. Chapter 5 will add more detail to the supply side of the market.

2.3   The Market

If we put the demand and supply mechanisms together, we begin to see an interesting, dynamic process in the market. Suppose our market is an apple stand located at the orchard. The apple grower will have to guess at a price (possibly based on yesterday's price) and will pick apples for sale today based on that guess. If the grower guesses a price that is too high, consumers will instead buy peaches at the stand up the road, and the apples that were picked won't be sold. That means the apple grower will have a surplus of apples at today's high price. Now, the grower will notice this and lower the price during the day so that she doesn't have to throw away too many apples. This lower price will carry over to

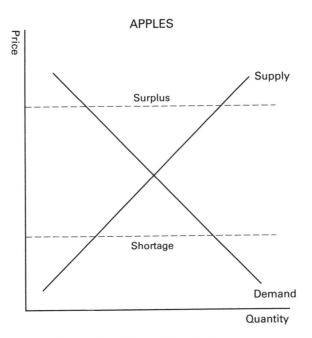

Figure 2.3   Supply and Demand for Apples

the next day, which will cause the grower to pick fewer apples tomorrow. This lower price of apples will also bring customers back from the peach stand. More apples are purchased, fewer apples are picked, and yesterday's apple surplus disappears.

Now suppose that on some other day, the apple price the grower guesses at the start of the day is too low. More customers will want to buy apples than the number of apples that were picked. The stand will start running out of apples sooner than the grower had planned. At the current price, there is a shortage of apples. Seeing this, some consumers (they're really good at bargaining) will offer a higher price to get some of the existing apples. This tells the grower two things: increase the price today *and* pick more apples tomorrow. The grower will pick more apples, consumers will want fewer apples at the higher price, and the shortage disappears. We can see this story when we combine the demand and supply line in figure 2.3.

We're making some assumptions for the model (economists do this a lot), but all of this human behavior—what economists call "market forces"—pushes the price of apples toward a price called the equilibrium price or *market price*. At this equilibrium price, apple production equals apple consumption. In a perfect world, this means no apples are wasted (no surplus) and no opportunities for sale are missed (no shortage). We say this market price "clears the market": it leads to a quantity supplied that equals the quantity demanded.

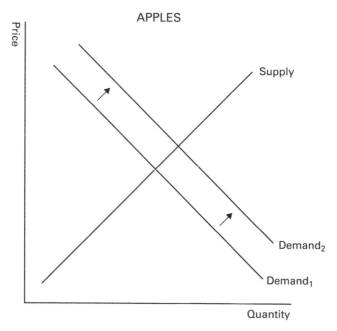

APPLES

Figure 2.4   Increase in the Demand for Apples

2.4   The Market Model and News: Necessary Curve Shifting

The market model also shows us how prices and quantities change depending on changes in these human processes—for example, how supply and demand respond to news. The supply and demand lines are where they are in figure 2.3 because of the current desire by consumers to eat apples and the current ability of growers to produce apples. But these things—the factors behind the lines' location—change, and the market model tells us how the market price and quantity will react to these changes.

Suppose a news report says that a new scientific study proves Ben Franklin's adage, "An apple a day keeps the doctor away." This news will cause people to want more apples than they did yesterday. To be precise, consumers will want to buy more apples at every price. The old demand line is no longer correct; the demand line that includes that news is now to the right of the old demand curve. We say that the demand for apples has increased because of this news, and the demand line shifts to the right (see figure 2.4). Notice that the shift to the right does indeed show that more apples, a higher quantity, are desired at every price.

Assuming the market forces that found the original equilibrium price and quantity still work, this shift will increase the price of apples, which will allow apple growers to pick

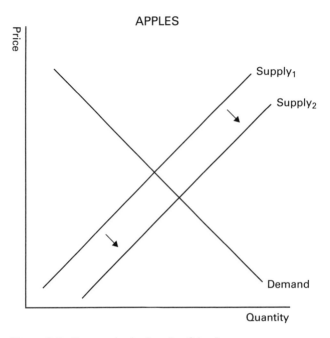

Figure 2.5   Increase in the Supply of Apples

more apples. The shift of the demand line to the right caused by the news story will move the equilibrium along the supply line, so the news story will increase both the price of apples and the quantity supplied.

We can tell a similar story when the news affects producers. Suppose there is unusually good weather in the apple-growing region of the country. More apples will grow on every tree without costing apple growers anything. Now, at every price, apple growers can increase the supply of apples they bring to market.

As was the case with the demand curve in the previous example, the old supply curve is no longer correct. This good weather means that the new supply curve will be to the right of the old supply curve. We say that this change in weather led to an increase in supply. We shift the supply curve to the right, moving along the demand curve (see figure 2.5). As we move to the new equilibrium, we see that market forces together with the change in weather have pushed the price of apples down, and at that lower price there is an increase in the quantity demanded.

The market model and its ability to iterate to a price that clears the market works as long as no producer and no consumer is big enough to manipulate the market. Manipulation can happen, but let's postpone our discussion of that for a while.

While the goal is to get a good understanding of economics without too many arcane precision points, there are things that economists talk about that allow people to talk more clearly about changes in the market. In showing how news and events cause the supply or demand lines to shift (increase or decrease), so that the market reaches a new equilibrium, we are also showing a change in quantity (assuming we are at equilibrium, that is, the quantity demanded matches the quantity supplied).

Looking at the increase in the demand for apples in figure 2.4, however, people sometimes say that the demand for apples increased, causing the supply to increase because the quantity supplied increased. That's very confusing because figure 2.5 shows an increase in supply and a shift of the supply line. But there is no shift of the supply line in figure 2.4; rather, there's a move along the supply line. So economists differentiate between a shift in a line and a movement along a line this way: if an external change occurs—news or a change in the weather, for example—that shifts the line, we say there's been an increase or a decrease in supply or demand (or on occasion, both). After the market reaches the new equilibrium and one line has moved along the other, we say there has been an increase or decrease in quantity supplied or demanded.

So, in figure 2.4, the news story caused an increase in demand—demand shifted to the right—which moves *along* the supply line and causes an increase in quantity supplied; but *not* an increase in supply. The supply line doesn't shift. Strictly speaking, there is an increase in both the quantity supplied and the quantity demanded, but our desire is to dissuade students from calling the increase in quantity supplied an increase in supply.

Sample Exam Question 2.2
When good weather occurs, as in figure 2.5, does that cause an increase in demand?

2.5   The Market Model and Time

Dozens of tweaks and complicating factors can be applied to the basic market model, and we discuss many of them throughout this book. One adjustment we can make right away, while the derivation of the model is fresh in our minds, is incorporating time into the model. By "time" we mean the time it takes for the market to adjust. Economists often refer to this time element as "short run" versus "long run."

Let's start with the supply curve. We said earlier that an increase in the price of apples would cause apple growers to pick more apples from their trees. The obvious limit to that process is the number of apples that are actually on the trees. In the short run, the supply curve relationship—an increase in the quantity supplied will require an increase in the price—is limited by the number of apples that have already been grown. If we extend the

Curiosity 2.2
The Difficulty of Finding the Exact Demand Line

The basics of the market model are pretty easy to understand. Ironically, the graphical application of the model (curve shifting) is a lot easier than actually deriving a market's supply and demand curves. After they are shown the basics, analytically minded students have occasionally asked me to give them the exact equation for each of the lines. I tell them that, in the real world, finding (estimating) the precise relationship that I'm calling supply and demand would require an almost impossible set of coincidences.

To actually map out any good's demand curve, we would need to have its supply curve alone shift several times, and trace out the demand curve. Similarly, to map out the supply curve, we would need demand alone to shift several times, and trace out the supply curve. In reality, what we observe in the market is a combination of shifts that we usually cannot discern perfectly. As such, in this book we will stick to the conceptual view of the market and not pretend that we know the exact equations.

process over time, we could say that if prices rise and stay high, apple growers will add inputs at the beginning of the growing season *next year*—water, fertilizer, and so on—to make sure more apples are available to be picked at the end of the next growing season. Extending this further, if prices are expected to stay high for a longer period of time, producers could even plant more apple trees. These measures all take effect in the longer run.

All of this means that the supply curve relationship gets more pronounced if we allow more time. Again, avoiding for a while some of the weeds (specifically, the problem with measuring "flat" and "steep," which is discussed later in this chapter), this means the supply curve is not very responsive in the short run but pretty flexible in the long run. In terms of the curves, this means that the supply curve is steeper in the short run and flatter in the long run (see figure 2.6). How long is the long run? In this example, it's how long it would take to grow (a long-term activity)—as opposed to pick (a short-term activity)—more apples.

A similar story can be told about the demand curve and its underlying relationship. We said consumers buy a smaller quantity of a good at higher prices because of the substitution effect. While that's true, it isn't automatic, and it can change over time. Our apple consumers might not know what are good substitutes for apples, depending on what they were going to use the apples for (apple pie versus fruit salad versus a fruit basket). Apple demand is almost certainly less responsive to price changes in the short run—a day or two—than if you give consumers time to find substitutes. That means the demand curve is also steeper in the short run and flatter in the long run, as shown in figure 2.7.

Let's combine our short-run and long-run market models and see how the impact of an increase in demand will change over time (see figure 2.8).

In the short run, an increase in demand will cause a bigger increase in price than in the long run. That makes sense since it is harder to change quantity on both sides of the

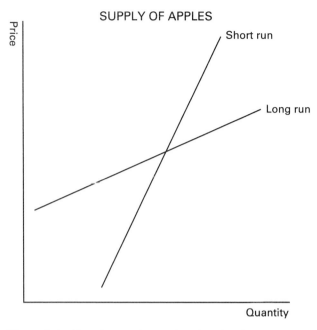

Figure 2.6 Short-Run and Long-Run Supply of Apples

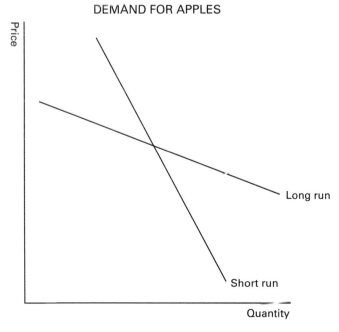

Figure 2.7 Short-Run and Long-Run Demand for Apples

APPLES

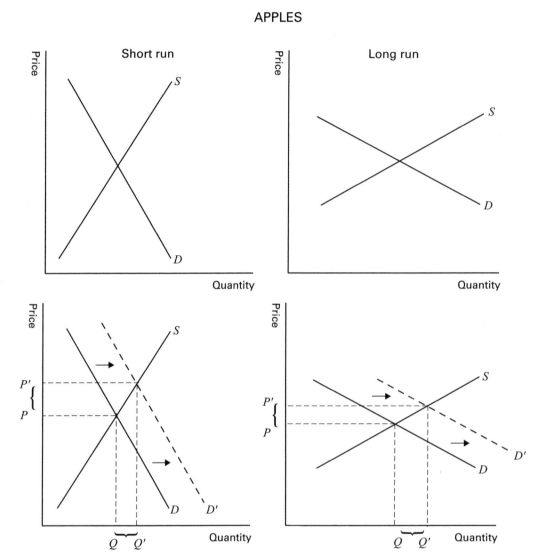

Figure 2.8   Increasing Supply in Response to Demand in the Short versus Long Run

market right away. Put differently, you can respond to an increase in demand by raising the price of the good with the stroke of a pen (or a few keystrokes on a computer), but picking or growing more apples will take days, weeks, or months.

As we discussed, changes in quantity for either the supply or the demand side of the market take more time. As a grower, you need time to pick or grow more apples, and as a consumer, you need time to find good substitutes. So, while we can say that, for most goods most of the time, an increase in demand will cause an increase in price and an increase in quantity, we know that prices tend to react more in the short run and quantities tend to change more in the long run. That is, prices are easier to change in the short run, while quantities take a while to change overall.

So, without having spent too much time on details, we can show how to apply the market model and how to discern microeconomics in news accounts.

> **Sample Exam Question 2.3**
> Why is the supply curve of Rembrandt paintings steeper than the supply curve of apples, even in the long run?

2.6   Measuring Flat and Steep: Elasticity

While it is easy to envision flatter versus steeper lines, developing a mathematical measure of the underlying relationship is trickier. Let's focus on the demand curve and its underlying relationship: an increase in price will lead to a decrease in quantity demanded. "Flatter" implies that the quantity change is bigger in the long run.

The steepness of a line is usually measured as the *slope* of the line. For a demand curve, the slope would be the change in price divided by the related change in quantity (old-schoolers called this "rise over run"). For the demand curve, the slope is negative, but our focus is on the absolute value of the slope. If slope were our metric for steep versus flat, we would say that a steep demand curve had a big slope (a bigger change in price than quantity) and a flat demand curve had a small slope. But the terminology of "big" and "small" slopes is problematic.

Consider the demand for eggs. Suppose we know two points on the demand curve. At $1 per dozen, the quantity of eggs demanded (per person per week) is two dozen, and at $2 per dozen, the quantity demanded is one dozen. The slope would be negative one: a price change of one divided by a quantity change of negative one.

Or would it? Suppose we stated the demand curve in eggs, not dozens. At $1 per dozen, the quantity of eggs demanded would be twenty-four, and at $2 per dozen it would be twelve. Now the slope (for the same demand curve!) is negative one-twelfth: a price change of one divided by a quantity change of negative twelve. Obviously, one is much bigger than one-twelfth, so does that mean the curve magically got flatter? No. It means that the units we use for our slope measure of flat versus steep dramatically affect the measure.

Economists have found a solution for this "units" problem. If we measure the changes as percentage changes rather than absolute changes, we eliminate this problem. This new measure is called *elasticity*: the percentage change in quantity divided by the percentage change in price.

A percentage change, in general, is an absolute change relative to or divided by some base (often the starting point, but sometimes the average of the two prices). The percentage change in price in both cases above is one. The price change for this increase is $2 minus $1, which is $1, divided by the starting price, $1: $1/$1 = 1.

The percentage change in quantity for this price change is also the same in both cases, but the absolute numbers are different. If we use dozens, the percentage change is one dozen minus two dozen divided by two dozen, or negative one-half. If we use eggs, the percentage change is twelve eggs minus twenty-four eggs divided by twenty-four eggs— again, negative one-half.

The elasticity in either case is negative one-half divided by one, or negative one-half. Elasticity purges the "steepness" metric of units. You'll also note that, compared to slope, we now have the quantity change in the numerator. That's more intuitive. We want to be able to say a price change is causing a quantity change.

When we use the term "elasticity," we don't speak of flatness or steepness; we say elastic and inelastic. *Elastic* means there is a big percentage change in quantity relative to the percentage in price. So elastic we can think of as a flat curve, or a big change in quantity for a given change in price. And *inelastic* means the percentage change in quantity is small relative to the percentage change in price, or a steep curve.

Most economists divide elastic and inelastic around negative one. If the elasticity of demand is two, then the percentage change in quantity is twice the percentage change in price. We would say that demand is elastic (flat); the price increase is causing a large percentage decrease in quantity. We talk about the implication of demand elasticity for businesses throughout the book.

Examples

Example 1   A freeze in southwestern U.S. and Mexican fields has resulted in damaged crops and inflated prices for produce such as lettuce, broccoli, and cauliflower.

How would this situation be interpreted on a supply-demand diagram?
At every price, the supply of produce is now less, so the supply curve shifts to the left. This shift causes excess demand at current produce prices, thus pushing them up.

Curiosity 2.3
The Elasticity of a Straight Line

Purging the measure of steepness of the units that we use when we describe a market is an important reason for using elasticity instead of slope to talk about the response of quantity to price changes by consumers or producers, but there's another, more subtle reason. Steep and flat are visual measures of responsiveness; alone, a steep demand line changes in price have little impact on quantity demanded. The units correction simply says that if our quantity is in millions of units, a change from one million to two million would show up as simply two, and would seem small, but if quantity is in units, that same change would be one million, and would seem big.

But while straight-line demand (or supply) lines have a constant slope, they do not have constant elasticity. That makes sense if you remember that elasticity is calculated using a change divided by a starting level for both price and quantity. The slope, the change, is constant but the starting point is not. So elasticity changes constantly along a straight demand or straight supply line. We can align this fact with our visual descriptors of flat and steep for any one good.

Suppose our demand line is represented by the formula:

$P = 500 - 10Q,$

which has a constant slope of −10 and would look steep if we graphed it. Suppose the market quantities over the past few years have fluctuated between twenty and forty units. Between forty and forty-one units, the price would have changed from $100 to $90 and the elasticity, e (as we increase quantity and decrease price) would have been:

e = % Change in quantity/% Change in price = ((41 − 40)/40)/(($90 − $100)/$100)
  = −0.25,

or a small (negative) elasticity, and our visual descriptor of steep demand would line up with our more accurate economic descriptor, inelastic demand. Between thirty and thirty-one units the price would fall from $200 to $190, and the elasticity of the demand line at that point would be:

e = % Change in quantity/% Change in price = ((31 − 30)/30)/(($190 − $200)/$200)
  = −0.67,

which is still less than one and inelastic. But as we move toward the high end of the demand line, things change. Between quantities twenty and twenty-one, the price falls from $300 to $290, and the elasticity is now:

e = % Change in quantity/% Change in price = ((21 − 20)/20)/(($290 − $300)/$300)
  = −1.5.

The line at that point is elastic. Elasticity of demand in this case goes above one after the price reaches $250 and the quantity falls to twenty-five. Along a demand line that looks steep and has a big slope, the best we can say is that it is inelastic for more of its length, not all of it.

In our discussion, we're interested in how sensitive quantity is to price, so we'll say the more precise inelastic and draw demand and supply lines that look steep.

Example 2   According to a story in the business section of the local newspaper, "The higher prices may make it possible for some producers who closed during the last two years to reopen."

How would this possibility be interpreted on a supply-demand diagram?
The higher price slides us along the supply curve to a higher output. Some of that higher output comes from new producers.

Example 3   There are still 2,500 vacant units in the city and just so many tenants to go around. Landlords will have to take measures to get people in their buildings.

What is the current status of this market?
There is an excess supply of rental accommodation.

What measures will the landlords have to take?
They will be forced to lower rents.

Example 4   A new low-calorie ice cream has hit the market and it's all the rage. Diet-conscious consumers are raving about this product on social media and it's flying off the shelf (in the freezer section of the store). In light of that, the price of this product is going up rather precipitously. Can we predict what will happen to the price of the product if other producers copy the recipe?

Use a short-run and long-run supply and demand diagram to explain these price changes.
The initial supply and demand curves for this product are inelastic, and the product's popularity will shift the demand curve to the right. Most of the market's short-run reaction will be to increase the price of the ice cream. Over time, the producer of the ice cream can ramp up production, making more product available and the supply curve flatter. In addition, other companies may copy this product, providing consumers with substitutes and making the demand line for the original ice cream flatter. Combined, this means that the price of the original ice cream should fall from its short-run peak.

Example 5   The radio commentator said, "As the summer vacation season shifts into high gear, gas prices are up, but according to recent data, gas consumption (quantity) is also up. I guess the law of downward-sloping demand doesn't hold for gas."

What contradiction does the commentator think he's seeing? What mistake is he making in his interpretation of the data?
The reference to the law of downward-sloping demand is our aforementioned norm that, from the consumer's perspective, higher prices should cause consumers to buy less of a good (lower quantities). What the commentator is missing is the "why" part of the price increase. In this case, the summer vacation season means an increase in demand for gas—a shift of the demand curve to the right. That would indeed raise both the price of gas and the quantity of gas supplied.

Example 6 **The expected price drop for cherries due to the bumper crop this year won't be as much as we thought, because of short supplies of pears and peaches.**

Explain why the price of cherries is expected to drop.

A bumper crop means that the supply of cherries is much higher than expected, shifting the cherry supply curve to the right. This shift creates an excess supply at current cherry prices, pushing cherry prices down.

Why should short supplies of pears and peaches inhibit the fall in cherry prices?

Short supplies of pears and peaches should lead to their prices being bid up, which in turn should cause people to demand more of alternative fruits such as cherries. This extra demand for cherries should inhibit their price fall.

Exercises

(B exercises are more challenging.)

A2.1   The headline reads "Heating Oil Prices Skyrocket As Temperatures Plummet to Record Lows." Explain this price change using one shift in the supply and demand model.

A2.2   The headline reads "Gasoline Prices Skyrocket after Explosion at Oil Refinery." Explain this price change using one shift in the supply and demand model.

A2.3   The newscaster says, "According to a study, eating kale at least once a day will increase your life span by an average of five years." What should this news story do to the price of kale? Explain using the market model.

A2.4   There's a popular expression down on the farm: "Good weather means bad prices." Use the market model to explain this expression.

A2.5   According to a commentator, "The one good result from the recent negative news stories about candy is that the price of candy has fallen recently." Explain this effect using the market model.

A2.6   The recent fungal infestation that swept across many strawberry fields was a public relations nightmare, chasing consumers away for the summer, as well as a supply shock. Strangely, strawberry prices didn't change. Use the basic supply and demand model to explain why.

A2.7   A fad is a sudden increase in demand for a good. The biggest beneficiaries of a fad are the producers that already had the product on the shelf. Explain using the market model.

A2.8 Over the past decade, several swanky hotels opened in Las Vegas featuring many new attractions. These new hotels increased the number of rooms by 20 percent, but room prices went up. Using the basic market model, give a possible explanation for this result.

A2.9 The worst possible combination of events for drivers happened in California. An explosion closed one of the largest oil refineries just as the summer driving season kicked in. Show what this combination of events would do to gasoline prices.

A2.10 The Affordable Care Act increased the demand for "health care" by giving more people access to health insurance. It did not do anything to increase the supply of "health care." Therefore, the Affordable Care Act made the price of "health care" do what?

B2.1 A recent study highlighted the dramatic increase in the price of new homes in California. The study noted that new home construction in California lagged that in the rest of the country. Use the market model to explain this price increase.

B2.2 The recent *E. coli* contamination of lettuce hit both sides of the market. Growers pulled lettuce from stores and consumers stopped buying lettuce. How could you use the market model to determine which of these shifts was bigger?

B2.3 According to a news story, the price of new homes in Squareville rose and the number of new homes sold rose. Also, the price of new homes in Roundville fell and the number of new homes sold rose. Using one shift in each case, explain these observations using the market model.

B2.4 Parents are more likely to pay excessively high prices for popular toys if they wait to do their shopping until a few days before Christmas. Why?

B2.5 If you are a price-conscious traveler, you should never pull off for dinner at a freeway exit that has only one restaurant. Why?

3   Applications of (and Interference with) the Market

The market model is elegant and relatively simple. It explains where things come from and how things get distributed in the competitive marketplace. Of course, there are other economic systems that produce and distribute things in different ways. In what are called "command economies," such as communist and socialist systems, the government is in charge of production and distribution. No economic system is perfect, and even the efficiencies that many economists like in the competitive marketplace come at the expense of some consumers or producers who cannot afford to buy or produce a good at the market price.

Governments often try to intervene when a market result feels unfair. If a price is so high that a substantial percentage of the population cannot afford to buy that good, governments often legislate a lower price. If a price is so low that many producers go out of business, governments can legislate a higher price. These and other government interventions in the marketplace allow us to apply the supply and demand diagram and get a better understanding of how markets work.

To some extent, working through the impact of government intervention in the marketplace will test your belief in the market. Specifically, if a price is artificially changed by government decree, will the outcome be unambiguously better? Or will the factors that determined the market price have adverse effects on consumers or producers after the imposition of a mandated price? Put differently, could government intervention in the market end up causing a worse result for the very people the government was trying to help?

On completion of this chapter, you should

- understand price ceilings and price floors,
- understand tax incidence, and
- be able to see how quotas and subsidies have different outcomes than price regulation.

3.1   Regulated Prices

The basic market model does a good job explaining how prices and quantities are determined in a competitive environment. The model assumes that consumers and producers incorporate all factors necessary in setting the market price, and in producing and distributing the good. Despite this, governments and regulators sometimes see issues and priorities (some of which we discuss in chapters 10 and 11) that they believe market participants have not taken into account. When this happens, these policymakers try to improve on market outcomes by mandating a price different from the market price.

When regulating bodies override the market with their own price, they are almost always doing so with an eye toward some concept of fairness. They believe that the market-determined price is inherently unfair to a segment of the population and (assuming some form of representative government is behind this regulating body) that their mandated price will correct this perceived unfairness. This is a noble endeavor. The question we need to address is, do these government-determined prices do more harm than good?

3.2   Price Ceilings

A *price ceiling* is a legally determined price set below the market price to help consumers. Let's use the market we described in chapter 2, the market for apples, to see how this works. In that example, a large number of consumers and a large number of producers determined a market price and a market quantity (we will address the regulation of uncompetitive markets in chapters 7 and 10). Suppose those values ended up being $1 per pound for apples and one million pounds of apples sold every day, as shown graphically in figure 3.1.

As described in chapter 2, the market price connects the desires of consumers with the cost of producing apples. Nowhere in the discussion of the apple market did we say that *everyone* would be able to afford apples. At any price other than zero, some people who might want an apple will not be able to afford one. Indeed, every nonzero price for any

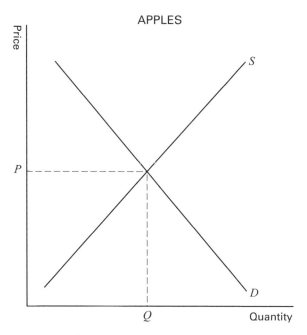

Figure 3.1   The Market for Apples

good will probably feel unfair to someone in the market. Enter governments and regulators. In an attempt to make apples affordable to more people (actually, more affordable to all people), the government decides to regulate the apple market and to set the price of apples at fifty cents per pound. The government imposes this price ceiling on the apple market at fifty cents per pound to help consumers. At that price, though, the quantity demanded exceeds the quantity supplied, and there will be a shortage of apples.

Does this price ceiling help consumers? We needn't look any further than our market model and the underlying factors that determined the supply and demand lines to answer this question. At the lower price, consumers would want more apples. On the graph, we move down and to the right on the demand line and see that at a price of fifty cents per pound, the quantity demanded increases relative to the market equilibrium (see figure 3.2). This is consistent with the income and substitution effects. This new lower price allows consumers at every level of spendable income to buy more apples, and it would cause consumers to substitute apples for other fruit whose price did not fall. If we looked only at the demand line, this policy would appear to work.

Unfortunately, the consumers who are represented on the demand line do not grow the apples. The apple growers are represented on the supply line, and they decide how much they can produce by comparing the price of apples to the cost of production. In chapter 2,

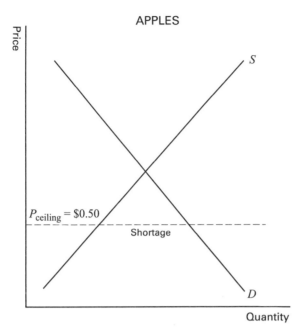

Figure 3.2   Price Ceiling on Apples

we said that as the price of apples increases, apple growers can afford more inputs and thus produce more apples. This works in reverse when the price ceiling is imposed. Faced with the lower price ceiling of fifty cents per pound, apple growers will not be able to afford as many workers, as much fertilizer, or as many delivery trucks. The legally imposed price will decrease the quantity supplied. We see that result on the graph when we apply the price ceiling and move along the supply line down and to the left.

This price ceiling has moved the apple market away from the previous equilibrium in which the quantity demanded equaled the quantity supplied. At fifty cents per pound, the quantity demanded exceeds the quantity supplied; there will be a shortage of apples after the price ceiling is imposed. Armed with this outcome, we can try to answer the question, does the price ceiling help consumers?

We could argue that it has helped some consumers. Those who were able to buy apples at fifty cents per pound are better off, right? Maybe not. Before the apple market was regulated, the one and only determinant of a consumer's ability to buy apples was money. If you had $1, you could buy a pound of apples. That price brought to the market the amount of apples that those able to afford them wanted. That is no longer true at fifty cents per pound. Many more people will want apples than there are apples available. Stores will regularly run out of apples, meaning consumers will have to spend more time shopping for apples. The apple market previously distributed apples based on money; it now distributes apples based on money *and time*. Depending on how people value their time (and irritation and frustration), this price ceiling might not have made anyone better off! This is an excellent application of the concept of opportunity cost that we discussed in curiosity 2.1. While the dollar price is lower, the opportunity cost—which includes time, among other things—might not be.

3.3 Rent Control

I don't think there has ever been a price ceiling imposed on apples in the history of the United States, but there are markets in which price ceilings have been imposed and are being tried today. One of the more controversial price ceilings is rent control. The political popularity of rent control is easy to understand. There are many more people (read: voters) who rent apartments than there are people (again, read: voters) who own apartment buildings. If the electorate was composed only of renters and apartment owners and you asked voters to determine rents, the majority would certainly want rents to be low. This isn't very different from the argument politicians make when they say college should be free in order to appeal to college-age voters.

But rent is a price that's based on costs. The apartment owner had to buy or build the apartment building and pay for the land it sits on, and now must maintain it as well. We'll discuss an unusual exception in chapter 10, but for the most part, rents are determined in a competitive market and are high if the costs of building and maintaining apartments are also high. If the government imposes a price ceiling on rents—rent control—the quantity supplied of apartments will fall, as we showed in figure 3.2 for apples.

In the real world, rent control is a bit trickier than the generic case that we made using the apple market as an example. At any one time, there are many apartment buildings that are already built and full of tenants. These buildings don't suddenly go away when rent control is imposed. This is another case in which there is a clear difference between the short-run and the long-run market. In the short run, the supply of apartments doesn't change much; the supply is inelastic. In the long run there will be more or fewer new apartments built, depending on the ability of builders to recoup their costs—and rent control will make it harder for apartment builders to do so. So, rent control will look as if its working—helping renters without decreasing the quantity of apartments available—but only in the short run. In the long run, rent control will decrease the number of apartments built (including those that would have replaced existing apartments) (see figure 3.3).

This is a case where the politicians espousing a price regulation look good in the short run, when they need to get elected, and simply aren't around in the long run, when the problems begin to manifest. As is often the case, the government is being asked to deal with a problem springing from a market, and in using rent control, it are trying to solve

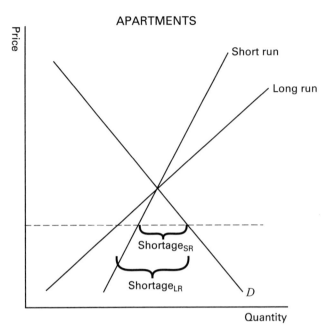

Figure 3.3   The Market for Apartments with Rent Control

the problem by ignoring the market. If rents are too high, a better solution is to find a way to build more apartments.

In the News: California: NIMBY Override

Nowhere is the housing shortage more obvious or more topical than in the state of California. If you Google the highest-rent markets in the United States, you'll see that more than half of the top twenty most expensive rental markets are in California. While rent control has been tried in many places, the reality of insufficient supply has sunk in for many politicians. But increasing the supply of housing is not actually a state-controlled issue. Cities and counties must grant building permits for housing, and they are often unwilling to do so for the kind of housing that would actually solve the problem: high-density housing. High-density housing means smaller homes and apartments that use less land and thus are cheaper to build. This is often housing for lower-income people and, by its nature, somewhat less glamorous than the mansions California is often associated with.

High-density, affordable housing is something everyone in California says they want—just not in their city (or as we sometimes say, not in my backyard—NIMBY). To counter the NIMBY attitudes, the governor and the legislature are considering changes that would

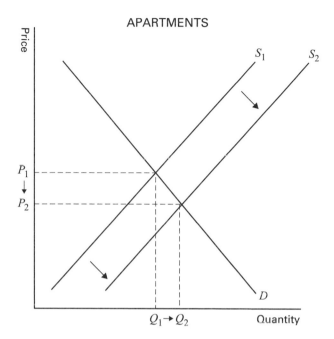

Figure 3.4 Using the Market Model to Solve the Problem of Increasing the Supply of Apartments

allow some housing to be forced on cities; that is, they would allow the state to override cities when cities decline to permit affordable housing. While the future of this movement will certainly involve litigation and controversy, it is a move in the right direction in that it addresses the housing shortage by shifting the supply of housing in a sustainable way (see figure 3.4).

3.4 Price Floors

There are two sides to every market. As such, there are two market participants who might not like the market price. Suppose many apple growers thought the market price was too low—unfair in some way—and they convinced a government regulator to set the regulated price above the market price. This would be a *price floor*, a legal minimum price put in place to help producers.

There are historical examples of price floors in many countries' agricultural industry. One justification goes something like this. Suppose the apple industry has many producers, some of which are much bigger than others. The large producers can produce and sell

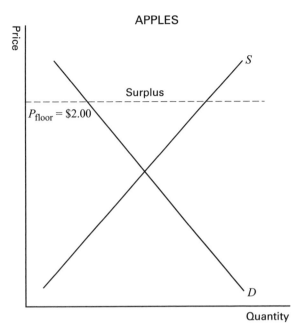

APPLES

Figure 3.5   Price Floor on Apples

apples at lower prices than the small producers (we discuss economies of scale in chapter 5). But rather than succumb to this size disadvantage, the small producers convince the government to apply price supports (a price floor) in their industry to protect their orchards and their jobs.

Returning to our earlier market equilibrium in figure 3.1, the unregulated price of apples is $1 per pound, but at that price, smaller growers would go out of business. The government sets a price floor at $2 per pound to help apple producers. At that price, the quantity supplied exceeds the quantity demanded or there is a surplus of apples. We see that result in figure 3.5.

We can go through the same exercise that we did for a price ceiling and ask whether this policy does what it was intended to do—help producers. Unless the demand for apples is very inelastic (which is unlikely), the higher price of apples as a result of the price floor will lead to a substantial decrease in apple sales. All told, apple growers likely will not be helped by this policy if only a price floor is implemented.

But that result can be changed with one small addition to the price floor. Suppose the government imposed a price floor and agreed to buy all the surplus apples. Growers would then be selling more apples at higher prices, and they would absolutely be better off. Price floors are different from price ceilings in this respect. Having created a market imbalance with the price interference, the government has an easy fix in the case of a price floor: it can simply buy the entire surplus.

The comparable fix in the case of the price ceiling would be for the government regulator to mitigate the shortage, that is, produce more apples. If it did that—if the government grew apples and thus increased the market supply—that action alone would lower the price and there would be no need for a price ceiling.

> **Sample Exam Question 3.1**
> Price ceilings and price floors are usually policies that look good to voters rather than policies that fix a problem in the market. If the correct market fix for high rents is for the government to build more apartments, why would voters settle for imposing rent control?

3.5   Minimum Wages

There aren't many market interferences that are better known and more controversial than the minimum wage. We will do a basic market model analysis of the minimum wage here and a deeper analysis in chapter 10 when we talk about input markets and monopsonies.

As with everything else, there is a market for labor. Wages—the price of labor—are usually determined by employers' demand for labor and the supply of labor offered by people entering the workforce. Highly technical job markets such as the computer industry have a high demand for labor these days and, because of the technical training requirements, a low supply. Together, those market forces mean high wages for people with computer training.

Low-skilled jobs, sometimes called entry-level jobs, are subject to exactly opposite market forces. Supply is high, since few skills are required, but demand, while ubiquitous, is comparatively low. Historically, many of these jobs have relocated to other countries. Correspondingly, wages for entry-level jobs are also low—too low, it is argued, for people to live on. Again, concepts of fairness are invoked, and in many countries the government steps in and mandates a minimum wage.

The minimum wage is a legal wage set above the market wage, so it is a price floor. As we saw earlier in the example of a price floor for apples, the only way suppliers of labor wouldn't actually be worse off would be if the government bought up the surplus (which does not happen in the U.S. labor market) or if the demand line were very inelastic.

It is sometimes argued that the demand for entry-level labor is, indeed, inelastic. The popular logic for this is phrased as "someone has to flip the burgers" or "someone has to sweep the floor." While that might be true immediately after a minimum wage is imposed (or increased), it certainly isn't true forever. This is another case in which we would want to consider the long-run versus short-run market, or the changing elasticity of demand over time (see figure 3.6).

The effects of high or increasing minimum wages are a good place to think about the market model. Some studies find that increasing the minimum wage does not decrease the number of jobs or the level of employment, but most studies find the impact is consistent with the market model, and only the magnitude of the job loss is under debate. Big or small, the magnitude is certainly bigger in the long run as employers replace labor with capital (stores put in self-checkout lines and robots flip the burgers and sweep the floors).

But how could an increase in the minimum wage *not* decrease the number of jobs? Using the market model, not ignoring it, reveals that the only way would be if the minimum wage caused an increase in the demand for labor: a *shift* to the right of the demand line (or the unlikely possibility that the demand line is upward sloping). When we derived the market model in chapter 2 and discussed the factors that cause the supply or demand line to shift, we specifically said that the price of the good for that market could not shift either the supply or the demand line. Those lines graph the *relationship* between price and quantity for consumers or producers. So while this argument in favor of high minimum wages is interesting, it is inconsistent with the market model.

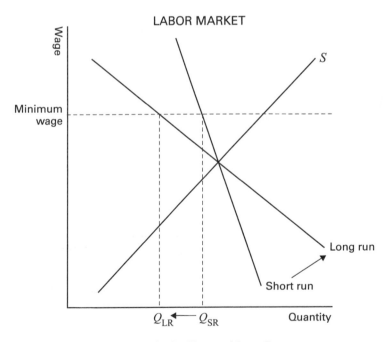

Figure 3.6   Minimum Wage in the Short and Long Run

Curiosity 3.1
The Underground Economy

The market model does tell us how some attempts to regulate the market will ultimately work out. A price ceiling causes the quantity supplied to decrease. At that lower quantity, according to the demand line, some consumers are willing to pay a higher price. So if there is no enforcement mechanism in place to prevent this, a price ceiling will actually lead to an increase in the price consumers pay!

In the same way, a price floor can work backwards. Mandating a price higher than the market price will, according to the supply line, increase the quantity supplied. At that higher quantity supplied, the price consumers would be willing to pay is actually lower than the original market price. This one is trickier. Normally the quantity supplied would increase only if producers were paid the higher price; the price floor. But we could imagine a high minimum wage attracting more people into the labor market through immigration. Once here, those people might be willing to work for a lower wage (see figure 3.7).

Figure 3.7   Price Floor and the Lower Price in the Underground Economy

Some argue that the market for labor is special because the price in this market, the wage rate, is income, and increasing people's income would increase people's demand for all goods. With that increase in demand, producers of all goods would increase output and thus need to increase the demand for labor. This logic falls apart when you realize that all prices would also have risen if the demand for all goods rose, so the higher minimum wage cannot buy more of all goods. If the circularity of that logic is hard to follow, we'll say it a different way. If raising the minimum wage magically increased the demand for labor, why wouldn't the correct minimum wage be $100 or even $1,000 per hour?

3.6   Subsidies and Quotas

The government doesn't always legislate prices when it wants to change a market result. Price is arguably the easiest thing for the government to mandate. Passing a law that sets a price doesn't require any change in production (supply) or tastes (demand) as long as the government doesn't care about surpluses or shortages. But mandating a price different from the market price doesn't always achieve the government's desires.

If the government wants to lower the price of flu shots so that more people can afford them, simply mandating a lower price will not achieve the desired goal; with no change in the supply line, a price ceiling would make fewer flu shots available. Instead of ignoring the market (the supply side, in this case), the government could effect change in the market. The government could increase the supply of flu shots.

One way for the government to increase the supply of something is to become a producer. There are situations where the government runs a business (the postal service and, in some municipalities, water and other utilities), but the government has no expertise in operating a business. An alternative is for the government to subsidize private production—allow private businesses to produce flu shots, but pay some of the cost of ramping up production. Suppose the government offered to pay flu shot companies $2 per shot for every shot they sold. This would shift the supply line to the right (or down by $2), simultaneously increasing the supply in the market while lowering the price to all (see figure 3.8).

One wonders why the government doesn't always use subsidies when it wants to increase availability and lower the price of a good, especially since policymakers usually have at their disposal market-based rather than market-ignoring ways to lower the price of a good.

Another nonprice intervention is a quota. If there is a good that the government does not want people to consume as much as the unfettered-market quantity (e.g., cigarettes or sugary soda), the government could mandate a production limit on all firms. Suppose the market quantity was one million units per day. The government could order producers to decrease that to half a million. That would decrease the quantity supplied (but not shift the supply line to the left) and increase the price of the good (see figure 3.9).

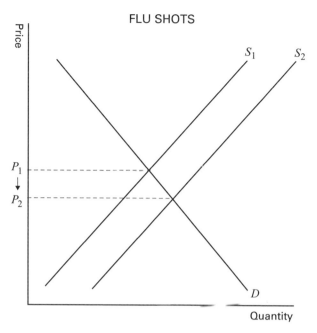

Figure 3.8   Government Subsidizing the Production of Flu Shots and Thus Lowering the Market Price

Why couldn't the government do this when it wanted more of a good—simply order producers to increase output? This is an important issue to understand. The supply line represents the cost of production (more details to come in chapter 5). Mandating an increase in production without subsidizing the cost of production would cause producers to lose money and ultimately leave the industry. The key is the price. The government can mandate a lower supply because it allows, and even wants, the price to rise. Mandating a higher supply (without a subsidy) would mean the price needs to fall—but the costs do not (see figure 3.10). Producers would lose money on every unit they sold.

Sample Exam Question 3.2
What would the difference in market outcomes be if the government imposed a production quota on cigarettes rather than run negative advertisements (assuming they reached the same number of consumers)?

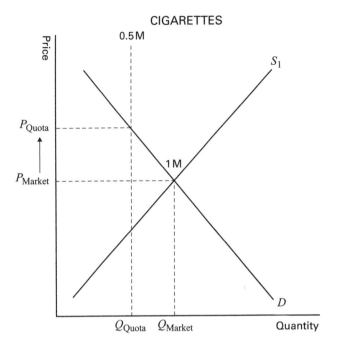

Figure 3.9   Quota on Cigarettes

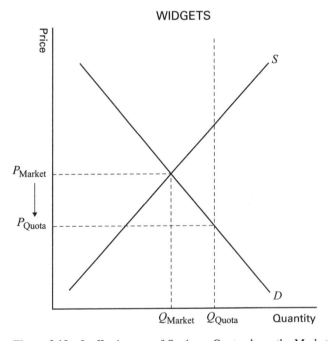

Figure 3.10   Ineffectiveness of Setting a Quota above the Market Quantity

Curiosity 3.2
Moving Demand

There are situations in which our society or the government believes that the market demand is problematic; the good is desirable but, perhaps, unhealthy. One possibility is to work with the market and market forces and provide information to consumers. The government can, and does, run public service announcements with the sole purpose of decreasing the demand for an unhealthy good. Stop-smoking advertisements featuring maimed cancer survivors and the famous "This is your brain on drugs" commercial are good examples. The idea behind these negative ads is to decrease the demand for the good and thus lower the market quantity (see figure 3.11). This policy is analogous to subsidizing something the society wants more of. Here the government uses market forces rather than supersede them.

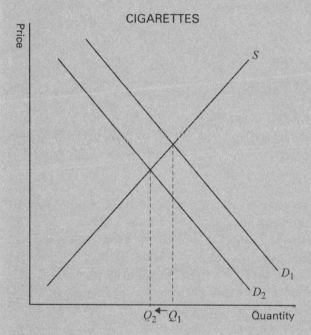

Figure 3.11   Falling Demand for Cigarettes with Negative Advertising

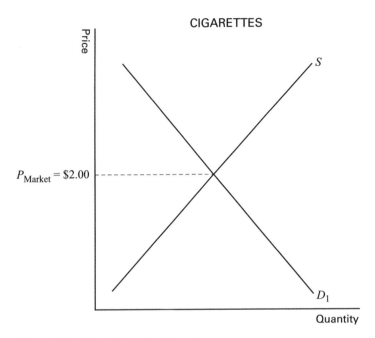

CIGARETTES

$P_{\text{Market}} = \$2.00$

S

D_1

Price

Quantity

Figure 3.12   The Market for Cigarettes

3.7   Tax Incidence

There are other applications and extensions of the market model aside from price interference. One interesting and useful extension is what's known as tax incidence. When a tax is imposed on a product (called an excise tax) such as cigarettes or alcoholic beverages or gasoline, the taxing authority often tries to apply the tax to only one side of the market. A tax on cigarettes, for example, might be charged to the producer—a per-pack tax charged to cigarette companies—hoping to force producers to pay the tax. But does charging the tax to producers mean cigarette companies actually pay the tax? Where the tax actually falls is known as the *tax incidence*, and the basic market model allows us to answer that question.

We show the market for cigarettes in figure 3.12 with the market price of cigarettes as $2 per pack before any taxes. The supply line reflects the costs associated with producing cigarettes: the cost of tobacco, paper, and so on. If a tax of, say, $1 per pack is imposed and charged to the cigarette company, how does that ultimately affect the price of cigarettes? The cigarette company would treat the tax as if it were a $1 increase in the cost of

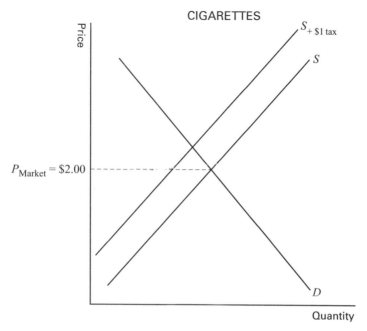

Figure 3.13   Effect of Tax of $1 Per Pack Charged to Producer

production (per pack). We can show that by shifting the supply line up by $1, as in figure 3.13.

The cigarette company might try to increase cigarette prices by $1, but that increase in price, according to the demand line, would decrease the number of packs of cigarettes bought by consumers. If neither the supply line nor the demand line is dramatically inelastic or elastic, then the shift up in the supply line together with the normal impact of a downward-sloping demand line should split the impact of the tax in half. The price will rise, but by something closer to fifty cents (rather than $1), and, when the dollar tax is subtracted from that price, the amount that cigarette producers get per pack will fall by about fifty cents. Even though the tax was charged to the producer, the tax is actually split between the producer and the consumer.

This allocation of a tax, the tax incidence, shows that the burden of a tax has less to do with where the tax is charged than it does with the nature of the market for the good. Building on that analysis, let's suppose the supply or demand line is less generic. In the more realistic cigarette market, cigarettes are addictive, so the demand for cigarettes is likely inelastic. Shifting the supply line up by $1 along an inelastic demand line gives us a different result. Unwilling to smoke (much) less, consumers willingly pay more of the tax.

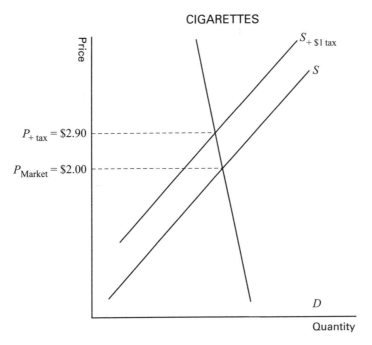

Figure 3.14   Tax Incidence with an Inelastic Demand for Cigarettes

The price of cigarettes after the tax is applied is close to the pretax price plus $1. At that price, producers will be getting close to the amount they got before the tax was applied and they will be able to produce close to the same quantity of cigarettes (see figure 3.14). If the demand for a product shows that consumers want to continue to consume the same amount of the good regardless of the price (what we've called an inelastic demand), then consumers will pay the tax even though it is charged to the producer.

This is a generalizable result. The more inelastic side of the market will pay more of an excise tax regardless of where the tax is charged. There's a simple logic to this beyond the shifting lines in the market model. Inflexibility usually has a price. If you want to keep quantities from changing regardless of market forces, you will ultimately have to pay for your inability or unwillingness to change. You can see a more complete graphical rendering of tax incidence in appendix 3.1.

Examples

Example 1   Price ceilings aren't always explicit; the government doesn't always say it is setting a legal maximum price. But the government, as operator of a large health insurer (Medicare), can simply refuse to pay a market price.

If the government (Medicare) pays a doctor, say, half of what the doctor asks for an office visit, how might that change the market?

Under that scenario, doctors might limit the number of Medicare patients they accept. They might shorten the time they spend caring for Medicare patients. Or they might be more inclined to send more Medicare patients to emergency rooms for many medical problems.

Example 2   Climate change is a social concern. The use of carbon-based fuels (oil and coal) has been implicated in creating the problem. Unfortunately, the alternatives (solar, wind, or nuclear energy) are currently more expensive than carbon-based fuels.

Taking market forces into account, what would be the most effective way to transition the economy from carbon-based to alternative fuels?

By taxing carbon-based fuels and raising their price. This would allow the market to find the best alternatives. The problem with subsidies here is the government has to pick a winner before innovations have occurred. If the government subsidizes any one of these alternatives over the others, it might be picking a less effective alternative based solely on lobbying or some other political pressure.

Example 3   Minimum wage increases are at the center of political debate these days. One observation that proponents of higher minimum wages point to is that several major employers have increased their own entry-level wage (sometimes erroneously referred to as the employer's minimum wage) during the recent economic expansion.

Why isn't this observation a justification for a higher national minimum wage?

Arguably, this is a reason why the current minimum wage is about right! If the government is trying to set a national standard without decreasing the number of available jobs, you would expect some employers to pay more than that on their own when they need to increase their workforce. The difference: an increase in the national minimum wage would apply to all employers and would be permanent (historically, the government has never decreased the minimum wage). When the economy cools off, employers need the ability to lower wages in order to keep people employed.

Chapter Summary

- Supply and demand represent the current ability to produce and the desire to consume a good.

- Mandating a price change without shifting supply or demand will cause a market imbalance, a shortage or surplus of the good.

- If the market result is not acceptable to society and the government, they can operate within the market—affect supply or demand—to get a more sustainable outcome.

- Taxes that are imposed on specific goods are not necessarily borne by the side of the market to which the tax is applied.

Exercises

(B exercises are more challenging.)

A3.1 **The idea that a price ceiling imposed on a competitively produced good will make people better off is a blatant disregard for the existence of the supply line. Explain.**

A3.2 **When intervening in the market, the government has only one straightforward way of lowering the market price and increasing the market quantity. Explain.**

A3.3 **One way in which governments have dealt with the shortages created by price ceilings is to combine the ceiling with some sort of voucher program whereby the government sends everyone a coupon that allows consumers to buy a certain amount of the good. How does that allocation system compare with the unregulated market?**

A3.4 **Price ceilings are an example of how governments do not understand opportunity costs. Specifically, governments frequently do not appreciate the value of people's time. Explain.**

A3.5 **Even when they accomplish what they are intended to accomplish, price floors make one side of the market unambiguously worse off. Explain.**

A3.6 **Milk price supports are an example of a price floor put in place to help producers in the dairy industry. The government buys large quantities of several different dairy products (cheese, butter, etc.) and thus keeps the price of dairy products higher than it otherwise would have been. This is bad for consumers in two ways. Explain.**

A3.7   Everything else being the same, a price floor is probably better for producers and worse for consumers in the long run, assuming the government always buys all the surplus created by the price floor. Why?

A3.8   Using the basic market model for labor, and thinking about any country (not just the United States), show the following: a high minimum wage (well above the market wage rate) combined with open borders for all immigrants will increase the labor surplus in a country.

A3.9   In the case described in the previous question, show why the underground market wage rate will be correspondingly lower.

A3.10 If an excise tax is imposed on Picasso paintings but charged to consumers, the sellers would actually pay most of the tax because Picasso is dead. Explain logically.

B3.1   Explain the following statement using an appropriately drawn supply and demand diagram: In light of the realities of cigarette smoking, a tax on cigarettes will perform far better at generating revenue for the government than at decreasing cigarette smoking.

B3.2   Between the Affordable Care Act and the aging of the baby boom generation, the demand for health care and prescription drugs is at an all-time high in the United States. Those market forces have also pushed up the price of prescription drugs faster than the prices of most other goods. In response, many policymakers—including the president—are calling for price controls (price ceilings) on prescription drugs. For generic drugs, which are priced by the basic market model, would that be a good idea *from the consumer's perspective?*

B3.3   True or false, explain: It's okay to impose a price ceiling on a good that has a completely inelastic (perfectly vertical) supply line in the short and long run because the ceiling will not have any market repercussions. So rent control would work if there was nowhere left in the city to build!

B3.4   One proposal for reducing skyrocketing medical costs is to cut physician reimbursements by government-run programs such as Medicare. If we analyze that proposal as a price ceiling on doctors' pay, this would cause a shortage of doctors. Why would that shortage be much worse over time?

B3.5   If the desired outcome is decreased cigarette use, which government policy would be more effective, a cigarette tax or a highly successful campaign to decrease the demand for cigarettes? Assume the demand for cigarettes is quite inelastic.

Figure 3.15   Relatively Elastic Demand: Producers Pay More of an Excise Tax

---

Appendix 3.1   Tax Incidence Redux

There are infinite possibilities for tax incidence, but we're focusing on essentials in this book, so let's keep it simple. In section 3.7, we discussed the cigarette example in which the tax was charged to producers but consumers were the more inflexible side of the market (demand was more inelastic than supply). Even though the tax was charged to producers, they were able to pass most of it along to the relatively inflexible consumers.

Suppose an excise tax is charged to producers, but demand is very elastic (demand is more elastic than supply). When producers try to pass the tax on to consumers, they find consumers unwilling to pay the higher price. The elastic demand means consumers would rather use less of the good than pay the higher price. Here, producers would pay more of the tax (see figure 3.15). The new price is only slightly higher, and, after subtracting the tax, producers would get much less per unit than they did prior to the imposition of the tax.

Of course, the government can charge excise taxes to consumers in the form of good-specific sales taxes. To analyze this situation, we have to imagine there are now two

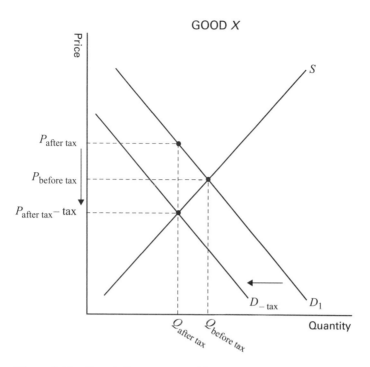

Figure 3.16   Generic Tax Incidence When Consumers Are Charged the Tax

demand lines: the demand line that represents what consumers pay and the demand line that producers get after the tax is subtracted. In the generic case in which neither side of the market is particularly inelastic or elastic, we can see that a $1 tax imposed on consumers is once again shared between both sides of the market. The consumer pays fifty cents more and the producer gets fifty cents less than in the pretax situation. The key here is that those producers don't get all the money that consumers pay; producers get only the after-tax amount. Producers therefore cannot pay for as many inputs and cannot produce as many units. At that lower output, producers get a lower price, as shown in figure 3.16.

We can now show how producers could pay taxes charged to consumers. Suppose the demand for this good is elastic, the supply is inelastic, and we once again charge a $1 tax to consumers. We shift demand down by the amount of the tax, but suppliers can't decrease their level of output. Since demand is elastic, consumers aren't willing to pay more for the good. So producers pay most of this tax in that they are getting almost $1 less per unit for every unit they sell, as shown in figure 3.17.

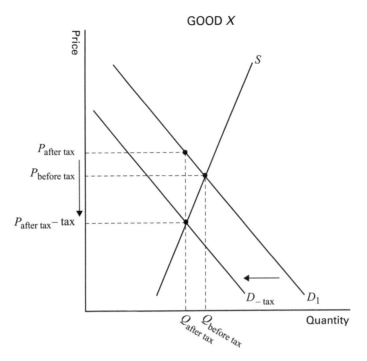

Figure 3.17   Inelastic Supply, Elastic Demand: Tax Charged to Consumers

As we said in the discussion of tax incidence in section 3.7, who actually pays taxes imposed on individual goods has more to do with the nature of the market—the elasticity of the market participants—than on where the tax is charged.

4   Behind the Demand Line: Consumer Theory

Economics begins with observation, and our observation of consumers is important to understand and model their behavior. For most consumers and most goods, we've noted their tendency to consume less of a good as its price increases. We said the intuitive explanation for this behavior is a combination of an income effect (one's (fixed) spendable income simply cannot buy as much at higher prices) and a substitution effect (consumers usually have many ways of satisfying a need or desire). While these factors are a good start toward understanding consumer behavior, economists have come up with richer and deeper explanations for our spending habits.

Once again driven by observations, there are more things we know about consumers than the simple price-quantity trade-off. We know that consumers tend to buy a variety of goods. We know that consumers need information in order to satisfy their needs. We know that binging, while a popular concept these days, is the exception rather than the rule (except at the all-you-can-eat buffet!). We bring all these observations together within a relatively simply model that's known as consumer theory.

Consumer theory is the product of many other disciplines. It draws from philosophy and the idea that we are constantly trying to satisfy needs and wants. It also draws from science and math to explain the process of maximizing happiness. And finally, it draws from other business disciplines (marketing in particular) to understand how we learn about product attributes. While consumer theory is often taught with calculus, we will use a more intuitive approach in the body of this chapter.

On completion of this chapter, you should

- understand the observations on which consumer theory is based,
- understand the critical concepts of marginal utility and diminishing marginal utility,
- understand the conditions that lead to utility maximization, and
- recognize the real-world problems that consumers face in trying to maximize their utility.

4.1   Utility, Utility Maximization, and How We Shop

For most people and most goods, we don't consume large quantities of any one good at any one time. If that feels as though we are hedging a bit, it's because we don't want you to immediately start thinking of exceptions. If you were to ask me why I don't eat, say, donuts all the time, I would say that beyond some point, I simply get tired of donuts. Doubtless you do too. You get tired of donuts and most other goods after you've consumed a few of them.

This observation about typical human behavior allows us to describe a process for achieving happiness that operates inside our head. (We might even call this happiness "*utility*," based on the ideas put forth by philosophers such as John Stuart Mill and Jeremy Bentham.) Inside our head, we feel that consumption of anything good leads to happiness. The sensation we get when we put a fresh, warm donut in our mouth is wonderful, but the happiness that we get from consumption follows a predictable pattern.

We notice that every additional donut we eat (at any one time, not over our lifetime) makes us happier, but the increment to our happiness gets smaller. The second donut isn't quite as amazing as the first; the third donut is less wonderful than the second, and so on. After a while, as wonderful as that first bite was, we start getting sick of eating donuts.

It's impossible to quantify happiness in a general way for everyone, but we can imagine a representative consumer—perhaps your donut-loving author—whose happiness we could measure with a happiness meter placed on his forehead that measures the jollies (the unit of happiness) every time he ate an additional donut. His jollies would diminish as shown in table 4.1.

The first donut gives him happiness, measured as ten jollies. The second donut makes him happier, but not as happy as the first one. By the sixth donut, he derives only one additional jolly. If we had to explain why the first donut gave him much more happiness than the sixth donut, we would simply say, "He's getting tired of donuts by the time he eats the sixth one." We call the increment to our happiness *marginal utility*: the change in utility as we change our consumption. And the pattern that we see in table 4.1, the pattern that we believe most goods display, is what we call *diminishing marginal utility*.

Table 4.1   Donuts and Jollies

Donuts	Jollies	Change in Jollies
1	10	10
2	18	8
3	24	6
4	28	4
5	30	2
6	31	1

Diminishing marginal utility explains why we don't consume just one good all the time. For any good, while consuming it makes us happier, the increment to our happiness gets smaller with every additional unit consumed. There are some goods that don't follow this pattern. Some goods, like drugs and alcohol, are famous for altering one's mental processes. They can make us want them more and more no matter how much we consume. These mind-altering substances are controlled by the laws and norms in our societies specifically because their use can lead to excess consumption and bad decisions.

There are other goods that make us happy only after we've acquired a certain amount, such as Lego blocks and Christmas lights. Still other goods' jollies depend on the consumption of a related good before they bestow happiness. I don't really enjoy gasoline if I don't own a car. We'll address some of these issues later in the chapter, but rather than looking for complications, let's use this concept of happiness to explain how we shop. (A graphical rendition of this process can be found in appendix 4.1.)

Suppose there are two goods, donuts and chewing gum, that have a similar magnitude and pattern of jollies bestowed (similar to table 4.1), and we are trying to decide how much of our limited cash—say, $3—to spend on each. To make life simple, let's suppose each donut and each pack of gum costs fifty cents. We could spend all our money on donuts. That means we could buy six donuts. The last donut would give us one jolly, according to the table. If chewing gum has a similar jolly chart, spending all our money on donuts would not be the best use of our money; I would be happier buying some units of both goods. Let's see why.

If we forgo that last donut and spend that fifty cents instead on gum, we would lose one jolly (from the forgone donut) but gain ten jollies from buying and consuming the gum. Giving up the fifth donut would feel the same. Swapping the fifth donut for another pack of gum would cost us two jollies but would give us eight jollies. The last iteration we could make that increased our happiness would be to trade the fourth donut and its four jollies for a third pack of gum and its six jollies.

This shopping process involves comparing the happiness from the last unit of each good that we buy with the price of that good. When this process is complete, when we can't make any more happiness increasing trades, what would our basket of goods look like? We would want the jollies per dollar (price) of the last unit of all goods to be about the same. Recall that the jollies from an extra unit, here the last unit, is called marginal utility. So we will have maximized our jollies when

$$\frac{\text{Marginal utility good } X}{P_x} = \frac{\text{Marginal utility good } Y}{P_Y}$$

for all goods X and Y. If another good costing fifty cents was available with a similar jolly chart, we would buy fewer donuts and packages of gum and buy a couple of units of this new good. When we shop, we simply try to combine goods in an affordable way to get the most possible jollies. The easiest way to do that is to compare the jollies we get from the last unit (or, in the case of something we might buy, the next unit) of all goods.

Since marginal utility falls as we consume more of any one good, that shopping rule implies we will usually buy a variety of things rather than a large amount of any one thing. When you look at your shopping cart at checkout time, that's generally correct. At some level, this process seems obvious, even if quantifying it is a bit controversial. But there are some well-known problems with utility maximization that need to be addressed before we move forward.

4.2 A Few Problems with Utility Maximization

The idea that we try to allocate our income to maximize our happiness seems obvious. But there are situations in which we cannot do that. One possible problem lies in our available information. To be precise, how do we know what jollies to expect from a product? If it's something we've consumed before, the answer is easier (though we still might not know the incremental jollies if we're considering a quantity we've never tried before), but what about a new product? Informing us what to expect when we consume a product is one of the reasons for marketing and advertising.

While some ads try to be funny or memorable without giving a lot of information about the product, most ads tell you how the product is better than the one you're currently using. If informing people about product attributes so that they can better maximize their jollies is indeed the point of advertising, then misinforming people must be problematic. Marketing campaigns and ads that simply lie about product attributes make utility maximization impossible. Aware of this problem, most countries have truth-in-advertising laws that outlaw such practices.

But advertisements aren't always informative in the strictest sense of the word. And they need not be. If a company hires a professional athlete or movie star to promote its product and I have a desire to align my tastes with that personality's (let's say I'm a big fan), then I will buy that product. I don't rationally believe that wearing basketball shoes promoted by the NBA's hottest star gives me his abilities on the court. Rather, they allow me to get jollies simply because I am a fan.

Utility maximization does not have to be boring and functional. We all get jollies in subtle, humanist ways. Connecting products with personalities is not lying about their attributes, and those ads do not prevent me from maximizing my jollies.

Sample Exam Question 4.1
Why do companies often give away free samples? They could advertise their goods to tell people about the goods' attributes. Why in some cases is advertising alone not enough?

Another problem occurs when we consider the available sizes of goods. The calculus version of utility maximization is given in appendix 4.2, and that rendition of the model highlights an interesting real-world problem. When we do the problem in the classroom and with calculus, utility maximization is easy because the changes we use (when we take a derivative) are infinitely small. The (usually unspoken) assumption in that version of the model is that we can buy very small sizes of all goods and thus ensure a perfect, utility-maximizing combination of all goods. Economists like this approach because it's elegant and clean. Unfortunately, it isn't correct. Nothing is sold that way.

In the real world, we have to buy large packages of most goods. We don't get to buy cookies one at a time; we buy a package of twenty or none at all. We can't open the jar and buy just a spoonful of caviar. We have to buy the entire jar. This "units" problem means our process of utility maximization is both hard and somewhat iterative. Consider the jar of caviar. Suppose you've allocated your $20 of spendable income toward a basket of, say, fifteen goods. As you are heading toward the checkout line you see a $20 jar of caviar on the shelf and you pause, because caviar is your single favorite good in the world. You look in your shopping cart, look at the jar of caviar, and walk toward the checkout line with your fifteen goods and no caviar. Why? It's your single favorite good!

Single favorite good means caviar gives you more jollies than any other single good. But buying the caviar would force you to give up fifteen goods, not just one. And the caviar does not give you more jollies than *everything* in your shopping cart. The available size of caviar, which costs $20—all your spendable income—makes it impossible for you to combine it with other goods, and so you rarely buy caviar, even though it's your single favorite good.

The most obvious place where sizes and utility maximization are a problem is at a warehouse store, such as Costco. These stores specialize in selling large quantities of goods: twenty pounds of rice or six cans of soup. A single person living alone has a problem trying to allocate her shopping dollar among a collection of goods that are all "too big." Storable goods with a fairly high turnover (e.g., paper products) might be okay, but many

Curiosity 4.1
False Advertising and Price Confusion

If advertising exists in part to help consumers maximize their jollies, other practices on the part of producers and retailers might be harder to explain. The ability of a consumer to buy more of one good and less of another in order to get as close as possible to the utility maximization rule (jollies per dollar for the last unit of all goods should be equal) assumes that the process is relatively simple. In the donut versus chewing gum example, the prices were the same, so the consumer had only to balance the incremental jollies. The caviar story introduced the "units" problem, which is really a price and units problem (the smallest available size was still so expensive that the consumer would have had to give up too many other goods to purchase the caviar).

But how does a consumer maximize her utility if she can't even figure out the price? Sometimes stores have sale prices that are truly difficult to understand. Canned tuna is on sale, seven cans for $10. What's the price per can? Many people can't divide ten by seven in their head. Not knowing the price per unit, much like being misinformed by false advertisements, makes utility maximization impossible. The odd thing about this price confusion strategy is it doesn't obviously lead to higher sales of the good. False advertising, at least in the short run, will allow the producer to sell more goods. Price confusion could go either way. Not knowing the correct price per unit, I might buy more than I wanted to, but I also might buy less.

food products get wasted. So even at the warehouse store's lower price, a single person doesn't shop there much.

The size of caviar problem also applies to collections of goods, such as the earlier mentioned Lego blocks or Christmas lights. As a rule, we don't buy Lego blocks or Christmas lights one at a time. We buy these goods in collections or pairs, and therefore at a higher price. That makes these goods harder to fit into a utility-maximized combination of goods, but that's the nature of those goods. Collections or collectibles are often cited as an exception to diminishing utility. It is argued that getting the tenth of a ten-part set of things does, in fact, give you more jollies than getting the ninth. That might be true, but one could argue the actual "good" is the set, not each part.

Sample Exam Question 4.2
Arguably, coins are among the lowest-cost and thus easiest to enjoy collectibles. Why?

4.3   Cardinal versus Ordinal Utility

The version of utility maximization we have followed so far is an example of *cardinal* utility: a ranking based on a specific number of jollies that we get from different levels of consumption. Many economists argue that we don't really know that; we don't know the exact number of jollies across all levels of all goods. The alternative that they prefer is *ordinal* utility: an ability to say that we prefer one thing to another, but not with exact levels of jollies. The difference is subtle and important to economists (probably more than to students and those looking to apply these concepts).

In an ordinal ranking of donuts and gum, we don't know the exact number of jollies associated with each, so we can't use diminishing marginal utility. Instead, it is argued, we feel a different desire to trade gum for donuts as our level of consumption changes. If we have a lot of gum and not many donuts, we would not be willing to exchange many of our scarce donuts for an additional piece of gum. In appendix 4.2, we relate this desire to exchange one good for another (called the *marginal rate of substitution*) to the marginal utility of each good.

Whether in its cardinal or ordinal version, utility is a model that tries to formalize the process we go through when we shop. That it is imperfect is not in question; all models are imperfect. But both the cardinal and the ordinal versions of the model fit the observations of consumer behavior that we're trying to explain.

Most economists agree with some version of the utility-based model. It is also true that we cannot compare one person's utility, measured cardinally or ordinally, to any other person's utility. Jollies are idiosyncratic. The donut-loving author's jollies in table 4.1 range from ten to forty-one. Your donut jollies might start with 100 or 1,000 and rise from there. The important thing for explaining consumer behavior is not where it starts, it is what happens as we change our level of consumption. Jollies rise at a decreasing rate, what we called diminishing marginal utility.

Since jollies are specific to one person and the goods that person is considering consuming, we can't compare jollies across people. If your jollies start at 1,000 and rise (across six donuts) to 1,041, one might assume you like donuts more than I do. We can't know that. Cardinal jollies are useful for seeing the pattern, but they can't be used to compare across individuals.

This is an important point. It means we can't look at one person—let's call him Bill—who has chosen to consume twenty donuts and another, Jane, who has chosen to consume two donuts and say anything about their comparative overall happiness; we can't say whether the consumer of twenty donuts is overall happier than the consumer of two. We simply don't know that. As such, we can't judge whether the two of them would be better off if we took one donut from Bill and gave it to Jane.

But we don't need to compare the exact number of jollies across different people in order to use this approach for understanding overall consumer behavior and the demand line.

All we need is the pattern of change of jollies to be the same across all people; we need happiness rising at a decreasing rate from whatever number or level happiness starts at.

4.4   Behind the Demand Line: How Utility Maximization Explains the Demand Line

Consumer theory and utility are how economists explain the observed inverse relationship between price and quantity demanded—a downward-sloping demand line—for most goods. Let's see how. We get jollies from consumption, and we try to allocate our spendable income so that we maximize those jollies. That process tells us to spend our money across all goods until the increment to our happiness—the marginal utility—is the same per dollar for all goods. Put differently, we would spend our last dollar on the good that we can buy for a dollar that gives us the most extra jollies.

Suppose we've done that allocation the best we can, taking into account the problems we discussed in section 4.2, and suddenly the price of good X falls. Good X now becomes a cheaper source of additional jollies. (We didn't highlight it in chapter 2, but along any demand line we're assuming that the only price that's changing is the price of good X.)

In our earlier example, the utility-maximizing allocation of our $3 was three donuts and three packs of gum when each cost fifty cents. If the price of a pack of gum fell to twenty-five cents (and the price of a donut stayed at fifty cents), we would give up the third donut and buy at least two more packs of gum. When we make that change, we lose six jollies from donuts and add six jollies from gum (four jollies from the fourth pack plus two jollies from the fifth pack), but we have twenty-five cents left over with which we can buy another pack of gum or any other jolly-producing, twenty-five-cent product.

Let's consider the caviar problem from section 4.2 again: every good becomes easier to buy and easier to buy more of when its price decreases. In appendix 4.3, we show how we can use consumer theory and the concept of utility maximization to incorporate the income and substitution effects that we described in chapter 2.

4.5   Substitutes and Complements

When we talked about the jollies that we get from donuts and chewing gum, we discussed the jollies that we get from either of them independent of one another. In doing so, we were treating these goods as substitutes. By that we mean the jollies we get from donuts are independent of the jollies we get from chewing gum. This is a different perspective on substitution than the one we invoked in the derivation of the demand line. There we said that other fruit was a substitute for apples. Here we're saying any other good we could spend our money on is a substitute for donuts from the utility-maximizing perspective.

The distinction we want to make here is between goods that are *substitutes* (independent sources of happiness) and goods that are *complements*. There are many goods whose consumption and corresponding happiness are interdependent: the jollies I get from X rise if I also consume some Y. For example, I don't need much (any!) gasoline if I don't own a car. However, I might enjoy my donuts more if I had them with a cup of coffee. Goods like these are known as complements. They tend to be consumed together, and the jollies that we get are from consuming a combination of them. Clearly, having some goods as complements makes utility maximization harder, or at least harder to explain.

The easiest way to deal with this is to return to the Lego set and shoe example from section 4.2. Some goods give us jollies only after we have a critical mass: a pair of shoes or a set of Legos. After allowing for that, we differentiate between which set of Legos or pair of shoes gives us the most initial jollies (and we pretty much require the pair of shoes be the same type of shoe). So our internal jolly calculator is capable of combining individual units into sets and determining the jollies of every combination (perhaps with some trial and error or other learning processes). Complementary goods can be analyzed in the same way. I get some jollies from the individual goods, but more jollies from certain combinations of goods. If they both cost the same per unit (say, $1), I might get more jollies from two donuts and one cup of coffee than from any other combination of those

Curiosity 4.2
Consumer Surplus

Another demand-side concept that we can describe is called *consumer surplus*. When the market finds its equilibrium price, as described in chapter 2 and now augmented in this chapter, it is finding the price that the marginal consumer is willing to pay. That is, there is usually one price for every good on the store shelf: the price at the intersection of supply and demand. But the demand line has many other prices. In particular, there are prices higher than the equilibrium price. This means there are consumers who were willing to pay more for the good but didn't have to because the equilibrium price represents only the jollies of the last consumer.

Every combination of price and quantity for prices higher than the equilibrium price represents a higher-value transaction that didn't take place because all consumers were able to buy at the lower, equilibrium price. We can show this value as the area under the demand line and above the equilibrium price in figure 4.1, and we call that area the consumer surplus. It's the value consumers were willing to pay for a good but did not have to pay.

The assumption behind the existence of consumer surplus is that all consumers pay one price. If the seller can customize the price and charge each consumer the price the customer is willing to pay, the seller can capture this consumer surplus. This practice is, curiously, both an old one and a new one. When retail was primarily individual proprietors, similar to today's farmers markets, a lot of haggling and bargaining went on. Prices might not have been publicly posted. Instead, the vendor would tell you an initial price, you would offer a lower price, and the final price would usually be somewhere in between. No two customers would pay the same price. The vendor was trying to capture more of the consumer surplus. Modern online retailers have tried to do the same thing by using your personal profile to guess at the highest price you are willing to pay.

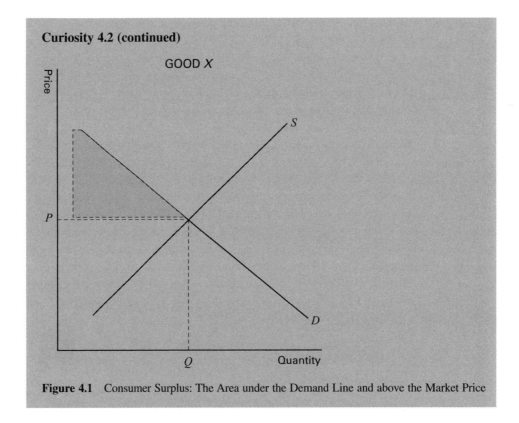

Curiosity 4.2 (continued)

GOOD *X*

Figure 4.1   Consumer Surplus: The Area under the Demand Line and above the Market Price

goods. So, if I've decided to spend $3 on coffee and donuts, that combination would be my choice. I would then compare the total jollies from two donuts and one cup of coffee to the total jollies from all other goods or combinations of goods that cost $3.

We all know many goods that have become staples of our diet by being complements to many other goods. Seasonings, condiments, and bread are all things we usually use with other goods. We learn how to combine goods and determine combined jollies. As is true of a lot of other aspects of utility maximization, dealing with goods that are complements is tricky, and the math behind the maximization becomes more complex, but the logic is relatively straightforward.

Examples

Example 1   The Federal Communications Commission allows most legal products to be advertised on television and in other public media, but not cigarettes. Cigarette television commercials have been banned since 1970.

Why cigarettes? There are commercials for beer, junk food, and other products on TV that are also arguably dangerous.

Some jollies are more problematic than others. The jollies people get from cigarettes often lead to future "bads" (negative jollies?), such as cancer. In addition, the nicotine in cigarettes is highly addictive, and the level of addiction appears to be stronger if you start smoking at a young age. The commercial ban is intended to stop children from smoking.

Example 2   A commercial aired recently that suggested coffee shops are a substitute for your internet service provider. The gist was that people with slow internet at home try to use the free coffee shop internet instead. The commercial was trying to get people to use a particular (supposedly faster) internet service provider at home.

At first blush, it doesn't make sense that a coffee shop should be a substitute for a home internet service, but if we focus on the attainment of jollies and opportunity cost pricing, that relationship makes sense. Explain.

There are many ways to get jollies. Think of all the things you could eat for dinner tonight; for example, all of which give you dinner jollies. The "good" in this case is the ability to access the internet. The commercial (aired by an internet service provider) suggests that the opportunity cost—the time, irritation, noisy atmosphere, and so on—associated with using the coffee shop's internet is actually higher than you think, and thus you should be willing to pay for its more convenient, just-as-fast home service.

Commercials often focus on the attributes of a good and try to convince you that one good gives you more jollies than another, but they may also, as in this case, remind you that an alternative you think of as free isn't really free.

Example 3   There's an old jingle for a brand of margarine that goes "Everything's better with Blue Bonnet on it." This is a catchy, rhyming jingle that certainly promoted brand recognition.

In addition to brand recognition, what other aspect of the jingle would promote sales?
"Everything's better." This ad is trying to make this product a complement to as many foods as possible. By doing so, the ad makes people believe that the jollies they get from "everything" they put this product on will increase. If this incentivization works, people would be willing to pay for the product, knowing there are extra jollies from consuming everything they put it on.

Chapter Summary

- We used the observation that consumers do not consume huge quantities of the same good at any one time to develop a utility model of happiness. This model posits that for most goods, happiness rises at a decreasing rate. We call this pattern diminishing marginal utility.

- Using this utility pattern, which is a normal part of consumer behavior, we determined that happiness is maximized when we consume all goods until the marginal utility of the last unit divided by the price of that good is equal across all goods.

- Precise utility maximization is difficult to realize in practice because we don't have perfect information about the happiness-generating attributes of all goods, and the available sizes of some goods make them harder to buy.
- While consumer theory and utility maximization are abstractions, they help us understand why we usually buy more of a good when its price falls.

Exercises

(B exercises are more challenging.)

A4.1 The hardest goods to introduce to the market are the ones that are completely new (i.e., have no close substitutes), offer limited ability to sample or test drive, and are expensive. Why?

A4.2 It's okay for advertisements to show a movie star drinking a particular brand of beer. It's not okay for the movie star to say, "Drinking this beer will make you a movie star like me." Why?

A4.3 It's not unusual for people to take things out of their shopping cart and substitute other things as they wander through the grocery store. Why do people do this?

A4.4 Government agencies like the Food and Drug Administration often ban food additives and other ingredients that are deemed dangerous. Why ban them? Why not just tell consumers that the ingredients are dangerous?

A4.5 Binge-watching the entire season of a streamed TV series would appear to violate diminishing marginal utility. Try to explain it (everyone else has seen it). Are you more likely to binge-watch things on weekends or on work or school nights? Why?

A4.6 Assuming you need the goods sold there, why might it be easier to maximize your utility when you shop at a dollar store (where everything costs $1)?

A4.6 To the user, drugs like cocaine and heroin seem to have increasing marginal utility. If that's true, why are some people who are addicted to such drugs often unhealthy and homeless?

A4.7 Once upon a time, the predominant method for distributing recorded music was in the form of a record album (or tape) that had ten or so songs on it. Now, songs are sold over streaming services one at a time. True or false, and explain your answer: It's easier for new artists to get people to pay for their music now.

A4.8   Why do people usually eat too much at an all-you-can-eat buffet? What price do we ignore when doing so?

A4.9   If laws against shoplifting are not enforced, honest customers will find it harder to maximize their utility. Explain.

A4.10   We observe that people save some of their income for the future. How can we explain this observed behavior using the concepts of utility and diminishing marginal utility?

B4.1   This morning, you consumed donuts and coffee at levels where the marginal utility of the last donut was ten and the marginal utility of the last cup of coffee was five. Donuts cost $1.00 each and coffee costs fifty cents per cup. Have you maximized your utility? If you don't know any more than this information (and that you have no extra money available for breakfast), describe a change in your purchase that should make you *happier*. *Note:* Given how little information you have, you should consider only a one-unit change in each good.

B4.2   Video streaming services and inexpensive, large flat-screen TVs are an enormous threat to movie theaters. Taking into account the price of watching and enjoying each movie, explain why.

B4.3   Several new online retailers have popped up trying to make the car-buying process easier. They claim you just pick out your car on the website and it is delivered to your door. This method probably works best for repeat buyers—people replacing a car with a new version of the same model. Why?

B4.4   When a company introduces a new cookie in the existing competitive, well-established cookie industry, it will have a better chance of success if the new cookie is initially sold in comparatively small packages or at lower prices. Why?

B4.5   When I ask students to suggest a good that does not have diminishing marginal utility, often someone suggests money itself. Consider Bill Gates, billionaire founder of Microsoft. While we aren't supposed to look at goods over time when we measure jollies, discuss the marginal utility of, say, $1,000 for Bill Gates now versus the same $1,000 dollars when he was a twenty-year-old college dropout in the 1970s.

Appendix 4.1   Utility Maximization Graph

The graphical approach to utility maximization begins with a new graph, the indifference curve. For any two goods, our earlier donuts and chewing gum will suffice. We can graph

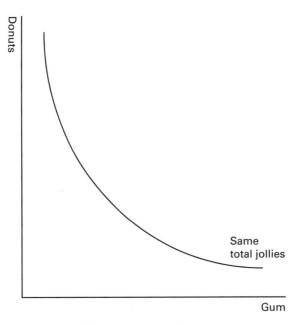

Figure 4.2   Indifference Curve for Donuts and Gum

all the combinations of the goods that give us the same total jollies. Suppose we wanted to find all combinations that gave us sixty-eight jollies, the total we'd have if we started with three of each good. We could stay at sixty-eight by giving up a little bit of a donut and adding a little gum, but if we gave up one entire donut, we'd have to add two more gums. The reason is diminishing marginal utility working in opposite directions for each good. As we give up a donut, we lose a lot of jollies, and as we add gum, we don't get many jollies back. The implication of this is the trade-off, which we call the *indifference curve*, and it is indeed a curve—not a straight line—as we see in figure 4.2

To derive the utility maximization condition, we need to know the slope of the indifference curve. The slope is the change in the good on the vertical axis, donuts, divided by the change in the good on the horizontal axis, gum. We know that total utility is constant along the indifference curve, so the jollies we get by (say) increasing our consumption of donuts must be balanced by the jollies we give up when we decrease our consumption of gum. For small changes, these jolly increments are the marginal utilities. So the slope of the indifference curve at any point on the curve is given by:

$$d\text{Donuts}/d\text{Gum} = -MU_{\text{Gum}}/MU_{\text{Donuts}}.$$

What we ultimately want is to reach the highest indifference curve that we can afford, so we need to map out what's affordable. For simplicity, let's assume we have a fixed

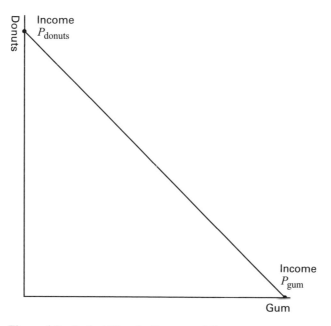

Figure 4.3   Budget Line for Donuts and Gum

amount of money—our spendable income—available for shopping today. Combining that spendable income with the prices of donuts and gum, we can derive what's called the budget line:

Spendable income $= P_{Donuts} \times$ Donuts $+ P_{Gum} \times$ Gum,

and graph this line to demarcate the combinations of donuts and gum that are affordable (see figure 4.3).

This graph is easy to draw. The endpoints are our spendable income divided by each price; then we simply connect those endpoints. The slope of the budget line is also easy: it's the ratio of the endpoints, which turns out to be:

dDonuts$/d$Gum $= -P_{Gum}/P_{Donuts}.$

Finding the highest affordable indifference curve means we find the curve that just touches (is tangent to) the budget line. When a curve is tangent to a line, they have the same slope, so the utility maximization condition would be to find the combination of goods where the ratio of marginal utilities equals the ratio of prices, and we've spent all our spendable income, as shown in figure 4.4.

$MU_{Gum}/MU_{Donuts} = P_{Gum}/P_{Donuts}.$

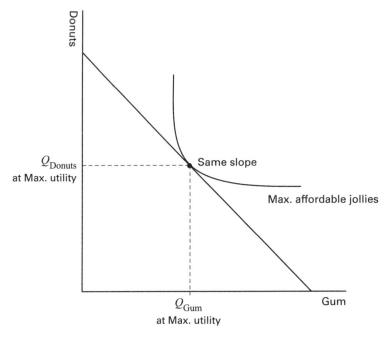

Figure 4.4   Utility Maximization

Spendable income = $P_{\text{Donuts}} \times$ Donuts $+ P_{\text{Gum}} \times$ Gum.

If we rearrange the first condition, we get the utility maximization condition from section 4.1:

$$\frac{\text{Marginal Utility}_{\text{Gum}}}{P_{\text{Gum}}} = \frac{\text{Marginal Utility}_{\text{Donuts}}}{P_{\text{Donuts}}}.$$

Sample Exam Question 4.3
Looking at the graphical version of utility maximization, and assuming you could always get away with it without having any guilt or regrets, doesn't stealing donuts and gum always increase your happiness?

Appendix 4.2   Utility Maximization Calculus

The mathematical version of utility maximization usually starts with an equation that calculates jollies; a utility equation. Everything about this equation is controversial if you get too specific. The fact is, we never know how people get their jollies well enough to write a formal equation. Our observations tell us that jollies rise at a decreasing rate, so that says something about the form of the equation. We're assuming the jollies for these two goods are independent. Beyond that we're guessing.

For donuts, we could guess:

Donut jollies = 10 Donuts − Donuts^2,

which has jollies that rise at a decreasing rate, but beyond a certain point (starting with the sixth donut), jollies actually decline as you eat more donuts. While that might be true, we can't say that we know that about any particular good.

It's usually safer if we don't get specific and instead write the utility equation in what's called its implicit form:

Jollies = U(Donuts),

meaning there is a calculation going on in our head when we eat donuts, but we don't know exactly what it is. We can say that this implicit equation has to have jollies that rise at a decreasing rate. That's a simple matter of saying the change in jollies—what we earlier called the marginal utility—has to be positive.

In calculus, we calculate a change by taking the first derivative:

dJollies/dDonuts > 0,

and we would calculate the change in that marginal utility by taking the first derivative of that equation or the second derivative of the utility equation:

d^2Jollies/dDonuts^2 < 0.

By saying the first derivative is positive and the second derivative is negative, we are saying that whatever the form of the utility equation might be, it has jollies that increase at a decreasing rate. These restrictions on the utility equation allow us to apply an important calculus result. In general, if you want to maximize an equation, you take the derivative of the equation and set that derivative equal to zero. That works because you want to find the last unit (remember, the derivative is a change, so an extra donut or gum) that makes your jollies rise. That last unit will add an infinitely small amount, approximately zero, to your jollies.

We can also use an implicit form for the utility equation for both donuts and gum:

Jollies = U(Donuts, Gum),

where, once again, we don't know the exact form of the equation, but we want it to have a positive first derivative and a negative second derivative for both donuts and gum.

We want to maximize this utility equation—take the derivative of it relative to both goods, and set both those derivatives to zero—but are constrained by our budget:

Income $= P_D D + P_G G,$

or

Income $- P_D D - P_G G = 0.$

(For simplicity, we'll assume income here is what we have to spend on these goods today, and we spend it all. Economists would say we're assuming the budget constraint holds perfectly.)

Maximizing the utility equation subject to the budget constraint can be done by combining the utility equation and the constraint into one new equation, like this:

$L = U(\text{Donuts, Gum}) = k(\text{Income} - P_D D - P_G G)$

(called a Lagrange equation, for the mathematician who invented this approach).

We maximize our utility by taking the derivative of this Lagrange equation relative to each good and setting both derivatives equal to zero:

$dL/d\text{Donuts} = dU/d\text{Donuts} - kP_D = 0,$

$dL/d\text{Gum} = dU/d\text{Gum} - kP_G = 0.$

We can rewrite each of these as:

$$\frac{dU/d\text{Donuts}}{P_G} = k,$$

and since they both equal k, they must equal each other:

$$\frac{dU/d\text{Donuts}}{P_D} = \frac{dU/d\text{Gum}}{P_G}.$$

This is the same condition (together with meeting the budget constraint) for utility maximization that we got in the graphical approach in appendix 4.1 and in the intuitive approach in section 4.1. We try to consume all goods such that the ratio of marginal utility to the price of the last unit of all goods is equal.

The controversy over ordinal versus cardinal utility and the reality that utility can't ever be measured for anyone has led many economists to shy away from even marginal utility as a measurable construct. Still, there must be something that we use when we shop and make choices. To this end, many economists prefer writing this utility maximization condition as:

$dU/d\text{Donuts} = P_D,$

$dU/d\text{Gum } P_G,$

where the marginal utility ratio, called the marginal rate of substitution between donuts and gum, is all we know. This marginal rate of substitution is a relative measure of jollies—how much we currently like donuts relative to gum—rather than an absolute number of jollies for either good.

One could argue that we don't really know the marginal rate of substitution either. All of this is abstracting from reality. We know (or we think we know!) the observation that consumers don't usually consume a lot of just one good at any one time. From that, the rest is a model that we can use to explain the demand line. Since our desire is to communicate the essentials of microeconomics, we'll leave that debate to others.

Appendix 4.3   Deriving the Demand Line and Inferior Goods

Using the graphical approach to utility maximization from appendix 4.1, we can derive the demand line for donuts. Recall that the demand line shows the relationship between price and quantity demanded for any one good. To get that for any one person, we start with that person's utility maximization for one set of prices and one level of income, as shown in figure 4.5.

We then decrease the price of gum, the good on the horizontal axis, from the initial price of P_1 to P_2 and then P_3. Recall the endpoint of this graph is Income/Price, so when we decrease the price, we move the endpoint of the line to the right (the line gets flatter.) As we did in appendix 4.1, we find the indifference curve that is tangent to each new budget line and observe the increase in the quantity of gum on the horizontal axis. Mapping these price-quantity combinations onto a graph, we get this consumer's demand for gum (see figure 4.6):

If we do this for every consumer and add up the quantity demanded at all prices, we get the market demand.

While we have this derivation in front of us, we can talk about another interesting concept. Suppose that instead of changing the price of either good, we increase the amount of income this consumer has to spend. That would shift the budget line parallel to the right, allowing this person to consume more of both goods. If the quantity demanded of a good increases when you get more income, we say it is a *normal good*. Recalling the description of the income and substitution effects in chapter 2, we can isolate the income effect by changing income and we can say that normal goods have a positive income effect.

Not all goods are normal goods, however. There are goods that we actually want less of as our income rises. Popularly in economics books, we say turnips are such a good. You may eat them when you are poor, but not when you are wealthier (arguably, economists are showing a certain amount of snobbery when they use this as an example). If the quantity demanded of a good falls as we increase income, we say that good is an *inferior good*. We can show an inferior good on our maximization graph. In figure 4.7 we've replaced gum with turnips to show how it's possible for the tangency to be further to the left after we increase income.

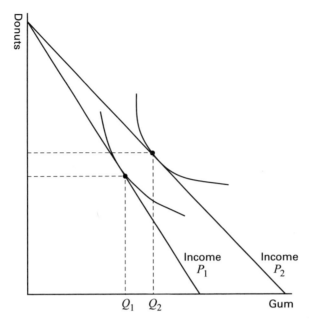

Figure 4.5   Decrease in the Price of Gum

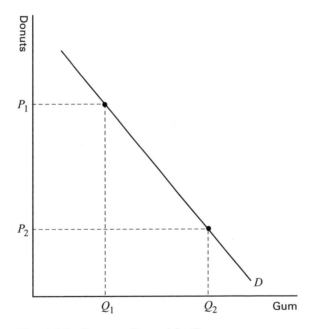

Figure 4.6   Consumer Demand for Gum

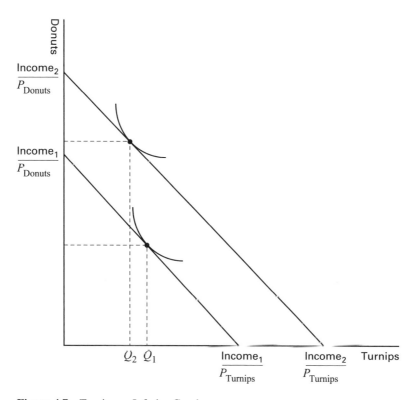

Figure 4.7   Turnips as Inferior Goods

For normal goods, the income and substitution effects augment each other. When the price of a good falls, the substitution effect always says you should consume more of it, and since that decrease in price will give the consumer more available income (because all the units you previously bought now cost less), some of that additional income will also be used to buy more of this good (and all other normal goods).

An interesting possibility exists for inferior goods. When the price of an inferior good falls, the substitution effect still says one should buy more of it but the income effect says one should buy less of it. That means, for any given price change, inferior goods have a small change in quantity demanded. It's even possible, though very rare, for an inferior good to have an upward-sloping demand line! When the price goes down, you actually consume less of the good. That would happen if the good is inferior and the income effect is actually bigger than the substitution effect. "Possible" isn't the same thing as "probable." There aren't any consistent cases of goods with upward-sloping demand lines out there.

5   Behind the Supply Line: Theory of the Firm

When we discussed the supply line in chapter 2, we said that producers usually increase their output as prices rise. The rationale was that producers could afford more inputs if they could sell their goods for a higher price. That intuition makes the critical connection between price and the cost of production. While the nuance of this connection needs fleshing out, most businesspeople know the simple reality behind this connection. If you ask the owners of a pizza parlor why the price of a pizza is a lot less than the price of an automobile, they would simply say it costs a lot less to produce a pizza.

But when we made that connection in chapter 2, we set aside a lot of the story. Most notably, which costs do producers use to determine the level of production? There are many ways to calculate costs. Since price is a per-unit measure, we should be looking for a measure of cost per unit, but there are a couple of ways to calculate that. We will zero in on the relevant costs for a firm's production decision and talk about how that decision depends on the time frame that decision-makers use.

In many microeconomics books, *theory of the firm* is famously confusing because of the multitude of approaches we can take for measuring costs. Add to that the tendency of microeconomics book authors to use confusing graphs to teach theory of the firm and you're looking at an important if rather intuitive set of concepts that gets lost in the mire. We will use a blend of graphs and charts to make the concepts resonate. But the easiest way to keep things straight is to remember a simple idea: firms should not make any production decision that actively increases losses or decreases profits.

On completion of this chapter, you should

- understand fixed and variable costs,
- understand average and marginal costs, and
- see why marginal cost, with some conditions, is the cost that firms use to determine production.

5.1   So Many Costs, So Little Time

As part of their production process, most businesses employ two distinctly different types of inputs. Fixed inputs, while not literally fixed forever, are ones that are hard to change quickly. They include things like the factory or other buildings, large machinery and equipment, and the field in which the crops are planted. These factors take time—usually years—to create and thus take time to change. In making immediate production decisions, the firm generally assumes these fixed factors cannot be changed.

Businesses also use many factors of production that can be changed quickly. Labor, utilities, such as electricity and water, and most raw materials can be added or subtracted in a matter of days. These variable inputs are the ones that a firm adjusts when it changes its output in the short run.

Associated with these fixed and variable inputs are fixed and variable costs. *Fixed costs* are the expenditures the firm makes when it builds a factory, acquires land, or buys machinery. In making the immediate decision about how much to produce, the firm views these fixed costs as, well, fixed. *Variable costs* include the cost of hiring more labor, the cost of electricity or water, or the cost of raw materials. By their nature, these costs rise and fall as the firm expands or shrinks its level of production.

Let's return to the farm, this time looking at a strawberry field, and try to sort out these costs and how the firm, or the farm, should use them to make production decisions. As we did in chapter 2, let's look at the last part of the production process, picking strawberries, and let's create a chart with the fixed and variable costs associated with various levels of strawberry picking. In table 5.1, we show fixed costs of one hundred for any amount (number of truckloads) of strawberries that are picked from our current field. This is the cost of the fixed inputs, such as the land on which the strawberries grow. When we are considering how many strawberries to pick, a lot of things are actually unchangeable. All the costs of planting and growing the berries have been paid and are now fixed. For reasons that will be clear when we discuss average cost, we focus on the cost of the land, but there are actually many costs that would be considered fixed costs when the strawberries are ready to be picked.

Table 5.1

Quantity	FC	VC	TC
1	100	10	110
2	100	30	130
3	100	60	160
4	100	100	200
5	100	150	250
6	100	210	310
7	100	280	380

Note: Quantity in truckloads; costs in $ thousands. FC, fixed costs; VC, variable costs; TC, total costs.

Unlike fixed costs, variable costs are shown in table 5.1 as increasing as we pick more strawberries. In fact, we've shown variable costs rising at an increasing rate. That's something we observe in most businesses; it's caused by the change in the productivity of labor as we increase the level of production.

In our strawberry field, the problem looks like this. Our field has seven truckloads of strawberries in it. When we pick the first truckload, laborers can move quickly down each row and pick the most accessible berries. Picking the second truckload will require more labor, but laborers will also have to take more time; the most accessible berries have already been picked. Picking the fifth or sixth truckload will take a lot more labor and time. The workers will have to pick berries that are much less accessible, and because there are so many laborers in the field now, they are getting in each other's way to some extent. Picking all the remaining strawberries for the last truckload of berries will take a lot of labor and time.

The observation that variable costs rise at an increasing rate actually results from an interaction between our variable factor and a fixed factor. For any field size (fixed factor), the productivity of labor declines as more labor (variable factor) is crammed onto the land. That decrease in labor productivity means that reaching capacity, producing the last feasible units, will require a lot of extra labor. This is a seeming contradiction, but the strawberry field helps us understand. Suppose there are seven truckloads of strawberries in the field, and six truckloads have already been picked. Picking the last truckload means looking at every plant to get every last strawberry. That would certainly take a lot of labor and a lot of time. We will revisit this explanation for increasing variable costs in chapter 10 when we discuss the diminishing marginal product of labor.

Increasing variable cost has some workarounds in the real world. It's possible that, as we add more labor, we can specialize the work that labor is doing. That would likely increase productivity initially. Similarly, we could change technology or add more of the fixed factor (a bigger field or more equipment) to increase labor productivity. We discuss

Table 5.2

Quantity	FC	VC	TC	AC
1	100	10	110	110
2	100	30	130	65
3	100	60	160	53
4	100	100	200	50
5	100	150	250	50
6	100	210	310	52
7	100	280	380	54

Note: Quantity in truckloads; costs in $ thousands. FC, fixed costs; VC, variable costs, TC, total cost; AC, average cost.

these things later in the chapter. For now, let's see how increasing variable costs helps us determine the firm's level of production.

5.2   Average and Marginal Cost

There are two ways we can imagine calculating cost per unit. One way is to calculate *average cost*. Average anything is calculated by dividing a total by the number of units used to create that total. In the case of average cost, we would add all fixed and variable costs together to get total cost and divide that total by the number of truckloads. Table 5.2 shows the total and average cost for our seven truckloads of strawberries.

As is the case for most firms' production, the average cost of picking strawberries (producing some number of units) starts high, falls to some minimum, and begins to rise again. So common is this pattern that economists have names for the falling and rising phases of average cost. If average cost is falling as the firm grows, we say the firm is experiencing *economies of scale*. If asked to explain this observation, we would say that the firm's fixed costs are being spread over an increased number of units. In our strawberry field example, the total cost of producing the first truckload berries includes all the fixed costs. When we expand to a second truckload of berries, the fixed costs are now divided between the two truckloads. So economies of scale happen during a firm's initial expansion because the firm can distribute overhead across more units.

The increase in average cost that occurs when the firm starts to reach capacity is called diseconomies of scale. These increasing costs are due to rapidly rising variable costs. More precisely, variable costs were rising even as the firm expanded from producing one truckload to two, but the cost saving the firm experienced in splitting its fixed costs over two truckloads overwhelmed the increase in variable costs. Closer to capacity, the cost saving from spreading fixed costs over more units of production is much smaller, and now variable costs are rising much faster, thus increasing average costs. Average cost is

Table 5.3

Quantity	FC	VC	TC	AC	MC
1	100	10	110	110	—
2	100	30	130	65	20
3	100	60	160	53	30
4	100	100	200	50	40
5	100	150	250	50	50
6	100	210	310	52	60
7	100	280	380	54	70

Note: Quantity in truckloads; costs in $ thousands. FC, fixed costs; VC, variable costs, AC, average cost; MC, marginal cost.

an important determinant of long-run output and optimum firm size, and a concept we revisit in section 5.4 and appendix 5.1.

The other way we can imagine calculating cost per unit is by figuring *marginal cost.* Marginal anything is the cost of the next (or last) unit. So marginal cost is the change in total cost as we increase our production. We've calculated marginal cost for our strawberry field in table 5.3.

Notice we didn't calculate the marginal cost of the first truckload of strawberries. That calculation is problematic. For every level of output after the first unit, marginal cost is simply the increment or change in total cost. For the first unit, it isn't quite that simple. If we haven't acquired the fixed cost yet, the marginal cost of the first unit would be the total cost of the first unit, or 110,000. If we have paid the fixed costs, then the marginal cost of the first unit is 10,000 (but that wouldn't look like the change from zero to one). For now, let's leave the marginal cost of the first unit blank.

Armed with these various measures of cost per unit, let's figure out how firms should determine their level of output. Suppose a buyer for a grocery store drove up to the straw-berry farm and offered to buy four truckloads of strawberries for $40,000 per truckload. Let's assume further that this store is usually your only customer. Would you accept this offer?

Looking at the costs associated with picking four truckloads, you see that the average cost is $50,000—higher than the price being offered, but the marginal cost is $40,000—the same as the price. If you pay attention to average cost, you would turn down this offer. If you pay attention to marginal cost, you would accept it. Which of these costs per unit do you use in making this decision?

Remember how we calculated these costs. Average cost includes fixed costs, which you've already paid. Marginal cost includes only variable costs. If you turn this offer down because average cost is higher than the price at that level of output, you're still out your fixed costs. If you accept the deal, knowing that marginal costs are rising, you are assured of breaking even on the cost of picking the last truckload *and* you are assured of making money on each of the first three truckloads.

Putting this together, if you say no, you lose $100 (all of your fixed costs). If you accept, you make a combined $60,000 more than your variable costs, minus the fixed cost of $100,000. Your loss is only $40,000. You're going to lose money on this deal. The way to minimize your loss is to produce every unit that covers its marginal cost and, in the short run, ignore average cost.

That result is powerful. It means, among other things, that marginal cost is the supply line. But the very logic that got us to that result also leads us to some exceptions and clarifications. Specifically, the firm would produce where price equals marginal cost in the short run because fixed costs have already been paid. If the firm knows before planting that price will not cover average cost, then it will not grow any strawberries. So marginal cost is the supply line in the short run, or only if fixed costs are already paid. And even that production rule might need amending. If we expand our concept of variable costs, we can get a short-run shutdown rule as well.

> **Sample Exam Question 5.1**
> You have worked all year to grow fifty pounds of organic tomatoes. They are ready to be picked. The fixed cost is $100. Your only customer is offering you $2 per pound for the entire crop. Should you accept the offer?

5.3   Average Variable Cost

Determining output based on marginal costs can be boiled down to two factors. First, your fixed costs are already paid, so they won't enter into your short-run production decision. Second, marginal cost is the extra cost of an extra unit. It comes entirely from variable costs. If we already know we're going to lose money this year (as is the case for our strawberry farm), our focus should be on decreasing that loss. We shouldn't produce any unit that makes the loss grow. Choosing to produce where price equals marginal cost does just that under normal circumstances (rising marginal costs). Or does it?

Suppose our variable costs started at a much higher level, as shown in table 5.4. Perhaps labor has a powerful union that has pushed labor costs up. Notice that while variable costs start higher, the increments to variable costs are the same. Since the increments are the same, marginal costs are the same, and the marginal cost rule would say that the firm should produce four truckloads of strawberries if the price is still $40,000 per truckload. But that level of output no longer minimizes the firm's loss. Let's look at the losses under two scenarios. If the farm sells four truckloads at a price of $40,000 per truckload, its revenue is $160,000. The total cost of producing four truckloads is now $300,000. Thus, selling four truckloads will result in a loss of $140,000. Not picking any strawberries at all will result in a loss of only $100,000. In this case, the firm should turn down the deal.

Table 5.4

Quantity	FC	VC	TC	AC	MC	AVC
1	100	110	210	210	—	110
2	100	130	230	165	20	65
3	100	160	260	87	30	53
4	100	200	300	75	40	50
5	100	250	350	70	50	50
6	100	310	410	68	60	52
7	100	380	480	69	70	54

Note: Quantity in truckloads; costs in $ thousands. FC, fixed costs; VC, variable costs, TC, total costs; AC, average cost; MC, marginal cost; AVC, average variable cost.

Our production rule needs to be amended. The firm should sell every unit whose price covers its marginal cost and whose price covers *average variable cost*, where average variable cost is simply total variable costs divided by total quantity (output units). Like marginal costs, average variable cost is avoidable in the short run simply by not producing the last unit.

With so many measures of cost floating around, confusion usually sets in at this point. But notice that the logic hasn't changed even if the rule has. All variable costs are avoidable in the short run. Fixed costs have already been paid; variable costs have not. If variable costs start at a high level, the firm might choose simply to shut down rather than produce any output. Indeed, a price less than average variable cost can be called a shutdown rule.

Doesn't that mean the farm would be better off plowing its crop under and not picking any strawberries? It does indeed, and this has been known to happen. Abstracting from the many definitions and production rules, it is entirely possible that the market price at which producers can sell their goods has fallen so low that the strawberry farm would lose additional money (remember, the farm owners—producers—are already paying all the farm's fixed costs) if it picked any strawberries. In that case, the farm owners would plow the field under and hope for something better next year.

The production rule at this point is the firm should produce in the short run up to the point where price equals marginal cost as long as price also exceeds average variable costs. In the long run, the firm will produce where price equals marginal cost as long as price exceeds (total) average cost.

Sample Exam Question 5.2
Manufacturing businesses that need factories and machines are more likely to experience short-term losses than service businesses that need only people (labor). Why?

Curiosity 5.1
Short, Long, and All Other Runs

A popular question at about this time in your class is, how long is the short or long run? The correct and often frustrating answer is that it depends on the business, but the better way to think about the timing and the cost definitions is with the intuition behind the production rules.

Frankly, no economist could tell you an exact number of days that defines the short run or that delineates short run from long run, but you can usually figure this out for your business by determining which costs have been paid and which costs have not. For example, suppose the high labor costs that we discussed in section 5.3 are because of a labor union requirement that the firm pay the workers' annual union dues at the beginning of each year. While that cost is associated with a variable factor, labor, it might have been paid before the firm decides how much to produce. In that case, it won't cause the firm to shut down, at least not this year.

This is the reality behind the euphemisms "short run" and "long run." While they are temporal by nature, they are actually practical. Short-run costs refer to any costs the firm can still avoid and long-run costs refer to any costs the firm cannot avoid.

5.4   Average Cost Redux

Average cost was defined as total cost divided by total quantity, at all quantities. We noted that average cost starts high, falls, then rises again as the quantity of units produced increases. This pattern, we said, leads to what are called economies of scale (declining average cost) and diseconomies of scale (rising average cost). If we expand our time horizon, we can get a richer, more useful understanding of average cost.

We said that the short run was defined as the time frame over which fixed costs are fixed. For our strawberry farm, the amount of land can't be changed in the short run. But the farmer can acquire more land in future years and expand her crop beyond this year's limits. Let's imagine the numbers that we used in our earlier tables were for a small farm. We saw that all the measures of cost depended on the amount of land we started with. Notably, the increase in variable costs (and thus marginal cost) was because labor became increasingly less productive as we added more labor to the small field.

Suppose the strawberry farmer wanted to grow ten truckloads of strawberries next year. We said that the current field's capacity is seven truckloads. So expanding beyond seven truckloads next year will require more land. With a longer time horizon, our fixed factor isn't necessarily fixed. If we, say, double the size of the field (and the corresponding fixed costs), our average cost will start much higher, but the variable factor (labor) will have many more strawberry plants available to pick strawberries from. That increase in capacity will slow the increase in variable and marginal costs. What all this means is that increasing the fixed factors and fixed costs will increase the cost of producing a small number

Table 5.5

Quantity	FC	VC	TC	AC
1	200	4	204	204
2	200	12	212	106
3	200	24	224	75
4	200	40	240	60
5	200	60	260	52
6	200	84	284	47
7	200	112	312	45
8	200	144	344	43
9	200	180	380	42
10	200	220	420	42
11	200	264	464	42
12	200	312	512	43
13	200	364	564	43
14	200	420	620	44

Note: Quantity in truckloads; costs in $ thousands. FC, fixed costs; VC, variable costs; TC, total cost; AC, average cost.

of units but will decrease the cost of producing a larger number of units. We can see all these relationships in table 5.5.

By increasing the size of the field, we have slowed the decreasing productivity of labor: there are a lot more strawberries that can be picked, and thus new labor will not be as constrained. This means that minimum average cost will occur at a higher level of output (ten truckloads as opposed to five for the smaller field). It also means that minimum average cost is lower ($42,000 as opposed to $50,000). Up to a point, this happens in most production processes. There will be long-term cost savings when the firm grows both its fixed and its variable costs. We can think of this situation as creating long-term economies of scale.

This process might occur as the firm moves from a small to a medium to, perhaps, a large field, but it can't continue forever. At some point the larger field becomes impractical to manage. Workers can't be supervised or some other inefficiencies creep in, and minimum average cost eventually starts to rise if the firm expands too much. The implication of this process is that, for many industries and at any one time, there is an optimal firm size: a firm size that existing technology allows to produce at a lower average cost than other firm sizes.

The long-run minimum average cost will determine what all the surviving firms will look like. Suppose that in the strawberry industry, long-run minimum average cost occurs using a large field (using the simplified small, medium, and large approach), and this field has an average cost of, say, $35,000. This means the large firm could survive in the long run at a price as low as $35,000, but smaller and larger farms would not survive.

Reality Check 5.1
Inventories

There are many real-world aspects of business that make applying the costs concepts that we've discussed tricky. One of these that's worth discussing in more detail is inventory. When we described variable and marginal costs, we made it sound as though those costs, and the inputs associated with them, are always per-unit transactions. That isn't always true, and it makes the allocation of variable versus fixed costs harder in the real world.

In designating an input as variable or fixed, we usually consider the nature of the input more than the way the input is actually bought. Factories and land are considered fixed; labor and fertilizer are variable. But our strawberry-farm owner probably buys fertilizer in bulk at the beginning of every week or month and uses it one day at a time. Is fertilizer a fixed cost or a variable cost? For our purposes, we'll still think of fertilizer as a variable input, but the timing of things and the nature of business inventories make that a harder call.

To get a sense of how important this is, consider the input inventory problems of a restaurant. The restaurateur needs to keep an inventory of all the ingredients of everything on the menu. If you have thirty entrées, all made with fresh ingredients, that inventory represents variable costs; at the end of the day, you trash what you don't use. Is it any wonder why startup restaurateurs often lose money? The problem we see in this example is that inventory is often variable costs that are paid in advance, not when they are used.

This is a highly stylized concept with many potentially unrealistic assumptions. It says that if technology were easily copied across firms (and note that more broadly, all sources of economies of scale are easily copied), we would expect industries to converge to a collection of similar-sized firms. We do observe that—sometimes. The U.S. domestic auto industry eventually converged to three firms (Ford, GM, and Chrysler) of similar size. There are probably as many exceptions to this convergence as there are examples.

One interesting and important note: economies of scale are not permanent. Technology and markets change in ways that make optimal firm size very much a moving target. To wit, in the 1960s, barbershops and beauty shops were a classic individual-proprietor small business. There are now national chains such as Supercuts that have thousands of shops. Similarly, the coffee shop was once a small business. Starbucks and Coffee Bean & Tea Leaf are now national chains.

Examples

Example 1   This story is true of every business startup. One of the major ride-sharing companies (Lyft) went public (sold stock or ownership shares to the public) recently.

As part of that process, Lyft management revealed that the company had lost about a billion dollars the previous year. Still, people paid about $70 per share for a new share of this company's stock when it was first sold to the public.

Why would people pay anything for a share of a company that's losing money?

While this might seem like a finance question, we can answer it in large part with our various definitions of cost per unit. Currently, the price of each ride is less than its average cost. That means currently, the demand line is below average cost at the current quantity of rides being sold. The belief (or hope) is that demand will rise over time so that price will exceed average cost. Suppose the company's average cost doesn't change, but currently the company is not producing at minimum average cost. If demand increases (the demand line shifts to the right), the company will experience an increase in price and a decrease in average cost. That will eliminate its losses and provide investors with profits.

Example 2   Among the most expensive individual goods in our economy is military hardware. Stealth bombers famously cost billions of dollars each, and some navy ships cost tens of billions of dollars each.

Why are these individual goods so much more expensive than every other good in the economy?

Because we don't make very many of them. When only a few goods are produced and sold, the combined fixed and variable costs must be paid by those few units. Since the government is willing and able to do so, it pays a price that covers average and marginal costs, but because so few units are produced, there aren't any economies of scale.

Example 3   Tech-based goods such as "apps" are notoriously hard to price. For many such goods, all the cost is in development (fixed costs), and there are no marginal costs associated with the last user.

How are these goods priced and paid for?

Many approaches have been tried over the years for pricing these high-fixed-cost, low- or zero-marginal-cost goods. One approach is to charge a one-time access fee that covers fixed costs but not to charge a fee for use. Another is to give away the service for limited use and "upsell" expanded services once consumers are hooked. Still another is to give away the service but sell user information to a third party (usually an advertiser). Even with these hybrid pricing approaches, you need to consider the lessons of marginal versus average cost pricing. You can't charge a high price to any one customer in hopes of recouping your fixed costs because that will lead to no customers. Similarly, you can't charge zero forever with no avenue for earning revenue. As tricky and idiosyncratic as these new products are, pricing needs to follow an economic logic similar to that for traditional goods.

Chapter Summary

- Fixed and variable inputs were associated with fixed and variable costs, which then gave us two distinct ways of measuring cost per unit: average cost and marginal cost.
- Average cost was described more thoroughly to get an understanding of concepts such as economies of scale.
- A short-run production rule was described according to which the firm should produce in the short run where price equals marginal costs as long as price is greater than or equal to average variable cost.
- Long-run average cost was described to encompass a situation in which the firm can change both variable and fixed inputs.

Exercises

(B exercises are more challenging.)

A5.1   One frustration that college students sometimes encounter is that a class they signed up for gets canceled after the registration period is over. Use the definition of marginal cost to explain why a college would cancel a class in which only three people registered.

A5.2   How does the concept of overtime pay line up with the upward-sloping supply line? Recall that the supply line is marginal cost as long as marginal cost is greater than average variable costs.

A5.3   Joan's Restaurant uses marginal cost pricing. Jim's Restaurant uses average cost pricing. Why is Jim's Restaurant closing a week after it opened, even though Jim is a better cook? *Hint:* It has nothing to do with the quality of the food.

A5.4   As a follow-up to the previous question, Joan is using the best pricing approach in the short term, but she needs more than a few customers every day to survive in the long term. Explain the connection between the number of customers, marginal cost, and average cost and her restaurant surviving in the long term.

A5.5   Why are you less likely to sell your strawberries at a loss if the bad news story that decreased the demand for strawberries appeared in the paper before you rented the land?

A5.6   You hear lots of stories about people starting a successful business in their parents' garage or basement. Use the concepts we discussed in this chapter to explain those stories.

A5.7   It is a lot easier to develop a profitable software company than a profitable cancer-curing-drug company. Why?

A5.8   You run a clothing store in the business district downtown and you're making a profit. One day your assistant manager suggests you keep the store open twenty-four hours a day. Why is this a bad idea?

A5.9   Given your answer to the previous question, what would you say if your assistant manager suggested you open an online version of your store?

A5.10   Using the concepts we've discussed in this chapter, explain why online college courses and degrees are cheaper than the traditional classroom version.

B5.1   With the recent decline in unemployment and increase in market wages, many strawberry growers have switched to a "you pick" business model. Why?

B5.2   Hundreds of new businesses have popped up recently that offer apps for smart phones. An app is notoriously hard to price. The development cost is high, but the variable cost after that is often negligible. If we strictly follow the pricing rules we learned in this chapter, what should the price be for using an app?

B5.3   The story in the newspaper said that about 20 percent of restaurants fail in the first year. That's probably because restaurant owners are often great cooks but not great economics students. Your parents, both great chefs, recently opened a new restaurant. Their upfront (fixed) costs were $200,000. To cover this, they decided to charge the first one hundred customers the cost of the meal and service plus $2,000 ($200,00 divided by 100). So, on the menu, a cheeseburger was priced at $2,010. No one ate at the new restaurant in the opening week. What should the price of the cheeseburger be?

B5.4   As noted in the "Reality Check 5.1" at the end of the chapter, some of the timing issues that economists discuss in differentiating fixed and variable costs are harder in the real world because production processes involve inventories of goods rather than goods purchased one at a time. For example, the variable and marginal cost of making an omelet should include the cost of two eggs, but those eggs are bought by the dozen at the beginning of the day. Given that, are eggs a fixed cost or a variable cost for the omelet?

B5.5   For many years, the Chicago Cubs played only day games at home because they did not have lights at their baseball stadium. That saved the team a lot of money for electricity and thus lowered the marginal cost of each home game. Eventually, however, they joined the rest of baseball and installed lights so they could play at night. Why?

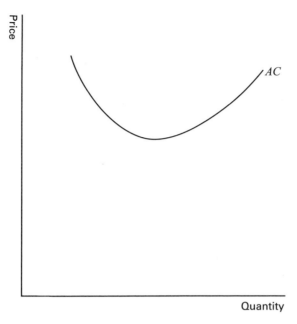

Figure 5.1   Average Cost

Appendix 5.1   Cost Curves

A picture is worth a thousand words, and it is with that adage in mind that we include the graphs that are commonly used in theory of the firm. Hopefully the thousand words are not all bad ones. Average cost, as we said in section 5.2, starts very high and falls as the firm spreads its fixed costs or overhead across more units. Eventually, the increasing variable cost increases begin to outweigh the overhead cost savings and average cost rises. Lacking specific numbers, we generalize average cost as having a U shape, as in figure 5.1.

Marginal cost, as we noted in section 5.2, is somewhat problematic to calculate for the first unit. If the firm is just entering the business, marginal cost could be said to include all of the fixed costs. That muddies the concept of marginal cost. We'll finesse this problem and begin counting marginal cost after fixed costs are paid (or, as accountants say, are sunk.) That means marginal cost is simply an upward-sloping line, representing the increasing variable costs of production (see figure 5.2).

The relationship between marginal and average cost helps us understand the two concepts. Marginal cost is the cost of the next unit; average cost is the average of all previous units. So if marginal cost is less than average cost, average cost is falling (we're adding a unit whose cost is less than the average cost of all previous units). If marginal cost is higher than average cost, average cost is rising. And if marginal cost is equal to average

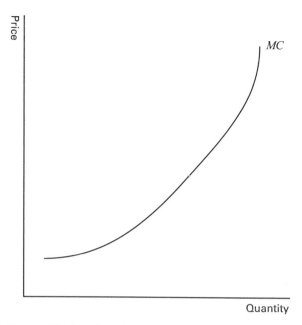

Figure 5.2   Marginal Cost

cost, average cost isn't changing. All of that means the marginal cost line goes through the average cost curve at the bottom, or minimum, of average costs, as in figure 5.3.

Average variable cost is a hybrid of these two concept in that we are calculating an average, not a change (as in marginal cost), but the thing we are averaging isn't fixed, it is rising. Average variable cost is still lower than average total cost since the latter includes fixed costs. Average variable costs can have many shapes. For our original strawberry business, table 5.3, average variable cost would be a rising line below average total cost. For table 5.4, with a very high starting value for variable costs, average variable cost would look U-shaped (see figure 5.4).

Finally, average fixed costs are always declining since we are spreading the fixed costs over an increasing number of units (see figure 5.5).

We can put them all together and get the abstract art that is theory of the firm (see figure 5.6).

Appendix 5.2   Economies of Scale in the Real World

The generic description of economies of scale—average cost falls as output rises—as coming from spreading fixed costs across an increasing number of units ignores the many other ways in which costs fall as a business expands. In fact, some of the cost saving that

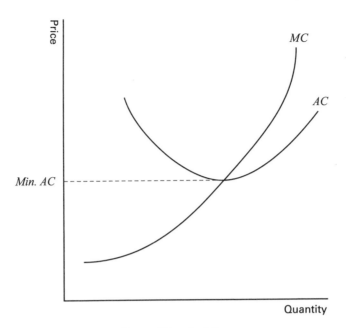

Figure 5.3   Average Cost and Marginal Cost

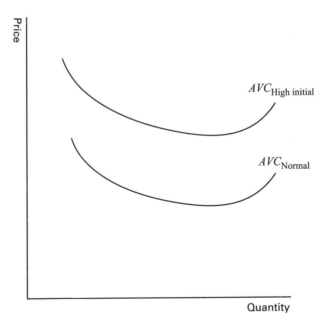

Figure 5.4   Average Variable Cost for Normal and High Initial Variable Costs

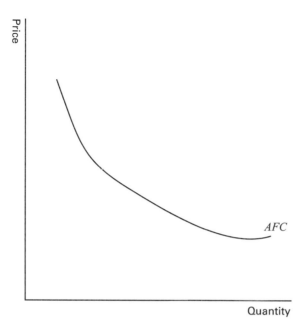

Figure 5.5   Average Fixed Costs

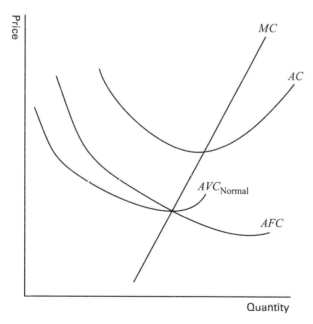

Figure 5.6   All the Cost Curves for the Original Business

we might get during the process we call achieving economies of scale might well be a saving in variable costs.

In the simple explanation of increasing variable costs in section 5.1, we focused on diminishing marginal product of labor as we added more labor to our fixed factor. That process should always occur, but it can be slowed, if not reversed on occasion, by changes in our labor force. Specifically, as we expand, labor might become more specialized in doing one particular task. Specialization would increase the productivity of labor, and, if it doesn't imply a corresponding increase in pay, the firm should experience a decline in average costs not through sharing fixed costs but by changing the expected increase in variable costs.

Specialization also has a well-known downside if it is taken too far. If workers' jobs become "overspecialized," they will often find the work tedious and unfulfilling. In that case, we observe rising costs as producers do not experience the increase in productivity with (over)specialization. In such cases there may be high turnover in the company's labor force, again increasing, not decreasing, costs.

Specialization is a labor-based example of producers changing how they do things as they grow. Our simple assumption earlier in the chapter was that productive technology was the same no matter how many units the firm produced. We know that's not true in the real world. Beyond some level of production, companies can employ assembly lines, robots, and many other innovations that change the relationship between fixed and variable costs and fundamentally change the source of economies of scale.

Anyone who has a home garden knows about this change in productive approach as output grows. A home gardener uses a shovel, a hoe, a pump pesticide sprayer, and a lot of her own labor. A farmer growing the same produce on hundreds of acres can use an enormous tractor and hire a crop-dusting plane. There's no way to use the approach taken by the big producer on the small home garden. The crop duster has no way to do a little crop dusting.

Economies of scale in the real world are achieved through a combination of changing variable costs, the spreading of fixed costs across multiple units, and changes in approach. Business school classes such as those on operations and strategy focus in detail on some of these real-world sources of economies of scale.

Appendix 5.3   Economies of Scope

Again focusing on the real world, there are many ways we can imagine expanding our business. We can produce an ever-increasing number of units of the same good (what we assumed earlier in this chapter) or we can take advantage of our inputs to produce related goods. The cost savings that a firm experiences as it increases production of related goods are called economies of scope.

Economies of scope are usually associated with concepts such as synergy. Basically, producers find they can produce *X* and *Y* more cheaply if they produce them at the same time (rather than individually and separately.) The two goods share fixed costs or required skills or have the same distribution channels.

It is easy to imagine how a producer might come up with economies of scope. A donut shop, as it expands, might find there are cost savings to be realized by buying its basic inputs (flour, sugar, butter) in bulk. But once the shop has fifty pounds of flour, sugar, or butter, it is easy to start making other, related products, such as muffins, scones, and cinnamon bread.

Certain sources of economies of scope for big businesses are familiar to most students. Marketing and advertising for a company's original product will usually lead to brand familiarity and brand loyalty. Having accomplished that, the producer can use the brand as an "umbrella" to more easily introduce and sell related products. A well-established toothpaste company will often introduce toothbrushes, mouthwash, and dental floss. This expansion in types of items produced decreases the average cost of the original marketing campaign that created the brand loyalty, which is the concept underlying economy of scope.

Umbrella branding also has risks. The company should not associate lower-quality products with its well-accepted brand. The end result would likely be lower sales of the original product as consumers began to doubt the quality of all the goods the company produced.

A similar story can be told about research and development, or R&D. When a company gets big enough to do its own internal R&D, it often finds new uses for existing products, or new products that are related to existing products. The popular office product Post-it Notes was the end result of an innovation, not very strong glue, thought to be useless. The well-known antibaldness product Rogaine was developed based on the observed side effects of the blood pressure medicine Minoxidil. Again, these new products help defray the costs of the original R&D and represent an economy of scope.

Finally, skills that laborers acquire often can be applied to creating more than one product. If a desktop computer manufacturer pays for a training program to teach its workers how to solder components onto a circuit board, those skilled workers could also solder components that go into DVD players or car radios.

There's an interesting reality in this story. When we talked about labor earlier in the chapter, we treated it as a generic, variable input, something we could add or subtract easily in the short run. That might be true of unskilled labor, but skills take time to acquire and are permanent once they are acquired (unless technology changes their applicability). In that sense, skilled labor is more like a fixed cost. And just as with other fixed costs, we can often use it as input for more than one product.

6   Perfect Competition

In the previous chapter we determined production rules for a firm in the short run and the long run that were based on price, marginal cost, and average cost. As part of that discussion, we didn't talk much about where that price came from. That's because we need to provide more detail about the structure of the industry in order to understand how the price is determined. Specifically, we need to know how many firms there are and how those firms compete with each other.

We will start this process with a highly stylized industry structure that was traditionally known as *perfect competition*. Microeconomists have recently shied away from that terminology because, well, nothing is perfect. The basic idea is that in some industries, there are so many competitors and so few firm-level differentiators that the individual firm has no real control over the price it can charge. Thus firms in industries that we used to characterize as experiencing perfect competition have more recently been called *price takers:* they must take the market price as a given and simply react to it.

As we'll see, in this environment the firm owner's goal ends up being not the achievement of fabulous wealth but rather breaking even; firms choose a level of output at which the market price covers both average and marginal cost. Students often find unrealistic the notion that some firms, because of the nature of their business, can never expect to do better than break even. And as we'll see, that isn't entirely true. We need to clarify what we mean by break even and we need to interject some reality checks about the timing and even possibility of what we will call excess profits.

We want to think of this model, like many in economics, as a roadmap. In this case the model is giving us a set of assumptions that, if they occur in the real world, would make profits very difficult to achieve. So, if the model seems unrealistic, we can think of it as an extreme case rather than the norm.

On completion of this chapter, you should

- understand the assumptions of perfect competition,
- understand why firms in these industries are price takers,
- see why these firms cannot make excess profits in the long run, and
- understand the dynamics and importance of easy entry and exit.

6.1 The Perfectly Competitive Environment

To better understand a firm's production decisions, we need to know more about the structure of the industry in which the firm operates. By that we mean how competitive the industry is, how many firms there are, how similar the outputs of these firms are, and how easy is it for new firms to enter this industry. The ability of any one firm to affect its own price depends on all these factors. To that end, we imagine perfectly competitive industries as ones in which the individual firm has no ability to affect its price. These firms are known as price takers because they must take the market price as given and make their production decisions accordingly.

The assumptions that we make for firms in perfect competition are famously extreme:

1. The industry is characterized by many small firms, and no one firm has the ability to affect the market price based solely on firm size.
2. All firms produce the same good.
3. All firms use the same technology to produce the good.
4. It is easy to enter and exit the industry.

The small firms know there are competitors everywhere producing the same good that they produce. If one firm tries to sell its products at a higher price, customers take their business to another, identical firm. As we'll see, if a firm tries to set its price below the market price, it will lose money on every unit it sells.

In the real world, perfectly competitive firms are likely to produce a basic commodity, such as an agricultural good. In some places, they might be strawberry farms that pop up on vacant lots all around town. These growers are producing perfect substitutes. The farms are all producing strawberries in the same way and the industry is very easy to enter. Any one strawberry farmer can look at the market and see that she is a small part of the market supply—too small to have any impact on it. The farm will have its own marginal and average cost, but since all farms are using the same technology, these costs will look the same for every farm.

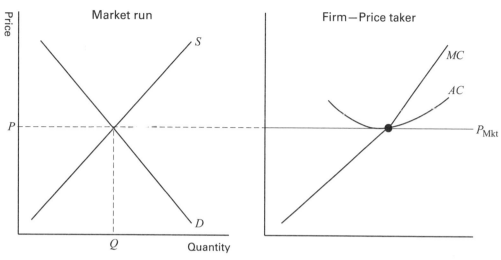

Figure 6.1 The Strawberry Market and Any One Strawberry Farm

Perfectly competitive industries are best analyzed by envisioning the market and the firm as wholly separate. The market, the aggregate of all the small farms and all consumers, is the supply and demand diagram. The firm—or, in the case of strawberries, the farm—has an average cost, marginal cost combination that looks exactly alike across all the small firms (see figure 6.1).

In figure 6.1, we show the market price as a horizontal line at the firm level. That's how it would appear to the firm because it has no ability to affect the market price; the firm is too small relative to the market. We also show that price as equal to (just touching) both marginal and average cost. That's one of the most important results of perfect competition: every firm operates at the break-even point in the long run. We should emphasize an important point here. This break-even result is not something we are imposing on each firm, it is not something that economists made up or want to happen. This break-even outcome is a result of the perfect competition model and its assumptions.

Sample Exam Question 6.1
There are a dozen strawberry stands within five miles of yours, so you know you shouldn't try to increase your price. Figuring customers won't bother to search for lower prices, you increase your price to fifty cents per quart higher than the rest of the market. You do have customers paying more for a while. Why isn't this a good idea?

Reality Check 6.1
Prices and Opportunity Cost in Perfect Competition

It's hard to know how literally we should take the results of some economic models. The idea that all firms in a perfectly competitive industry sell their goods at exactly the same price and that no firm makes profits in the long run are results that students might argue they have seen exceptions to. You might have seen strawberries selling for $2 per quart at one stand and $2.50 per quart at a stand a few miles away. How do we align that observation with the predicted results of perfect competition?

One possibility that lies outside the strict set of assumptions of the model is that input costs vary across producers. The land closer to houses and apartments (and customers) might be more expensive, so the higher price still represents a break-even result (Price = Average Cost). What economists would predict is that the more expensive land will probably be used for something other than growing strawberries (e.g., more houses and apartments) in the long run, but while it's vacant, it can be used to grow strawberries.

Another reason why real-world firms in perfect competition might not have exactly the same price all the time is that consumers don't always have the time or inclination to search for the lowest price. This reality is related to curiosity 2.1, on opportunity cost. We said that in the real world, dollar price is not the only thing we pay for a good. We also "pay" time, ease of use, and other things, all of which combine to produce a good's opportunity cost. If we allow for the fact that finding the absolutely lowest price for a perfectly competitive good is not effortless, then we would expect to see some variability in real-world, perfectly competitive prices.

Aligning that with profits is a matter of creating appropriate expectations on the part of the individual firm. Might an individual strawberry producer be able to sell at a price that's slightly higher than the other producers' prices and make excess profits because customers won't always search for a lower price? Yes! But you can't be sure of that, so your best guess is that your strawberry farm will break even most of the time.

6.2   Profits: Excess and Otherwise

A cornerstone of the perfect competition model is that firms do not—and cannot—make profits in the long run. The assumptions of the model make sure of that. But some of the discomfort that students have with this "zero profit" result comes from the fact that "profits" are defined differently in different disciplines.

Accountants usually define profit as earnings that accrue to business owners. To them, profit is what's left after the business owner has paid for all other inputs (including debt borrowing). Using that definition, profit is the compensation for owning a business. That might be compensation, which is necessary. Business owners need to receive compensation for the time, effort, and so forth involved in owning a business. Economists would consider this compensation a cost. If the business doesn't produce an acceptable amount of accounting profit, the business owner would probably do something else.

With that in mind, economists often define *profit* as returns above and beyond what is necessary to keep all factors employed by the business. We don't want to create or exacerbate confusion on this point; economists are correct that some of what accountants call profit is, in fact, cost. We'll follow an approach that many economists have used over the years and call any profits above and beyond what is necessary to stay in this business "*excess profits.*"

Sample Exam Question 6.2
Use the concept of opportunity cost to explain the following statement: If some of what accountants call a "profit" wasn't a cost, no one would open a business.

6.3   Price Increases: Short Run versus Long Run

Most of the important results that we get from this model are seen when we look at the industry over time. We can imagine starting from the break-even situation that was described in figure 6.1, in which the market determined the price and the individual firm simply found a way to survive (meaning Price = Marginal Cost = Average Cost). We said each firm is too small to affect the market price. But market-level things still happen. For example, good and bad news can still shift the supply or demand lines the way we described in chapter 2.

Suppose the strawberry industry got some unexpected good news: a new study has found that strawberries cure the common cold (yay!). This would certainly cause an increase in demand for strawberries at the market level and, following the dynamic we discussed in chapter 2, an increase in the market price of strawberries (see figure 6.2).

At the firm level, this is also good news. The increase in price will allow all firms to increase output and, *in the short run*, make excess profits. This must be true if we started this process where $P = MC = AC$. Recall from our cost curve discussion in chapter 5 that $MC = AC$ can only occur at minimum AC. At a higher price, the firm would still produce where $P = MC$, but now $P > AC$; therefore, firms are making profits in the short run.

At this point, the assumptions of easy entry and same technology kick in: realistically, anyone can grow strawberries. Here's the kicker: if the increase in demand is perceived as permanent, new firms will enter the industry. Firms that are breaking even growing *other* fruits and vegetables (or anyone else who is so inclined) will start a new strawberry farm. On the other hand, if the demand increase is only temporary, then the profits will go away as soon as demand returns to its previous level, and other firms won't have time to enter the market.

At this point we see the difference between the impact of one firm on the market and the impact of many firms on the market. These excess profits will attract many new strawberry

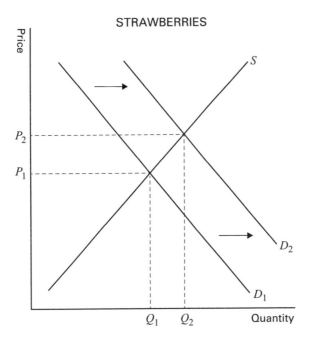

Figure 6.2   Increase in Demand for Strawberries Following Good News

growers to enter the industry, and that will affect market quantity. Specifically, the increase in strawberry farms will cause the supply of strawberries to increase—to shift to the right. This increase in supply pushes down the market price and ultimately eliminates the excess profits in the long run (see figure 6.3).

This excess-profit-eliminating dynamic helps us answer a few questions about the perfect competition model in the real world. For example, it's easy to say things like "short run" and "long run," but what exactly do we mean? How long is the long run compared to the short run? (We also pondered this question in curiosity 5.1 in the last chapter).

Having chosen an industry, strawberries, in which to discuss perfect competition, we can answer the question based on that industry. The long run is however long it takes a firm to enter the industry and begin production. To hazard a guess, that's probably about a year: a year to acquire land, plant, and grow strawberries. For some industries the long run is a year, for others (e.g., Uber drivers) it may be a week. If entrepreneurs are profitably selling bottled water on hot days in downtown Los Angeles, entry probably takes no more than a day. So we describe and define long run based on the specifics of the industry.

Another issue we can address by looking at this process is whether prices have to return to the same level in the long run after a change in the market. Figure 6.3 shows the profitable prices returning to their original, break-even level. But what is necessary

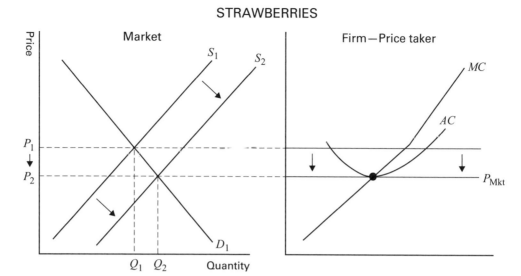

Figure 6.3 Profits Eliminated as New Firms Enter the Industry and Prices Fall

to stop entry is that profits go away completely. There are two ways that can happen. On the one hand, prices can continue to fall while firm-level average costs stay constant until we return to $P = MC = AC$.

On the other hand, we can also imagine that new firms entering the market push up fixed costs—the cost of land, perhaps—so that average cost at the firm level *rises* in the long run. If we combine falling market prices with rising average cost, we would get higher prices without profits in the long run (see figure 6.4).

6.4   What Goes Up Could Go Down

News isn't always good. Suppose we get bad news in the strawberry market. Like most agricultural products, strawberries have had problems in the past with *E. coli* contamination. This food-borne pathogen causes an illness that is dangerous, even potentially deadly, to humans, and announcements of *E. coli* contamination cause people to decrease their consumption of the product involved.

Suppose there is a highly publicized *E. coli* outbreak and strawberries are found to be the source, but the exact farm hasn't been identified yet. People would decrease demand for all strawberries, and, following the dynamic we described in chapter 2, this would cause a decrease in the market price of strawberries.

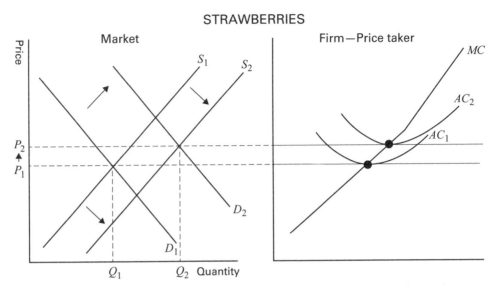

Figure 6.4   Falling Market Prices with Rising Firm-Level Average Cost

Reality Check 6.2
Short-Run Profits

Arguably, this model was created to describe industries in which excess profits couldn't exist. The assumptions purposely remove every source of excess profits that economists could imagine. For that reason, some economists say that excess profits cannot occur in perfect competition even in the short run.

But eliminating profits in the short run requires things that are completely unrealistic, such as having a market that was never surprised by demand shifts or where entry is instantaneous. Since every model's results are contingent on the underlying assumptions, we could add those assumptions to say that there are no excess profits in perfect competition. But what would be the point?

As it stands, the perfect competition model is similar to models for profits in other highly competitive spaces. The efficient market hypothesis in finance allows for the possibility of excess profits in the short run based on such things as luck (unexpected good news). In addition, excess profits can always exist if there are transaction costs. The time needed to get into a market with excess profits is a type of transaction cost.

So we'll stick with the version of the perfect competition model that allows for profits in the short run. It simply makes sense to say, "Being in the right place at the right time can make you a few extra dollars, but don't expect it to last."

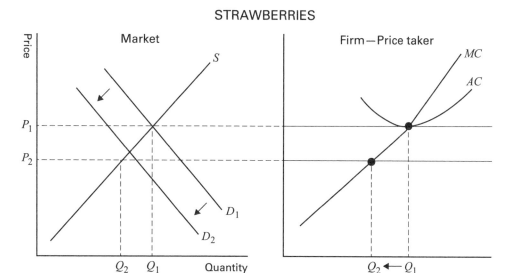

Figure 6.5   Decrease in Market Demand and Short-Run Losses at the Firm Level

Down on the farm, this price decrease will mean that *all* farms are now losing money in the short run (see figure 6.5).

Now, remember the assumption of easy exit: some farms will close, and this will cause market supply to decline (the supply line shifts to the left). This decrease in supply will cause the market price to rise until all the remaining farms break even.

This dynamic might occur even faster than entry. Arguably, closing a business is easier than opening one. There's an additional downside possibility. Recall from chapter 5 that the firm will shut down (produce zero units) if price is less than average variable cost. Average variable cost is always smaller than average (total) cost, so this situation would involve a dramatic decline in the market price. Still, the shutdown rule is for short-run production decisions. If prices fall so much that price is less than average variable cost, production will stop immediately at all firms (see figure 6.6).

6.5   What's So Special about Perfect Competition?

Perfect competition is an extreme model in many ways, and few if any industries fit the model perfectly. But perfect competition isn't just an extreme model that we use as an endpoint on some sort of competitive continuum, it is also the industry structure that produces most goods at the lowest possible price. In that sense, it is why economists tend to promote competition as the best possible outcome for consumers.

STRAWBERRIES

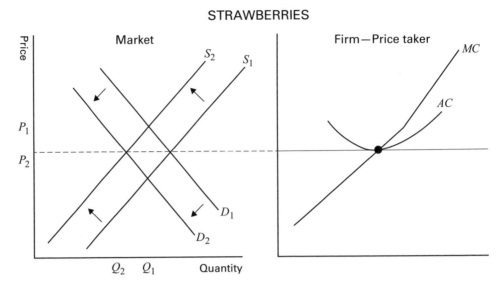

Figure 6.6 Market Supply Decreasing When Firms Exit Until Losses Are Eliminated

This lowest-cost outcome follows from the assumptions of the model. One assumption is that all firms use the same technology. This implies that technology must be easy to observe and replicate. Another assumption is that there is easy entry into the industry. The implication of these two assumptions is that all firms have the same average cost curve. In addition, firms are price takers, so they perceive a flat demand for their product at the firm level. That means all firms produce at minimum average cost. When we put all this together, we see the good is being produced at the lowest possible cost.

Of course, there could be innovations even in perfectly competitive industries. Like an unexpected increase in demand, a technological change (an innovation that lowers average cost at all or even some firms) would lead to short-run profits at some firms. But easy entry and easily replicated technology mean that these profits will be fleeting. Soon, all surviving firms will be using the new technology and breaking even, and we'll be back to zero excess profits.

If the focus of our economy is on producing goods at the lowest possible price, policymakers should strive to require all industries fit the assumptions of perfect competition. As a matter of fact, policymakers do not do that. There are goods and situations in which other industry structures prevail. As we explore these other industry structures in the next chapters, we will see what new things we get in exchange for producing goods that are more expensive.

Examples

Example 1   On the popular television show *Shark Tank*, potential investors query entrepreneurs about their new product and the extent to which the market for the new product is protected from entry.

The panel of investors on Shark Tank certainly understand the perfect competition model. Explain.

They understand that easy entry means no excess profits. These investors are specifically looking for excess profits. Their investment strategy is to help finance (invest startup money in) several different businesses, knowing they will not make money on all of them but hoping they will make excess profits on a few of them.

Example 2   Headlines from California and several other states: "Legal Pot Is More Expensive."

Let's assume marijuana is a perfectly competitive market, legal or not. Why would the legal product sell at a higher price?

The marijuana industry does fit many of the assumptions of perfect competition. There are many small firms, the product is close to homogeneous, production technology is the same across most firms, and there's easy entry and exit. One big difference between the legal and illegal product is that the legal product pays the costs of permits and other government-imposed, upfront costs. The fixed costs, and therefore the average cost of legal weed, are higher, so all firms selling legal weed will sell at a higher price. Given that, the government will still need to enforce drug laws in the pot industry to make legal pot competitive with cheaper illegal pot.

Example 3   A recent news story reported on legal action being taken against generic drug companies for collusion and other anticompetitive practices.

Since perfect competition eliminates excess profits, this behavior on the part of firms is predictable. What aspect of the model shows how this might work?

We said that no one firm could affect market price, but we also said, as part of the profit-eliminating dynamic, that when enough firms enter or exit the market, prices do change. That dynamic means that if enough firms could coordinate, they could affect, or in the case of generic-drug makers increase, market prices.

Example 4   Perfectly competitive agricultural firms can produce and sell goods at low prices in part because they don't have excess profits. But because there are many small firms, they also don't have the economies of scale that larger firms do.

If that is true, could we say that perfect competition does not always produce goods at the lowest possible price?

If there are technological changes that allow larger farms to have lower average cost (economies of scale), we would expect to see those farms outcompete smaller, more inefficient farms. So-called corporate farms and even farm cooperatives are examples of large-scale, lower-price producers. But increasing the size of the farm does not necessarily prevent the industry from being perfectly competitive. There still might be a large number of (now larger) producers that are all still price-takers.

Chapter Summary

- The model known as perfect competition—exemplified by an industry in which all firms are price takers—was described and the assumptions that would make an industry perfectly competitive were laid out.
- The industry dynamic was described in which excess profits or losses could exist in the short run but would be eliminated in the long run.
- The disciplinarily different approaches to profits were discussed, and we stated that perfectly competitive firms could not make excess profits in the long run.
- The importance of competition in producing low-cost goods was discussed.

Exercises

(B exercises are more challenging.)

A6.1   As businesses go, perfectly competitive ones have some benefits, especially for first-time businesspeople. Explain.

A6.2   Good news has caused an increase in the demand for strawberries, and the market price has risen. All existing strawberry farms are having an unexpectedly good year. You've been in the business for a decade, but Fred, the farmer next door, just started growing strawberries this year. Fred told you he was going to celebrate his good fortune by moving into a bigger, fancier house. How would you advise Fred regarding that move?

A6.3   The good news that the price of your strawberries has permanently risen because of the move toward healthier eating habits has been tempered by the fact that the rent on your land has increased. Why?

A6.4   As a follow-up to the previous question, if profits are eliminated in part by rising fixed costs, market quantities will not increase as much as in a perfectly competitive industry in which costs do not change. Why?

A6.5   Bad news has caused the market demand for strawberries to fall, and you and all your strawberry-farming friends will lose money this year. A few of your friends told you they plan to move to Florida and try to open an umbrella stand next year instead. While you might miss them as friends, you aren't entirely unhappy to see them go. Why?

A6.6 A few years ago, a decline in demand for strawberries was caused by an erroneous report of food poisoning connected to strawberries. The corresponding decline in strawberry prices meant that strawberry farmers lost money that year. Despite that, no strawberry farms exited the industry, and normal profits returned the next year. How is this outcome possible?

A6.7 At the beginning of the year, you got together with a bunch of your strawberry farmer friends and paid for a billboard to promote the benefits of strawberries for the coming summer. It worked, and the demand for strawberries increased. But you didn't make any greater profits this year than you did last year. Why?

A6.8 Anyone who survives in a perfectly competitive industry for many years has probably learned to do one thing: save some of the excess profits if market demand unexpectedly increases one year. Why is this a good long-run success strategy in this type of industry?

A6.9 Both strawberries and fresh-cut Christmas trees are perfectly competitive industries. Curiously, short-term profits last for a couple of years in the Christmas tree industry but only a year in the strawberry industry. Why?

A6.10 Strawberries have been correctly implicated in an *E. coli* outbreak that has driven strawberry demand and market prices to the lowest level in two decades. In fact, demand has fallen so much that no strawberries have appeared on grocery store shelves for most of the strawberry season. Why?

B6.1 You own a strawberry farm. True or false, explain: If your strawberries are already grown and ready to be picked, you will sell them at any market price because losses are a well-accepted possibility once you have paid your fixed costs.

B6.2 Suppose you tried to protect the short-run profits that you experienced after an increase in the market demand for strawberries by buying up all the available land on which strawberries could be grown. Having thwarted some entry, will you have protected your profits?

B6.3 An increase in demand for widgets (well known to be produced by price-taking firms) has led to short-run profits for all existing firms. Even though the widget industry is perfectly competitive, no firms entered, and the profits remained for a second year. How is this possible?

B6.4   You discovered a way to grow strawberries cheaper by putting plastic on the ground around each plant, saving water, and keeping the lowest berries from being eaten by insects. This innovation will allow you alone to make excess profits this year. Should you assume your profits will last forever and make a down payment on a mansion?

B6.5   The tomato market is perfectly competitive and, based on beginning-of-the-year projections of costs and price, entry is not profitable. When it comes time to harvest this year's crop, the market price is $20 per box, and at the output (Q') where $P = MC = \$20$/box, $AC = \$18$/box. Are these perfectly competitive firms making profits or losing money this year? Based on your answer, should all existing firms increase, decrease, or not change their output (from Q') this year?

7 Monopoly

When an industry structure becomes so familiar it has its own a board game, you know you're dealing with something important. For more than a century, economists and policymakers have discussed the social and economic problems that occur when one firm dominates an industry. Such a firm has the ability to impact both sides—supply and demand—of the market. As for any other firm, the monopolist's output choice will determine its costs. But unlike smaller firms, monopolies know that their production decision will also affect the market price. As such, many economists have started referring to monopolists as *"price setters,"* analogous to perfectly competitive firms being called price takers.

If a firm can affect both sides of the market, it does not approach its production decision in the same way that smaller firms in perfectly competitive industries do. Monopolies know that their costs rise as they produce more, but they also know that the price at which they can sell their output falls. That knowledge will lead monopolies to produce fewer units than firms in perfectly competitive industries. By decreasing industry output, monopolies can increase the price of their good, and in most cases, this so-called market control will allow these firms to make excess profits.

Monopolies present a problem for policymakers. The ability to control industry output and price has negative implications for consumers. As we will see, unfettered, monopolies produce fewer units and sell at a higher price than competitively produced goods. The easy solution is to make sure industries stay competitive. But some industries, by their nature, cannot have competition. For example, a city's water company is one of these "natural monopolies" because it is impractical to run competing pipes to every house. We'll see that these natural monopolies are usually either regulated by the local government or owned by the government outright. We'll also see that neither of those solutions works perfectly.

On completion of this chapter, you should

- understand how monopolies differ from perfectly competitive firms,
- see how a monopoly's market control gives it the ability to affect both costs and prices,
- see how this market control usually leads to excess firm profits, and
- see the problems in regulating these firms.

7.1   What Is a Monopoly?

Monopoly is an industry structure in which one firm dominates the entire market. The obvious question is, how much of the market does one firm have to serve for it to be a monopolist? Economists and courts have settled on 75 percent or more, and for our purposes that works fine. The recent litigation over the proposed merger of AT&T and Time Warner (both large providers of television programming) has shown that the concept of monopoly is still something of a moving target (see curiosity 7.1). Percentages of the market are probably less relevant than a pragmatic definition: if the firm dominates the industry and it can effectively ignore all other producers, we'll consider it a monopoly.

For our purposes, there are two categories of monopolies. First, some monopolies exist because of technical practicalities. We call these *natural monopolies*. The utility company that provides your drinking water or your electricity are natural monopolies. Historically, it was impractical to have more than one set of pipes or wires coming into your house providing these goods. Sometimes the local government decides these firms shouldn't be traditional for-profit companies; they should be owned and operated by the government. We discuss that possibility in section 7.5 when we discuss regulating monopolies.

Industrial monopolies, on the other hand, date from the early twentieth century. Standard Oil and US Steel, for example, dominated their industries, and to a large extent their unchecked ability to move markets led to the antitrust laws that made industrial monopolies illegal. In the 1960s, AT&T was forced to break up because it was deemed to be a monopoly; more recently, Microsoft and Google were accused of monopolistic practices. Some biotech firms are also monopolistic. That is, the only producer of a wonder drug has an innate ability to control the market. This monopoly is actually granted to the biotech firm by way of a patent. As we'll see, firms that are monopolies are usually more profitable than firms in more competitive industries. In the case of biotech and other firms with high R&D costs, those profits pay for the costs and risks of lengthy R&D processes. In fact, patents protect the monopoly for a certain period of time.

Curiosity 7.1
Natural Monopolies: Regulation versus Innovation

Natural monopolies are businesses with very large fixed costs, and therefore average costs that are falling for all levels of output in the existing market. In that case, only one firm can survive, and it will have the ability to affect the market price. Utilities such as the water company are natural monopolies because their fixed costs include installing water pipes to reach every customer (and, as is typical for a natural monopoly, we can't imagine competing water pipes vying for a homeowner's business).

But monopolies, even natural monopolies, don't last forever. Sometimes their end of life is related to government regulation, but it can also be due to technological change. In 1982 the U.S. government determined that AT&T was a monopolist, and the company was forced to break up into smaller telecom companies. No one would consider AT&T a monopoly today in that industry (though its merger with Time Warner Cable is currently being reviewed under antitrust regulations for other reasons), but that's not only because of the breakup. We can make phone calls now using cell phones and the internet, in addition to landlines. Technology helped create more competitors. The mechanism looks something like this: the profits that a monopoly generates are a strong signal to the market that innovation in that space will be rewarded, technology gets developed, and competitors start to emerge.

Like the water company, the electric company is usually considered a natural monopoly because you cannot run competing power lines to every house (strictly speaking, the production and the distribution of electricity could be considered different businesses). However, technology is changing how people get electricity. Solar power and other small-scale sources of electricity could do to the electricity industry what innovation did to the telecom industry.

All monopolistic firms have shared attributes. Economists describe a monopolized industry as one with one dominant firm that has the ability to affect the industry price. Firms in these industries are sometimes called price setters (instead of monopolists) because they can affect the industry price. There is no entry, so competitors cannot get into the industry, and the good being produced has no satisfactory substitutes. This last assumption isn't always included in the description of a monopoly, by the way. In reality, close substitutes are competitors

In chapter 2 we said that a producer in an industry with few substitutes will face a relatively inelastic demand curve. This means that monopolists have considerable power to raise their prices by restricting output. Some economists refer to a monopoly with no close substitutes and an inelastic demand curve as an "effective" monopolist. We'll stick with the notion that close substitutes are the same as competitors and that a monopolist has neither. We will discuss the hybrid case of monopolist with substitutes in chapter 8 when we talk about monopolistic competition.

7.2   Marginal Revenue

In chapter 6 we discussed small competitive firms that cannot affect the price of the good that they produce. Those firms choose to produce where the price of the good is equal to the marginal cost of the last unit produced. Monopolies are different because they know that their output decision will determine price. Monopolies "see" the demand curve, unlike perfect competitors, which can only make an educated guess at it. Suppose the demand for the monopoly's good is represented by the figures in table 7.1.

This is a simple, downward-sloping demand curve, like the ones we discussed in chapter 2. One important note should be added here: the monopolist can set its own price, but there are obvious limits. It has to pick a point that exists on the demand curve. A monopoly cannot simply make up a price-quantity combination. For this firm, the available price-quantity combinations are those listed in table 7.1, and those are the only choices.

In addition, this firm has to consider that it must pick one price for all the goods on the shelf. As described in chapter 2, the demand curve whose values are given in table 7.1 assumes the firm cannot sell unit number one (unit refers to quantity of 1000) for $70, unit number two for $60, and so on. We discuss this behavior, known as price discrimination, in appendix 7.1. Now, however, we assume that all units on the shelf go for the same price.

If this monopolist wants to sell five units, it will have to price all of them at $30. If it wants to sell six units, the price of every unit will be $20. That particular price-quantity choice has an interesting ramification. If the firm wants to increase its production and sales from five units to six, it will have to lower the price from $30 to $20—for all units! The revenue it would get at six units would be $120 ($6 \times \$20$), but its revenue at five units is $150 ($5 \times \$30$). The firm's revenue actually falls when it increases the quantity it sells. That might seem counterintuitive, but it always happens eventually because there's one price for all units. In order to sell one more unit, the firm has to lower its price. It wasn't already selling five units at $30, but to sell an additional unit, it has to lower the price. That means it will sell one more unit at $20, clearly a positive for revenue, but it will also

Table 7.1

Quantity	Price ($)
1	70
2	60
3	50
4	40
5	30
6	20
7	10

Note: Quantities in thousands.

Table 7.2

Quantity	Price ($)	Revenue ($)	MR ($)
1	70	70	70
2	60	120	50
3	50	150	30
4	40	160	10
5	30	150	−10
6	20	120	−30
7	10	70	−50

Note: Quantities and revenue in thousands.

have to sell the previous five units at $20, down from $30, so that will decrease revenue by $10 times five units, or $50. The net effect of this combination of higher sales but lower price is a change in revenue of negative $30 ($20 − $50).

This revenue change is called *marginal revenue* (*MR*). When a firm is big enough to affect the price of the good, it has to consider how its revenue will change when it changes output and sales. Small firms in perfect competition were also using marginal revenue, but their output decision did not affect the price of the good, so for them, marginal revenue was the same as price.

We can show all of the price, quantity, revenue, and marginal revenue combinations for this demand curve (see table 7.2).

Notice that after the first unit (where *MR* = Price), marginal revenue is always less than price. That is the one-price-for-every-unit problem showing its face again. When the firm wants to sell two units, it has to lower the price at which it (would have) sold unit one alone. So it sells two units at a price of $60 each, but it effectively lost $10 on unit number one's revenue ($70 − $60) when it increased the number of units sold. The marginal revenue of unit two is therefore $60 − $10 = $50.

Sample Exam Question 7.1

Real-world versions of marginal revenue and how it differs from price are easy to find. The local donut shop owner is tired of throwing away the donuts at the end of the day. He usually has to toss about twenty donuts that normally sell for $1 each. So he decides to sell all remaining donuts in the hour before closing for half price, fifty cents. After all, $10 (if he sells all of them) is better than zero. How might this pricing strategy actually hurt the donut shop's revenue?

7.3   Production for a Monopoly

In chapter 6 we saw that small competitive firms could sell all the units they wanted to at the same price, so they chose to produce where price equaled marginal cost in the short run. Monopolies have to consider marginal revenue, not price. They know that when they sell additional units, that will decrease the price of every unit so their marginal revenue is less that price. If we combine table 7.2 with the cost structure that we introduced in chapter 5 and used in chapter 6 to determine the output of a firm in perfect competition, we get a very different story for monopolies:

The breakeven output for the small competitive firm was at four units and a price of $40. At that point, total revenue equaled total cost ($160 each), and there were no excess profits. A monopolist would look at these same numbers and notice that the marginal revenue of unit number four was not its price ($40) but rather $10, because the firm had to lower its price to sell four units. That means the monopolist actually decreased its profits when it produced unit number four. The marginal revenue was $10 but the marginal cost was $40. The monopolist would have seen its profit fall by $30 when it produced that unit.

Instead of equating price and marginal cost, the monopolist would equate marginal revenue with marginal cost. That would occur at unit three. And at that output level, the monopolist would have a total revenue of $150, a total cost of $120, and an excess profit of $30. (Its profit would also be $30 if it produced two units, but this is another case of the "downside of simple numbers.")

The important distinction between monopolies and perfectly competitive firms is that monopolies decrease their output, which allows them to increase the market price (moving along the demand curve, not just making up a price). We know that the competitive firm was producing at a break-even point: $P = AC = MC$. Recall from the discussion of profits in chapter 6 that one of the costs in average cost is a "fair return" on ownership, or what accountants call profits. It stands to reason, and we can see in table 7.3, that the monopoly's ability to increase its price will allow it to make excess profits: $P > AC$.

Table 7.3

Quantity	Price	Revenue	MR	FC	VC	TC	AC	MC
1	70	70	70	60	10	70	70	—
2	60	120	50	60	30	90	45	20
3	50	150	30	60	60	120	40	30
4	40	160	10	60	100	160	40	40
5	30	150	−10	60	150	210	42	50
6	20	120	−30	60	210	270	45	60
7	10	70	−50	60	280	340	49	70

Note: Quantities, revenue, fixed cost, variable cost, and total cost in thousands.

Sample Exam Question 7.2

The monopoly story is compelling. Firms that can control their price can make excess profits. Most students memorize this fact and assume monopolies are always profitable. Not true! But you have to remember all the moving parts that are involved in making profits. Suppose I gave you a monopoly: you are the one and only producer of eight-track tapes. You might need to ask a grandparent what they are, but in 1972 they were the way people listened to music. You have the monopoly for producing eight-track tapes today. Are you rich?

Reality Check 7.1
Monopolies and Market Dominance

Whether the concept of monopoly is taught with calculus, graphs, or charts, we try to communicate this difference: some firms, by changing their output, have the ability to change the market price, and other firms, regardless of how much they produce, do not. In chapter 6 we called the firms that have no ability to affect the market price perfectly competitive firms or price takers, and in this chapter we are calling the firms that have the ability to affect the market price monopolies or price setters.

But there's a subtle reality. In the tables in this book or in the more elegant calculus derivations found in many microeconomics books, we show perfectly competitive firms as too small to affect the market price and monopolies as so big that their production decisions do affect the market price. But does that mean the exact same production change has a different impact in these different industries? Probably not.

If we are talking about a one-unit change—one more widget—produced by either a perfectly competitive firm or a monopoly, we don't really think the price falls in one case and not the other. There is a stated but often underemphasized size difference for the firms in each of these industries. The best way to think about it is this: in perfectly competitive industries, firms are so small relative to the market that they can't produce enough to change the market price. Monopolistic firms, on the other hand, are so *large* relative to the entire market that their production decision will eventually change the market price. The tables in this book show a one-unit change having a different effect on the market price in these two industry structures. In the real world, the exact same one-unit change probably wouldn't have any impact on the market price. The point is, monopolies will eventually be able to affect the market price with their production decisions; perfectly competitive firms never will.

7.4   Regulating Monopolies

If an industry can be monopolized (and if the demand for the product is higher than its average cost), the monopoly firm will be better off—it will be able to make excess profits—but that good's consumers will generally be worse off. Compared to the production of goods in perfectly competitive firms, the monopoly will be producing fewer units and selling them at a higher price. Since the profits that monopolies generate are what we called excess profits (more than the profit necessary to keep the firm operating), governments usually consider regulating monopolies.

In chapter 11 we discuss in more detail the role of governments in the economy. For now, let's just say that governments generally try to take care of the majority of their constituents. In the case of monopolies, that usually pits the firm and its owners against consumers. The firm wants excess profits; the consumers of the firm's goods don't want to pay more to get less. For most goods, there will be many more consumers than there are people involved in production, so the government usually sides with consumers and tries to control the monopoly's pricing power.

There's good news and bad as far as regulating monopolies goes. The good news is, we can use the perfect competition model to inform the regulation. The bad news is, that's a lot easier said than done. Taking a step back from both models, we can see that monopolies take advantage of their market power to hold back some units relative to what a competitive market would produce, and thus raise the price that consumers pay. As described for the market model in chapter 2, a competitive industry produces where the supply and demand curves cross. In chapter 6 we said that at that price, firms make a fair return—profits sufficient to keep the firm in business—but no excess profits.

When all of these concepts are combined, regulating a monopoly is as simple as stopping the monopoly from being able to raise the price of its good beyond the perfect competition price. With reference to chapter 3, the "perfect regulation" would be a price ceiling set at the competitive market price. Knowing it cannot raise its price above the price ceiling, the monopoly would now follow the same production rule that perfectly competitive firms do: price (at the ceiling) equals marginal cost, which is where the supply line crosses the demand line. And that will correspond to the same level of output that the competitive market would produce.

In practice, this simple regulation is hard to get right. How does the regulator—the government—know where any of those lines are? In most cases monopolistic industries have been monopolies for all of most of their existence. So the regulator has no competitive market data on which to base its price ceiling. In the case of what we called natural monopolies, such as the electric company, the government usually asks the firm for data on costs and consumption. In effect, the monopolist is asked to help regulate itself. In practice, we can see why this might not work very well.

The monopoly certainly has an incentive to overstate its production costs and be less than forthright about demand. The monopoly would likely try to keep some of the excess profits, so it might try to get the price ceiling to be above the price that would prevail in perfect competition. It gets worse. The government regulator knows about this incentive, so it likely won't believe all of what the monopoly tells it. But not having perfect market data puts the regulator in the position of having to guess the "right" price—the price that would have prevailed had the industry been competitive. Suppose the regulator guesses too low and sets the price ceiling below the market price. As we saw in chapter 3, that would also hurt consumers. While the monopoly sets a price higher than the perfectly competitive industry's price and sells correspondingly fewer units, a "too low" regulated price would cause a shortage. At a price ceiling set below the market equilibrium price, the producer would decrease the quantity supplied but consumers would want to increase quantity demanded relative to the competitive equilibrium. We said in chapter 3 that this would only benefit the consumers who could find the good on the shelf. Many consumers would simply waste time shopping for the good.

> **Sample Exam Question 7.3**
> The electricity provider in many places is a regulated monopoly. It needs permission from a government agency to raise its price. Once that price is set, it usually can't change it for many months. Why, then, do electric utilities often run advertisements asking customers *not* to increase their demand for this product? Most advertisements try to get customers to use more of a product.

Examples

Example 1   The monopoly profits granted to biotech firms through patents are supposed to pay for R&D (which entails high upfront costs that accrue before the product can be sold to the public). This monopoly power can be difficult to manage and controversial. Wonder Drug Inc. developed the first and only cure for a fatal disease. Not knowing what to charge, the firm set the price at $100,000 per dose for its one-dose cure, and people were appalled. Even if the price the firm set covers legitimate costs, such as R&D, the firm's monopoly position in the market will make it look greedy.

What could Wonder Drug Inc. do to deal with this problem?
Pricing is hard for every new product. In this case, a combination of information (marketing and public relations) and price assistance for those who can't afford the drug (see appendix 7.1 on price discrimination) might help. But it's also possible that the price is

wrong, that it's too high. Even if the medicine cures a fatal disease, you can't charge a price that no one can afford. Wonder Drug will have to consider price and quantity in order to get the desired profit-maximizing result.

Example 2 Antitrust laws came into existence because of the dual problem of monopoly pricing power and the regulator's problem in finding and setting the perfect competition price.

What aspect of competitive markets inclines them to produce more units at lower prices? Small, competitive firms do not perceive that they have an ability to produce enough units to affect the market price. Put differently, to competitive firms, marginal revenue is the market price. So smaller competitive firms will produce any unit whose price exceeds marginal cost. As such, they will produce units until the market reaches the intersection of supply and demand.

Chapter Summary

- Monopolies differ from perfectly competitive firms in that they control the market supply for the good.
- Having the ability to control market supply gives the monopoly the ability to pick the best (i.e., profit-maximizing) price for the market demand.
- Monopolies use marginal revenue rather than price in determining their output because they are aware of the impact their production decision has on the market price.
- The monopoly's ability to control output and price, together with the assumption of no entry, gives the monopoly the ability to make excess profits in the long run.
- Governments often regulate (break up) monopolies that cannot be induced to compete. This regulation is problematic because the regulator rarely has accurate information about market supply and demand.

Exercises

(B exercises are more challenging.)

A7.1 Ed's donut shop has an interesting pricing strategy. Donuts are $1 each, or a dozen for $10. What is the marginal revenue of the twelfth donut to Ed's shop?

A7.2 A monopoly's ability to control the market and potentially make profits is well known, but has limits. In their early years, the cable TV providers were local monopolies. Given that, why didn't they charge $5,000 per month for cable TV?

A7.3   Microsoft has something of a monopoly on computer operating systems. From the company's current level of sales, its marginal cost for producing an additional ten thousand units is $20 per unit. They can sell the additional units to high school students for $25 per unit. The current price of their product is $50 per unit. Can you see any reason why Microsoft should not produce and sell these units?

A7.4   Congratulations—you inherited a monopoly from your grandfather! You are now the only producer in the entire country of VHS-based camcorders (large tape-based video cameras). Will you be able to get rich by owning this monopoly? Explain.

A7.5   Suppose the demand for widgets has only two points. If widgets sell for $1, five thousand widgets will be sold every day. If widgets sell for $5, two thousand widgets will be sold every day. Would the widget producer ever increase output from two thousand to five thousand?

A7.6   It would be easier to regulate a monopoly that came into existence after several competitive firms merged or closed as opposed to a natural monopoly that has always been the industry's only producer. Explain.

A7.7   Suppose prices were never publicly posted. Everyone would pay the most they were willing to pay, and no two people would necessarily pay the same price. Now suppose the firm has sold twenty units so far at an average price of $5 each. The next customer is willing to pay $4 for a unit. Why is the marginal revenue for the eleventh unit higher in this case than it would normally be?

A7.8   Kit Kats sell for $1 at the Dollar Store, for $1.50 at the grocery store, and for $2 in the vending machine at work. If marginal revenue isn't going to be a "problem," what must be true about the customers?

A7.9   Suppose the monopoly's government regulator sets a price ceiling above the monopoly's chosen price. How would that affect the market?

A7.10   Everything else held the same, why would a monopolist prefer the demand for its product be very inelastic?

B7.1   Charlie's Hamburger Stand has a monopoly in Smallville. There are no other hamburger stands in town. Charlie is the mayor, and he won't let any other stands open. There are a few other restaurants and grocery stores. Charlie is currently selling one thousand hamburgers per day at $2 per burger. It would cost Charlie $1,000 to increase his burger production by five hundred burgers per day. Given all of this information, Charlie almost certainly will not expand his burger production. Why not?

B7.2   The government's antitrust regulator has the ability to stop any corporate merger that it deems monopolistic and potentially harmful to consumers. Suppose the department stores Macy's and JCPenney announce they are going to merge. Do you think the government would stop the merger? Explain.

B7.3   While a drug is protected by its patent, it can only be produced by the company that invented it. When the patent expires and the drug can be sold in generic form, it can be sold by anyone. Patent protection is supposed to compensate companies for the high cost of invention. Explain how this lines up with the economic models we have discussed.

B7.4   A profit-maximizing monopolist is selling five thousand units per day at $20 per unit and making profits of $50,000 per day (thus the average cost at five thousand units is $10). The government regulator tells the firm it *must* sell five thousand units for no more than $10 per unit. What would a monopolist do?

B7.5   Suppose the hundreds of firms in a perfectly competitive industry formed a cooperative and tried to act like a group monopoly, with every firm restricting output so that prices and profits would rise. What could go wrong?

Appendix 7.1   The Graphical Approach to Monopoly Pricing

The graphical representation of monopoly price and production (figure 7.1) can be gleaned from the numbers in table 7.3. Notice that marginal revenue (*MR*) is downward sloping like demand but it is steeper—the changes in *MR* for any change in quantity are bigger. That happens because of the one price for all assumption. When the monopolist increases its output and lowers its price, it has to lower the price of all the units; even the units it could have sold at the recently higher price.

For the mathematically inclined, we can also show another explanation for the steeper *MR* line. Using the numbers from table 7.3, the demand for this good can be written as $P = 80 - 10Q$. The slope of demand is the change in price divided by the change in quantity, which is -10.

Revenue is defined as price times quantity, so $Rev = 80Q - 10Q^2$. Marginal revenue is the change in revenue as we change price, which is the first derivative of the revenue equation: $MR = 80 - 20Q$. The slope of *MR* is the change in *MR* as we change quantity, which is -20, exactly twice the slope of the demand curve.

The monopoly's production rule is to set output where $MR = MC$. That means monopolies produce less than perfectly competitive industries do (competitive industries produce where supply equals demand), and this decrease in production allows them to increase their price.

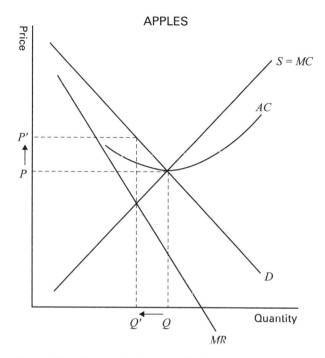

Figure 7.1   Monopoly Output and Price

Appendix 7.2   Price Discrimination

The running assumption in this chapter is that all consumers pay the same price. Indeed, the importance of marginal revenue comes from this assumption. A firm knows that if it increases output, it must lower its price for all its customers. But a quick trip to the movie theater tells us that this isn't always the case. Some businesses charge different prices for different customers. That is known as *price discrimination.*

Apart from the question of legality (price discrimination isn't always allowed), there are two important factors that a business considers when it tries to price discriminate. First, can the market be segmented into different groups, such as children and adults, men and women, business travelers and tourists? There are many ways to divvy up the market. Second, do these segments have different demands for the good? If there is no difference in demand, there is no point in setting different prices, but let's consider the ticket price for movies shown in a theater. Adults have more money and less time; children have less money and more time. Applying those factors to our demand curve, adults probably have a more inelastic demand and one that is further to the right. Kids have a lower, flatter demand. Those differences would imply a higher price for adults and a lower price for children, and that's what we see in the marketplace.

Like monopolies, firms that can price discriminate must have some ability to affect their price, and there are some mathematical conditions that must be satisfied for discrimination to increase firm profits. But an interesting new problem appears when a firm tries to price discriminate. The lower-price side of the market becomes something of a threat to the higher-price side. If the firm cannot maintain separation between the market participants, it will end up selling all its units at the lower price. If this happens, the firm will unambiguously have lower profits.

8   Imperfect Competition and Oligopoly Models

Somewhere in between the break-even world of perfectly competitive firms and the potential long-run profits of monopolies are the majority of businesses in the real world. Few, if any, industries are legitimately and wholly monopolized or perfectly competitive. The models and results from these extreme industry structures help us sort out how these real-world, in-between industries will turn out.

The nice thing about the perfect competition model and the monopoly model is that they provide us with straightforward results based on a rigid set of assumptions. When we consider the assumptions of perfect competition, it is no surprise that excess profits won't exist beyond the short run. There is nothing unique about any individual firm. Similarly, monopolies have the ability to make profits because, by assumption, they are protected from all of the forces that eliminate profits.

With those models and assumptions in hand, we can describe industry structures that are in between but are more closely aligned with one end of the spectrum or the other. That is, we can model industries as "closer to perfect competition" or "closer to monopoly," using those models as a template.

That works reasonably well, at least as far as economics is concerned. But, as we loosen the assumptions of our extreme industry structure models, we can also loosen the approach that we take in analyzing long-run profits. To that end, we will touch on other approaches in this chapter, such as strategy, which springs from economics but helps by adding nuanced business realities.

On completion of this chapter, you should

- understand monopolistic competition, and how the long-run results in these industries are close to perfect competition,
- see how oligopolies (industries with only a few firms) could cooperate and act like a group monopoly,
- see how noncooperative oligopolies might observe each other and react in the Cournot and Bertrand models, and
- understand the concept of price cooperation.

8.1   What's In Between?

Economists and regulators have used various approaches and measures to determine whether an industry is closer to perfect competition or closer to monopoly. This matters because without competitive forces, prices can be driven up and consumers hurt. Of course, there could be many firms in an industry, but also some degree of cooperation or collusion that results in monopolistic pricing. We'll address that in section 8.3. There are also economic models and real-world situations in which there are only a few firms, possibly just one firm, yet the competitive market price prevails. But most of the time, we believe, there is a positive relationship between the number of firms and the level of competition, and we'll assume that this competition pushes the ultimate price toward the market or equilibrium price that we described in chapter 2.

Measuring the level of competitiveness in an industry has generally involved determining the number of competitive firms in an industry. One such measure is called the concentration ratio. This measure calculates the sum of the market share represented by the top firms, usually for the top four or eight firms. For example, in the 2007 Economic Census (available at factfinder.census.gov), we find that the top four firms in the "camera and photographic supply stores" category represent 66 percent of the total market. The top four firms in the "fruit and vegetable markets" category represent only 7 percent of that industry. Based on these concentration ratios, we would expect the fruit and vegetable market industry to be more competitive.

While concentration ratios are widely used by the government, they have a well-known flaw. If the top firm within the grouping (four or eight) captures market share from the others, it will make the industry less competitive, but it will not change the concentration ratio. Given that, economists sometimes prefer a more complicated but more accurate measure for industry competitiveness, the Herfindahl index. The Herfindahl index (HERF) is the sum of the square of the market share of each firm. To get a sense of how that index works, suppose there are ten firms with equal market share (10 percent each). In this case, HERF = $(0.1^2) \times 10 = 0.1$, or 10 percent. If instead we looked at an industry with ten firms, but the top firm had virtually all the market, that industry's HERF would be approximately one.

We see that if an industry's HERF is closer to one divided by the number of firms, it is more likely to be competitive, and if the industry's HERF is closer to one, it is likely to be monopolized. Regardless of how we measure this, we need new models to describe the production rules, pricing, and profits for the firms in these in-between industries.

8.2   Closer to Perfect Competition: Monopolistic Competition

When we think about familiar industries and how they differ from the assumptions of perfect competition, one obvious change would be the assumption of homogeneous goods. We see industries with many firms (no one firm able to dominate the market), all firms using the same technology, and easy entry and exit, but each firm produces a good that's somewhat different. This is a highly competitive industry with heterogeneous goods.

Each firm has some pricing power; there are people who prefer one version to another. But there are many substitutes. Effectively, that means each firm is like a small monopolist with an elastic demand line. From here the model requires a story: a dynamic.

One way to see *monopolistic competition* in action is to look at an industry that fits the assumptions and then work backward from the observed (usually long-run) result. We can do that with restaurants. I specifically like to look at restaurants on a large highway close to my office: Main Street in Collegetown, USA. Right now there are ten restaurants within two miles of each other on that street. But there must have been a time when there was only one.

Suppose Jay's Diner was the first restaurant on Main Street. As the first restaurant, it had lots of business. Eating out at a restaurant always has substitutes (people can cook at home), but Jay's Diner was the only restaurant for many miles. We can think of Jay's Diner as a local monopoly. As such, it could make profits by producing food where marginal revenue equaled marginal cost, raising prices above a perfectly competitive firm, and having its prices be higher than average costs.

The problem is, these profits—this success—are easy to observe. Jay's Diner is always crowded; the parking lot is full; there are lines outside waiting for a table. A restaurant's popularity is never a secret. So other restaurateurs began looking at Main Street in Collegetown. A Mexican restaurant moved next door, a sushi place across the street, a French bistro opened half a mile away. All these restaurants are different from Jay's Diner and from each other. All are local monopolies of their *type* of restaurants, and they try to make profits. But with each new restaurant, the demand for all the previous restaurants falls a bit. Profits at Jay's Diner (and all the early restaurants) are being eaten away by the new competitors.

The reason why profits can't last is that, heterogeneous products aside, the industry has easy entry. Short-run profits bring in new restaurants until there are no more profits.

Just as it did with perfect competition, easy entry eliminates profits in the long run in monopolistic competition.

There are several interesting results that spring from this model and its long-run results. First, and sadly, there's no guarantee that the first business (Jay's Diner) survives in the long run. In a simplistic classroom version of the model, the new restaurants decrease demand at all previous restaurants and entry stops when there are no profits left at any existing restaurant. In the real world, the first restaurant often does things during its boom time that make it unprofitable in the long run. Thinking the profits will never go away, Jay's Diner expanded too much, added a parking garage, and grew its menu to increase average cost. When demand fell with new entrants, Jay's Diner found itself without enough demand to cover its average cost.

Sample Exam Question 8.1
How could Jay's Diner have expanded with less long-run risk?

Reality Check 8.1
Entry Deterrence

In both monopolistic competition and perfect competition, we see that easy entry eliminates profits in the long run. Regardless of the model, entry is a threat to excess profits. But entry is something that firms have some control over in the real world. As the industry structure moves closer to monopoly (where we assume there is no entry), one change is the existing firms' ability to slow or stop entry by competitors.

Some entry deterrents are legally granted, such as patents and trade secrets. These legal deterrents exist to compensate businesses and inventors for the substantial upfront cost of R&D. The logic is that a business is allowed to make excess profits for a number of years (usually around twenty) to recover the sunk costs of innovation. There are many issues and controversies involved in patents, but the logic is reasonable.

Entry deterrence does not always involve legal protections. Branding and brand reputation are traditional forms of deterrents. Entering a market that already has a well-accepted, brand-named product is daunting. The extreme example of this is a brand that has become the name of the product, like Kleenex or Band-Aid. A new competitor has to convince the market that its version of the product is just as good. That will involve information provision (marketing and advertising), short-term strategies such as giving away free samples, or simply selling the new product at a lower price. In all cases, making excess profits is clearly harder if the incumbent product has an established brand reputation.

A well-known strategy that is outside the purview of most economics classes is to tie up the means of distribution. For many products, their success depends on getting onto store shelves. While that might sound simple, existing firms often try to use up the "shelf space" with a wide variety of flavors, shapes, and sizes of their already popular goods. This limits a new entrant's ability to get its product on the shelf.

Another possibility for maintaining initial profits is to offer customers something that no other restaurant has. For example, Jay's Diner might have tried to keep customers from going to one of the new restaurants by hiring a fancy French chef. We can even imagine Jay's chef is the best chef in town. That would keep some customers, but it wouldn't keep Jay's profits. The chef would know he's the reason for the profits and he would want to be paid more in order to stay on at Jay's Diner.

Another interesting observation that springs from the monopolistic competition model is that prices in the long run at each surviving firm are not at any firm's minimum average cost. That's at odds with what we learned about the model of firms in perfect competition. There, price equaled average cost at minimum average cost in the long run. That means that prices in monopolistically competitive industries are higher than prices in perfectly competitive industries. This result can be interpreted as the cost of variety. Customers are willing to pay more for variety and choice, but variety also costs more to produce.

Sample Exam Question 8.2
Suppose there are four (somewhat different) gas stations on the four corners of an intersection, but the northeast corner is the best one for traffic and thus has more customers. Wouldn't that gas station make long-run profits while the others just break even?

8.3   Oligopoly: Cooperation

Closer to monopoly are industry structures with only a few firms. Such a structure is known as an *oligopoly*. There are many models and approaches in this area of business. One important dividing line is cooperation. If the number of firms is small, they might be tempted to coordinate their output and pricing strategies with an eye toward maximizing industry profits.

An industry with a single (monopolist) firm will make decisions that maximize firm and industry profits. An industry with a small number of firms could therefore maximize industry profits by acting like a "group monopoly": each firm could produce a fraction of the monopolist's output, charge the monopolist's price, and share the monopoly profits. We call this group a cartel, and we say these firms are colluding (or practicing *collusion*).

This sounds relatively simple, but there are a few problems with execution in the real world. First, in many countries, including the United States, collusion is illegal and the laws against it are vigorously enforced. That's true in most of Europe as well, and several tech giants (e.g., Microsoft, Google) have been scrutinized and penalized in Europe in recent years for anticompetitive practices. But some countries do not strictly prevent all forms of cooperation. In the Japanese system known as keiretsu, companies own shares in each other and individuals have seats on the board of directors of firms in related businesses. In less formal ways, businesses in China and Russia are thought to collude.

Collusion may also occur between countries and among what are called state-owned enterprises. The Organization of Petroleum Exporting Countries (OPEC) is a collusive group of fourteen countries that represents almost half the world's oil production. Since the 1960s, OPEC has coordinated and controlled oil production among its members. This quasi-monopolistic supply manipulation keeps world oil prices higher than a fully competitive world market would have brought forth.

Second, cartels have a tendency to fall apart because individual firms have incentives that are not consistent with maintaining industry profits. Suppose our cartel consisted of five firms, all producing one-fifth of the monthly monopoly output, one million units, all selling at the monopoly price, $10, and all making one-fifth of the monopoly profit, or $5 million per month (so average cost is $5 and profit per unit is $5).

The operators of firm three (this could be any of the firms) might say to themselves, "If our firm (alone) increases output a little, say, by 100,000 units per month, that wouldn't affect the price at all (much), and our firm could make an additional $500,000!" The reasoning is sound as far as it goes. Total industry output is five million (five firms, one million each), so this firm's increase of 100,000 would be an increase of 2 percent. Even if prices fell a few cents, firm three would make close to a half a million extra dollars each month.

But every firm would think that! Every firm would try to "cheat" a bit, thinking it is the only one doing so. And when they all cheat, prices fall, and they all make lower— not higher—profits. Cartel agreements are notoriously hard to enforce in the real world. (For a good read on this topic, check out the article online at https://www.nytimes.com/1988/04/24/weekinreview/the-world-opec-isn-t-the-only-cartel-that-couldn-t.html.)

OPEC's relative success and longevity are usually thought to be related to its having one very large producer, Saudi Arabia, and many other smaller producers. In that case, unless Saudi Arabia is the one that overproduces (which it has the least incentive to do, since overproducing would lower the price the most), the impact of small amounts of overproduction by the other members is minimal. Saudi Arabia as the largest producer also has the ability to enforce the production rules on other cartel members.

8.4 Oligopoly: Cournot Competition

Since overt cooperation is both problematic and illegal in many cases, we need to consider models in which firms do not cooperate. But not cooperating does not mean they ignore the other firms in an industry with only a few firms. What we imagine is that firms observe and react. There are two well-known noncooperative models that are structured this way (and several others that spring from them). The first is called *Cournot competition* or quantity competition. Here, firms observe each other's output and base their own output on this observation.

In the easiest version of the Cournot model, a firm observes other firms' output and assumes other firms' output is fixed. Suppose there are only two firms, firm A and firm B, and each firm can observe the other's output. Suppose they are each initially producing half the (break-even) perfectly competitive output. Each of them will notice that it can do better. Firm A will observe firm B's production (half the market) and assume that is fixed. Firm A would then monopolize its half of the market, decrease output, raise prices, and make profits.

Both firms would do this under this set of assumptions, and, after some iteration, they would each produce a share of the market that is less than half. Total output would then be less than the output in a perfectly competitive environment, and both firms would make a profit.

With a few more simplifications, we can get precise results for the Cournot model. Suppose there are two firms, each producing the same good (so consumers are indifferent), and each with straight (linear) demand. Suppose further that marginal costs are constant for all levels of output. As we recall our definitions from chapter 5, that assumption means that marginal cost equals average cost (because every unit costs the same). A linear demand will also have a linear marginal revenue, but with twice the slope (see the derivation in appendix 8.1).

Suppose the perfectly competitive output is one million units per day, and initially each firm is producing one-half of that. When they observe and react à la Cournot, they will each monopolize their share of the market. That means they will each reduce output to one quarter of the market, reducing total output to one-half of the market. That production decision—that each firm produces half its perceived share when they monopolize—is specific to this setup, in which we have a linear demand and constant marginal cost (see appendix 8.1). It helps us see the basic idea that each firm, acting like a residual monopolist but not cooperating or colluding, will choose to decrease output.

But that level of output won't be the final equilibrium. Each firm will look at the other's new output (now one quarter) and realize its calculation is wrong: if firm B is producing one quarter of the market, firm A's (residual) share is three quarters of the market, and their monopoly output would be three-eighths (one half of the residual). Iteration, or calculations, would ultimately lead both firms to the final equilibrium: firm A and firm B would each produce one-third of the market. Total output would be two-thirds of the market, prices would rise, and each firm would make profits.

We see that if there are two firms in this stylized version of the model, they each produce one-third of the market; total output is two-thirds of the market; and both firms make a profit. The simplifying assumptions (constant marginal cost and linear demand) mean that each firm, when it equates its marginal revenue to its marginal cost, will always produce half of its market share (half of the residual market). That rule allows us to scale up the model for additional firms rather easily. Suppose there are three firms, firm A, firm B, and firm C. Equilibrium would occur when each firm produced one quarter of the market.

Total market output would rise to three quarters, prices would fall, and all firms' profits would fall a bit.

Let's jump to, say, seven firms. Notice that when there were two firms, they each produced one-third of the market; when there were three firms, they each produced one-fourth of the market. If you see the pattern, you'll know that when there are seven firms, they will each produce one-eighth of the market (the fraction of the market is one plus the number of firms), total output is seven-eighths, and both prices and profits will fall a lot.

One interesting result of the Cournot model is that the industry gets closer to perfect competition as the number of firms increases. Aside from that result, we don't see a lot of real-world uses for the Cournot model (although it is a famous precursor to game theory, as we'll see in chapter 10). The assumptions often seem unrealistic, and the Cournot model is more of a template for noncooperative, oligopoly models' approach of observation and reaction than a directly applicable model (but see curiosity 8.1).

The approach that each firm takes in the Cournot model is actually a precursor to the so-called Nash equilibrium, which we'll describe in chapter 9 when we discuss game theory. Notice that each firm is maximizing its profits given the output of the other firm (assuming the other firm's output is fixed).

8.5   Oligopoly: Bertrand Competition

A more familiar (and applicable) noncooperative form of competition is for firms to observe each other's price and set their own price accordingly. This is known as *Bertrand competition* or price competition. The simplest version of price competition is what we call a price war. Suppose there are two firms producing identical goods, initially setting their price at, say, $8 per unit for a good with a constant marginal cost and an average cost of $4. Both firms sell one thousand units per day, and both make profits of $4,000. Either firm could start this price war, but let's say it's firm 1. Firm 1 observes firm 2's price of $8, assumes it's fixed, and decides to cut its own price to $7 in order to capture more market share. If firms can increase output easily in this case, firm 1 could capture the entire market with this price cut. But firm 2 would assuredly not keep its price at $8 if all its customers disappeared. Firm 2 would respond by undercutting firm 1. The end result of this is both firms end up setting their price at $4 and both firms break even. This price war eliminates profits.

There are a couple of ways that firms using Bertrand competition might avoid this result. One possibility is that the firms don't produce exactly the same good. If we introduce some product differentiation, we give each firm some ability to raise its price without losing all its customers. Let's see how this works out in a simple example, where we'll create differentiation just by changing the demand equations a bit:

Curiosity 8.1
Why Would a Firm Produce Its Own Competition?

There's an interesting phenomenon in the marketplace that's hard to explain. Companies sometime sell different brands of the same product. That is, companies sometimes produce their own competition. We can use the Cournot model to explain why. Suppose the demand for laundry detergent follows that shown in table 8.1. Suppose further that marginal cost is $1 and constant (so average cost is also $1). If the industry were in perfect competition, it would produce three hundred units per day, sell them for $1 each, and have no profits.

Table 8.1

Price ($)	Quantity	Price ($)	Quantity
1	300	6	175
2	275	7	150
3	250	8	125
4	225	9	100
5	200		

Now, let's say there are three products that equally share shelf space in the store—Red, Blue, and Green—and they are Cournot competitors, each producing one quarter of the market. One quarter of three hundred is seventy-five. There are three products, so total output is 225, which would make the price $4. Profits can now be calculated precisely:

Profits = (Price − Average Cost) × Quantity.

(Price minus average cost is what is sometimes called markup.)

So each firm will make profits of $225 per day (just a coincidence that this is the same as total output). Industry profits can also be calculated at $675.

But Red and Blue are both being produced by the same company, Acme (Green is produced by United), and no one at Acme can remember why the company is doing this. So management decides to combine the company's two products into one, called Purple. There are now two products in the market still being Cournot competitors. So each would now produce one-third of the market, or one hundred units. Total output would fall to two hundred units and the price would rise to $5. Industry profits would also rise to $800 ((5 − 1) × 200), which would be split evenly between Acme and United; each firm would get $400. But wait! When there were three products, two of which were produced by Acme, Acme's combined profits were $450! By producing Red and Blue, Acme took shelf space (and ultimately profits) away from Green.

In a world with a fixed factor such as shelf space, it's sometimes better to produce your own competitor and get a bigger percentage of smaller industry profits. Curiously, this well known competitive practice might go away as we move more toward online retailing. Online retailers warehouse their inventory in massive fulfillment centers and have no obvious shelf-space constraints.

Suppose the demand for each good is:

$Q_1 = 200 - 3P_1 + P_2,$

$Q_2 = 100 - 2P_2 + P_1,$

and each company has constant marginal and average cost:

$MC = AC = 20.$

Recall that profits are markup times quantity:

$\text{Profit} = (P - AC)Q.$

So firm 1's profit would be:

$\text{Profit}_1 = (P_1 - AC)Q_1.$

Substituting in firm 1's demand equation and the average cost of twenty:

$\text{Profit}_1 = (P_1 - 20)(200 - 3P_1 + P_2).$

Then multiplying:

$\text{Profit}_1 = 200P_1 - 3P_1^2 + P_1P_2 - 4{,}000 + 60P_1 - 20P_2.$

We can now use calculus to tell us how firm 1 thinks about its own price. We imagine a firm wants to increase its price as long as that price change increases its profits. If this process is orderly, the firm will increase its price until the change in profits is zero (the next price increase would make profits fall). In calculus, the first derivative of this equation shows how profits change when we change any of the terms on the right side of the equals sign. The firm's focus is on its own price, so the first derivative we're interested in is:

$d\text{Profit}_1/dP_1 = 200 - 6P_1 + P_2 + 60 = 0.$

And we set this derivative equal to zero in order to find the last price change.

Rearranging this equation to get firm 1's price:

$P_1 = 260/6 + 1/6P_2,$

$P_1 = 43.33 + 0.167P_2.$

Notice that firm 1 cannot set its price independently of firm 2. They are substitutes; but not perfect substitutes.

We'll do the same thing for firm 2m starting with substituting firm 2's demand equation:

$\text{Profit}_2 = (P_2 - 20)(100 - 2P_2 + P_1).$

Then multiplying:

$\text{Profit}_2 = 100P_2 - 2P_2^2 + P_1P_2 - 2000 + 40P_2 - 20P_1.$

And firm 2 will also want to increase its price until profits stop rising:

$d\text{Profit}_2/dP_2 = 100 - 4P_2 + P_1 + 40 = 0.$

which we can rearrange to get firm 2's price:

$P_2 = 140/4 + 1/4P_1,$

$P_2 = 35 + 0.25P_1.$

In practice, what probably follows is a series of price changes and responses over a short time, since each firm has the other's price in its own pricing equation. We can determine where this iteration will end by simply plugging one firm's pricing equations into the other's:

$P_1 = 43.33 + 0.167(35 + 0.25P_1),$

$P_1 = 43.33 + 5.833 + 0.04167P_1.$

$P_1 - 0.04167P_1 = 49.17.$

$0.9583P_1 = 49.17.$

$P_1 = 49.17/0.9583 = 51.31.$

Plugging that into firm 2's pricing equation:

$P_2 = 35 + 0.25(51.31) = 47.83.$

Both firms end up with a price that's higher than average cost, so both are making profits. But the math has a deeper intuition behind it. In thinking about pricing: when there are two firms that are not perfect substitutes, each firm realizes that it won't get all the other firm's customers by lowering its price. Some customers just prefer the other company's version of the product. So lowering your price has two opposite effects on your profits—you draw a few customers away from your competitor, but you lower the profits realized from all your existing customers. The calculus result finds us the prices at which those two effects balance out for each firm.

Sample Exam Question 8.3
Check that this is the profit-maximizing price for firm 1. Use the demand equation for firm 1 to calculate its sales at these prices. Then use that to calculate its profits. Now recalculate firm 1's sales and profits if it lowers its price to $50. Note that you'll need to use firm 2's pricing equation to calculate firm 2's new price.

8.6   Price Cooperation

Another way that firms can avoid a price war is to specifically incorporate a time element and the predictable response of the other player into the decision to cut prices. Subtly, when we discussed the price war earlier, we assumed that our price cut would not be met with any response (the other firm's price was perceived as constant)—basically, that our price cut would garner our firm the entire market forever. We know that's not realistic.

So let's first incorporate a time element about price changes into the mix. Let's say prices can be changed once a month. Now we can make the more realistic assumption that our price cut gets us the entire market, but only for a month. Using our earlier numbers, recalculated for months, the firms each start at a price of $8, making profits of $4 per unit (recall that average cost was $4 and fixed), and selling 30,000 units (one thousand per day for thirty days.)

Either firm could cut its price to, say, $7.50 and capture the entire market, but only for one month. After that they would be in a price war that would drive the prices of both to average cost, $4, and eliminate profits forever.

We can quantify this choice. Suppose sales increased by 10 percent, to 33,000 per firm per month, if the price were dropped to $7.50 (we're assuming this good has a downward-sloping demand line, so quantity rises if price falls). Let's say that firm 1 cuts its price to $7.50 and captures the entire market—66,000 units (33,000 times two firms)—for one month. That would mean profits of $231,000 for one month for firm 1. That sounds like a lot, but let's look at what firm 1 gives up.

At a price of $8 for both firms, each makes a monthly profit of $120,000. If the price cut by firm 1 leads both firms to break even forever after this month, firm 1 is comparing making $231,000 for one month to making $120,000 per month forever. Our intuition tells us that this is a bad trade-off: after only two months at $8, firm 1 makes profits of $240,000.

But we can formalize this intuition to make this comparison more obvious. In finance class, we learn a concept called *present value*. That's the value today of money in the future. The formula for present value is:

PV = Future money/(1 + Interest rate).

The logic behind present value is simple. If you wanted to recreate some amount of money in the future, you could put money in the bank (invest money) at some interest rate. If you wanted to have $1,000 in one year and the interest rate at the bank is 4 percent, you could put X dollars in the bank at 4 percent and have it grow to $1,000:

$1,000 = $X(1 + 4\%) = $X(1.04)$.

If we solve for X, we get:

$X = $1,000/(1.04) = 961.54.

So, if we put $961.54 in the bank at 4 percent interest, we'll have $1,000 in the bank in one year. So $961.54 is the present value (the value today) of $1,000 in one year at an interest rate of 4 percent.

In a somewhat harder derivation, we can determine the value of a sum of money that we get every period forever. Finance people call that kind of asset a "perpetuity" because the payments are perpetual. The present value of a perpetuity is:

$$PV_{\text{perpetuity}} = \text{Future money/Interest rate},$$

assuming the future money and the interest rate are constant every period.

We can apply this formula to firm 1's pricing problem. If firm 1 cuts its price to $7.50, it will make a profit of $231,000 for one month, but it will lose $120,000 dollars every month forever after that. Even if we use a rather high interest rate, say, 1 percent each month (a little more than 12 percent per year), the present value of the lost profits would be:

$$PV_{\text{lost } \$120,000/\text{mo.}} = \$120,000/0.01 = \$1,200,000.$$

The lost profits far exceed the one-month profits from capturing the entire market:

$$\$231,000 < \$1,200,000.$$

Even without cooperating or colluding, firms can determine that highly competitive pricing strategies such as price wars are not profitable in the long run.

Of course, it doesn't hurt to signal to your competitors that you've done the math and it's better for both of you to share a profitable market than to compete away both your profits. That signal is both simple and familiar. Both firms put a big sign in their window that reads, "We'll match our competitor's prices" or "We won't be undersold." While consumers might think these signs are speaking to them, they are in fact telling the competition, "If you cut your price, I'm guaranteeing that I'll cut mine." This is, in effect, telling the competition that price cuts will only work in the very short run. And ironically, this keeps prices high!

This strategy is known as *price cooperation*, but we caution that it is still a noncooperative (and therefore perfectly legal) strategy. Firms are not talking to each other or coordinating their pricing decisions. They able to see that the short-run gains from price cuts aren't worth the long-run losses.

There are some factors that make price cooperation more likely. If the industry has a small number of firms, as was the case in our example, the short-run gains from price cutting are likely to be smaller than the long-run losses. If there are two firms of about the same size, the most you can expect is to double your profits in the short run. That's usually not enough to compensate for losing all profits forever after. It also stands to reason that price cooperation is more likely if the industry has frequent and easy price changes. In that case, competitors could respond to your firm's price change very quickly, meaning your short-run gains could be negligible. And the nature of this form of competition requires

The Sears Catalog

Before the behemoth of Amazon.com, the online shopping giant, appeared in the world, there was a dominating retail force called Sears, Roebuck and Company, the mail-order store. Instead of browsing for items online, people waited for the enormous catalog to arrive in the mail three times a year (spring, fall, and Christmas). While that is indeed a curiosity, one wonders whether the different formats—catalog versus online—have any ramifications for how these two retailers compete. Specifically, which is more likely to price cooperate and which is more like to price compete?

Of the factors we've identified, the one that stands out is the ability to quickly change prices. Amazon.com can change prices instantaneously, as can its online competitors, so there's very little point in price competition. Sears, with its catalogs, had to stick with one set of prices for three to four months at a time. Ironically, that means Sears should have been more of a price competitor than Amazon.com.

that prices be easily observed. That means that stores that regularly put sales circulars in the newspaper are as likely to be price cooperating as they are price competing. After all, competitors as well as customers will know the sale prices.

Examples

Example 1   Nabisco has dominated the cookie and cracker business in the United States for many years. The company has strong brand familiarity, with products such as Oreos, Chips Ahoy, Ritz Crackers, and Saltines. Still, it does get competitive pressure from other cookie and cracker makers, such as Keebler and Sunshine. In recent years, Nabisco has used its brand familiarity to introduce mini, thin, and various flavored versions of all its aforementioned products.

That strategy is, among other things, an excellent entry deterrent according to the Cournot model. Why?

This is an example of a company that produces its own competition in order to use up the shelf space in the store. With multiple versions of popular cookies and crackers, Nabisco has likely expanded its market share so that even if the company had to lower prices on some of the original versions, its overall profits have risen.

Example 2   Dairy Queen and Baskin-Robbins are ice cream chains that compete with a combination of price and product differentiation. Both have been in business since the 1940s. Dairy Queen's most popular product is a mix-in dessert in which different candies and flavors are mixed with soft serve vanilla ice cream.

Baskin-Robbins features a wide variety of ice cream flavors. Both companies have a combination of loyal customers and price-sensitive customers (those who switch more easily when prices change), and let's assume they were in Bertrand equilibrium. Enter Cold Stone Creamery in the late 1980s, featuring an ice cream product in between these two original competitors; Cold Stone offers ice cream with mix-ins, just as Dairy Queen does, and a large flavor variety, just as Baskin-Robbins does.

How did Cold Stone change the equilibrium in the ice cream business?
Since Cold Stone provided a product in between, it probably took some loyal customers from both. In addition, it gave price-sensitive, less loyal customers another place to purchase ice cream when it was cheaper (with coupons and during promotional periods). In both cases, one would guess that Dairy Queen and Baskin-Robbins had to cut their price somewhat in response to this in-between competitor.

Example 3   Amazon came into existence as a low-price alternative to traditional bookstores, record stores, and other bricks-and-mortar retailers. Having put many retail competitors out of business, Amazon now shares the retail space with Walmart and Target, both of which have an online presence.

Assuming Amazon, Target, and Walmart will all survive for the foreseeable future, would you expect them to price compete or price cooperate?
Price cooperate. They can all easily observe each other's prices and they can all adjust prices almost instantaneously. They all have versions of price match guarantees so none of them has an incentive to undercut the others' prices going forward.

Chapter Summary

- We discussed industry concentration and other ways to describe industries that are in between perfect competition and monopoly.
- We learned about monopolistic competition, an industry structure that allows for product differentiation but still has easy entry and exit and thus has no long-term excess profits.
- We discussed the profit possibilities when firms cooperate or collude.
- We discussed output-based Cournot competition, which allowed us to explain why firms sometime produce their own competition.
- We discussed price-based Bertrand competition, which showed us that product differentiation and even a simple understanding of industry dynamics can lead to long-term profits.

Exercises

(B exercises are more challenging.)

A8.1   There are a couple of new sub shops opening up around the country. One of them promises to make a contribution to first responders for every sub it sells. That sub shop always has lots of police officers and firefighters eating there. The owner of that sub shop is probably making excess profits, right?

A8.2   The restaurant industry is still barely profitable in Boomtown, USA, and there's one plot of land left for opening a new eatery. You open a restaurant on that land, but at the end of the year, you are not making excess profits, even though you quickly got as many customers as the rest of the eating establishments. Why aren't you making profits?

A8.3   Cooperation or collusion is a familiar strategy for controlling output, increasing market prices, and making long-term profits. Arguably, it is easier for a small number of firms—two or three—to successfully cooperate in the long run than for, say, eight or ten firms to do so. Why?

A8.4   There are two firms in Cournot competition, each producing about one-third of the competitive market output, so total output is two-thirds of the competitive market output. Knowing they could sell more units, why isn't it in either firm's best interest to produce all the remaining third of the market output?

A8.5   Product differentiation allows firms that are price competing to keep some customers in the long run even if their prices are higher. There is an interesting trade-off, however. Suppose you flavor your cola with kale to appeal to the recent kale-crazed consumer and you increase your price to 20 percent higher than the other cola producer. You have a loyal customer base, but you do end up making lower total profits. Why?

A8.6   Coke and Pepsi are somewhat differentiated Bertrand competitors that usually sell for different prices in the grocery store. Coke usually has a higher price. If Coke were to cut its price, the company would capture some market share from Pepsi. Why doesn't it do this?

A8.7   Kellogg's and Post dominate the breakfast cereal industry, featuring many varieties that are popular among children. They have created brand loyalty over the years with cartoon characters, bright colors, and different flavors. They also feature high (compared to generic cereals), profitable prices. The German deep-discount grocery chain Aldi recently opened across the United States, selling primarily its own store brand of many products. Aldi's breakfast cereal names and packaging are very similar to Kellogg's and Post's, but Aldi cereals sell for half the price. Why mimic the packaging of a competitor?

A8.8   After many years of product differentiation to allow each firm to maintain different and profitable prices, the widget industry eventually had eight high-priced niche producers following the approach of the Bertrand model. Along came a low-price, generic widget producer, which captured a big chunk of the market almost overnight. Why?

A8.9   Best Buy and Circuit City were price-cooperating competitors for many years until Circuit City began to fail. During its last year, Circuit City was more likely to cut prices than it had been in previous years. Why?

A8.10   Once upon a time, stores had to put price stickers on every product so the cashier would know what the price was when you checked out of the store. Changing prices was slow and cumbersome; old stickers had to be peeled off and new ones applied to every unit on the shelf. Now, almost all retailers use bar code scanners, and prices are electronically stored in a computer. Based solely on this change in pricing technology, is price cooperation more likely or less likely now?

B8.1   There are many different family-owned restaurants on Main Street in Anytown, USA. Currently, no new restaurants are considering entering that market because there are no excess profits. In most cases, the owner of the restaurant hires outside help to do all the work in the restaurant. But Jay's Diner is different. Jay Jones, the owner, is also the cook; his wife waits tables; and his kids bus the tables and help with the cleaning. The Jones family makes more income than any other restaurant owner on Main Street. Why wouldn't this be considered excess profits?

B8.2   There are a dozen different restaurants along a two-mile stretch of the main highway nearby. One of them has changed owners and cuisine three times in the past two years, and there's a "For Rent" sign in the window. You always wanted to open a restaurant but you're not sure you should quit your lucrative job as an investment banker. Based on the monopolistic competition model, should you open your restaurant in the available space?

B8.3   You own one of many art galleries on Melrose Boulevard. The galleries are all a little different, and entry is no longer profitable. You have a particularly good eye for popular art. You are especially good at spotting young, up-and-coming artists, from whom you buy their comparatively affordable artworks, which you then sell for a handsome profit. You are earning a higher income than the other art gallery owners. Why? Is your art gallery making long-run excess profits?

B8.4   **Gillette and Schick controlled the highly profitable men's shaving industry using a combination of Bertrand competition (product differentiation and price cooperation) and Cournot competition (using up most of the retail store shelf space to prevent entry). Then along came the lower-price, online competitor Dollar Shave Club, which reached consumers in a new way and offered its products at half the price. If we assume this is a harbinger of the future for many brand-name products, how will the entry of Dollar Shave Club affect the profitability of companies like Procter & Gamble and Colgate-Palmolive, which produce many iconic brand-name products?**

B8.5   **When stores have been successfully price cooperating for many years, the biggest threat is a new competitor that doesn't play by the rules. The major national grocery chains (Kroger and Safeway-Albertson) run weekly newspaper ads, which allows them to price cooperate. When Costco became a major competitor in the grocery industry, it did not run weekly ads. How would that have affected prices at the major chains? Specifically, not knowing for sure, what would the chain stores have to assume about prices at Costco?**

Appendix 8.1   Cournot Graphs and Math

The keys to the simplified, but interesting result that we got in section 8.4 are the assumptions about the market. If demand is linear, then the related marginal revenue is also linear, and it has exactly twice the slope. Let's see why. Suppose demand is:

$Q = 100 - 4P,$

where Q is quantity demanded and P is price.

We can rewrite it as:

$P = 25 - 1/4Q.$

to allow for the fact that price is on the vertical axis in our market model. The slope of this line is the change in price for any change in quantity, or negative one quarter.

To determine marginal revenue, we must first determine the equation for revenue. Revenue is defined as price times quantity, so:

$Rev = P \times Q = 25Q - 1/4Q^2.$

Marginal revenue is the change in revenue as we change output or the first derivative of the revenue equation with respect to Q:

$MR = 25 - 1/2Q.$

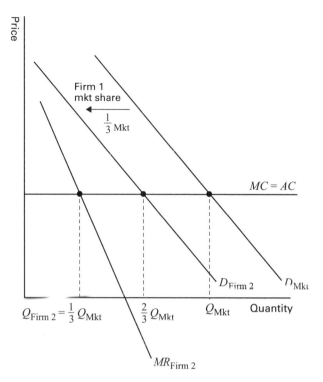

Figure 8.1 Monopolistic Output with Linear Demand and Constant Marginal Costs.

The slope of the marginal revenue line is negative one-half, exactly twice the slope of the demand line.

We also said that marginal cost was constant, meaning it is a horizontal straight line. If we draw a linear demand and a linear marginal revenue and add a horizontal marginal cost, we see that $MR = MC$ exactly halfway between the intersection of demand and marginal cost—the market equilibrium—and the vertical axis. Finally, remember that each firm is conceding the other firm's market share, so its perceived demand is the market demand minus the other firm's demand. When we put all this together, we see that each firm in Cournot competition will produce half its share of the market when it monopolizes that share. When both firms do this, the equilibrium would be each firm in a two-firm Cournot competition producing one-third of the market, and one-third of the market does not get produced by either (see figure 8.1).

9   Game Theory

In many ways, this chapter is a poster child for this book. No other topic is so obviously represented in the media as the one that was the subject of the Best Picture Oscar-winning motion picture *A Beautiful Mind*, the stylized story of mathematician-turned-economist John Nash. In line with the topics addressed in our other chapters, game theory has a very mathematical incarnation and a more intuitive, applicable way of looking at it.

Despite its name, game theory is actually an approach (more than a theory) to a broad set of problems. As early as the nineteenth century (In the Cournot and Bertrand models that we discussed in chapter 8), economists have been aware of the problems and differences in decision-making when more than one entity is involved in the process. If there are two cars at a four-way stop, the outcome depends on both drivers' choices; neither driver can determine the outcome alone. Game theory is a collection of models and approaches that address that situation.

After the real John Nash and others formalized the area we now call game theory, many disciplines began incorporating these models. In international relations, Cold War strategists used it to determine the scenarios under which the United States would end up in a nuclear war against the Soviet Union. One could argue (although precariously) that our ability to avoid World War III was due to the breakthroughs that had been made in game theory. As we will see, while that's a bit of an overstatement, game theory does help us understand how we can avoid unwanted outcomes.

On completion of this chapter, you should

- understand the scenario in which we apply game theory,
- understand how game theory can be used to solve a set of difficult problems, and
- be able to show how the setup of a game theory problem and its solution both inform a game's final result.

9.1   What Is Game Theory?

The best way to define game theory is to describe the situation in which we need and use it. We are aware that the outcome of some situations in life involves decisions and choices made by more than just the individual. When two people play tennis or chess, winning a point or the game depends on each player's ability to incorporate the other player's choices. These are examples of situations in which we use game theory.

Game theory is strategic decision-making, the process of making choices when the decision-maker is aware of the fact that other decision-makers' choices will affect the ultimate outcome. But emphasis is important in understanding this situation. In the discussion of perfect competition in chapter 6, there were many firms making simultaneous decisions, but we didn't need or use game theory. In that case, the individual small firm knew there were other decision-makers involved, but they all knew they were too small to affect the market. So the existence of other decision-makers is not by itself a reason the use game theory. We need other decision-makers and the mutual knowledge that all of their choices will determine the outcome. We need a known interdependence that affects the decision-making process.

To make that situation happen, we need to pay special attention to the setup. We describe not only the choices being made but also the relationship between the decision-makers, their choices, and the outcome. In many situations, this is a size thing. Simply knowing there are other decision-makers isn't enough in perfect competition because all participants know they are too small (relative to the entire market) to affect anything at the market level. The size of the decision-makers *relative* to the game is critical. A similar situation exists when people vote in a U.S. presidential election. Everyone knows that his or her vote alone has no impact on the final outcome (except perhaps in Florida in the 2000 presidential election), but the popular vote is still an important factor in the outcome.

So game theory is the approach we need when decisions are known to be actively interdependent. It is the set of choices all of which look, to some extent, like an intersection with a four-way stop sign.

9.2   Setup

While underlying assumptions are important in all economic models and to all results, game theory and its results are intimately related. In every situation we will take care to describe the setup of the game carefully. In most cases, our outcome will be as much an exercise in game theory as it is a commentary on the setup of the game. As we will see, most games have rules that we determine. As such, if we don't like the outcome, we can often change the rules that got us to that outcome.

What situation requires the use of game theory? What do we mean by a game?

1. There must be more than one decision-maker and an awareness that each decision-maker's choice will affect the outcome.

2. The choices available to each decision-maker must be clearly defined.

3. Outcomes based on these choices must be known to the decision-makers.

4. The decision-making process must be described and known to all players.

5. The decision-maker must be rational.

The first of these characteristics of situations in which game theory is useful is obvious. As stated earlier, this is when we need to use game theory—when there are multiple decision-makers who are all aware of the interdependency of their choices. If I know I can make a choice with no consideration of the choices made by others, I don't need game theory.

Once we are clearly in a game-theoretic setting, the participants need to know what their choices are. Everyone has been in interpersonal situations (relationships) in which the decision-making process is clearly interdependent but one or both players don't know what choices are available. The game, we would say, is poorly defined and as such won't be easy to solve. (This is what people sometimes call a no-win situation. Not knowing all the choices, we can't get the game to its optimal result.)

Similarly, we must have a known set of outcomes, which we call in game theory payoffs. Even if the choices are known, we can't make a decision if the outcomes based on those choices are poorly defined. This is a more difficult part of the setup than one might think. In classroom examples, we usually fill our payoff matrix with dollars or something equally ubiquitous and say that each player bases her choice on maximizing that payoff. That's fine if all the players care only and equally about money (or whatever is in the payoff matrix), but we know that what people care about is complicated and nuanced. Ultimately, what we want in our payoff matrix is whatever the players are using to make their decisions.

Certain procedural aspects of the game matter as much as choices and outcomes. For example, are choices made simultaneously or sequentially? All of our games need to specify the timing of choices. Similarly, we need to specify the cooperative nature of a game. Most of the time, we will talk about the most interesting games for us—noncooperative games. These are games in which the participants do not have the ability to cooperate or coordinate their choices. Cooperation is a bit trickier than one might think. The ability to successfully cooperate, as we will see, has a lot to do with the overall setup of the game.

Like payoff, rationality is a complicated concept. Ask a dozen economists or philosophers for their definition of rationality and you'll get two dozen answers at least. Oddly, a well-structured game theory problem has a built-in rationality. As previously stated, the payoffs in a well-structured game must be things that most decision-makers would chose in an orderly, rational way. So if all players care about money equally, I can structure my game's payoffs in dollars and get the right results (observable results for such players in the real world). If some players care about money while others care about, say, image, I have to structure my payoffs accordingly. After that has been accomplished, rationality can simply be defined as consistency: faced with (exactly) the same potential outcomes, players make the same choices.

9.3   The Nash Equilibrium: Hot Dog Stands on the Beach

A classic example of game theory involves location decisions in a strictly limited context. Suppose there are two hot dog stands on a one-mile stretch of beach. The stands are the same in all important ways, and customers always walk to the closest stand. Beachgoers are equally distributed along the beach, and there aren't too many people in total on the beach (we don't want long lines to form at either stand). Where along the one-mile stretch of beach will both stands locate?

Most people would say they would naturally space themselves out and locate around the one-quarter-mile and three-quarter-mile location. That would be best for all beachgoers since it would minimize the distance anyone had to walk (at most, one would walk a quarter mile to get a snack). The problem is, this is not an equilibrium location. In this context, equilibrium means stable, or a place where, once reached, no one would want to change.

Knowing customers walk to the closest stand, either stand would see it in its best interest to move. Suppose, at the end of the day, stand 1's owner closed up and went home to bed. Stand 2's owner, thinking strategically, packed up his umbrella and mustard and moved his stand right next to stand 1 (giving him three quarters of the beach on the next day). Stand 1 would almost certainly respond the next night by leapfrogging over her competitor in order to capture more of the market. This process would continue until we reached equilibrium, a place where neither stand owner would find it in her or his best interest to move. That would be in the middle of the beach (the one-half-mile point) and right next to each other. From there, neither could get more customers by moving, and each stand would have half the beach as its market. Notice that each stand would have exactly the same number of customers as it did at the one-quarter-mile, three-quarter-mile location, but from this location they do not risk losing any customers if their competitor relocates.

Curiosity 9.1
The Median Voter Model

Among the places that we see the hot dog stand result in our day-to-day lives is in politics. If we reimagine the setup, letting the beachgoers be the voting population and the hot dog stands be the candidates of two different political parties, we get an interesting, predictable result about elections. If voters are equally distributed in their political views (from far-left liberals to far-right conservatives), candidates will gravitate toward the center politically by the time the election is held. The rationale is, each candidate tries to get more than half of the political center plus everyone to one side or the other. That result means that in most elections in a two-party system, the candidates are more alike than different, and most elections are close (if the parties choose their candidate wisely). (For the 2018 U.S. presidential election, see media example 1 at the end of the chapter.)

Some people bemoan the lack of choice that the two-party system ultimately provides and call for more parties (à la many countries in Europe). But when we apply the hot dog stand model and the notion of Nash equilibrium to three hot dog stands, or political parties, we find there is no stable equilibrium. The stands never stop relocating!

This result is what John Nash noticed and formalized in what's called the *Nash equilibrium*—each player is doing the best they can, given what the other player is doing. No player can change their choice unilaterally and make themselves better off. Notice how important the setup is in reaching this result. Customers always walk to the closest stand, there is an equal distribution of beachgoers, and so on. Change any of those factors and you might get a different result.

This strategic result didn't change the idea of profit maximization, it augmented it. If my business decisions are truly independent of other businesses' decisions, I don't need game theory, but often that is not the case. If firm A thinks about cutting its price to capture market share from firm B, it needs to consider how firm B will respond, and how both firms' choices will determine firm A's original decision. We saw this dynamic in the section in chapter 9 on Bertrand competition.

9.4   Prisoner's Dilemma

For sheer range of application, no game beats *prisoner's dilemma*. The setup and scenario will be familiar to fans of cops and robbers television shows. Two suspects are caught after a bank robbery in which there are no good witnesses or other evidence. The police have one well-known avenue to solving the crime: get one or both of the suspects to confess.

The police question each of the suspects separately and offer both the same deal. If you confess and your accomplice does not, you will get one year in jail and your accomplice will get ten years (you will testify against your accomplice). If both of you confess, we won't need the testimony of either of you against the other, so you'll both get five years. If neither of you confesses, we still have you on possession of a firearm (or some lesser charge) and you'll get three years in jail each.

Looking at the situation, you might think neither person would confess, but each suspect's thought process is complicated by not being sure what the other person will do. Either suspect would think about what he should do in either circumstance, if the other person confesses or he doesn't. If each player cares most about minimizing his own prison sentence, he will go through the following process:

If the other guy does confess, I'm going to prison for either five years or ten. Clearly, five is a lot better, so I should also confess. If the other guy does not confess, I'm going to prison for either three years or one. Again, if I care most about minimizing my prison time, I would confess. Notice that no matter what the other guy does, my best choice is to confess. Confessing is called the player's *dominant strategy:* a choice you make regardless of the other player's choice. Both players, if they care most about minimizing their own prison sentence, will actually confess, and thus they will both get a five-year prison sentence (see figure 9.1).

Here's the part that boggles people's minds. Had they both not confessed, they both would have been better off! The game-theoretic result—namely, they both confess—is actually inferior to neither of them confessing for both players, but getting to that better outcome is hard. If you can't be sure what the other player is going to do, you have to confess.

This famous result is usually interpreted as the inferior outcome we attain when we act independently rather than cooperatively. If the two players could have cooperated in their decision process, they both would have chosen not to confess, and both of them would have been better off. Actually, the only way for two people who are making independent choices to achieve the superior outcome is for each person to care about the *other* person's result when they make their choices.

Prisoner's dilemma and its result has broad applications. The notion that individualistic decision-making often leads to bad results for the group will turn up later in this book when we talk about international trade and public economics.

SUNDANCE

		Confess	Not Confess
BUTCH	Confess	B gets 5 years S gets 5 years	B gets 1 year S gets 10 years
	Not Confess	B gets 10 years S gets 1 year	B gets 3 years S gets 3 years

Figure 9.1 Prisoner's Dilemma Choices

9.5   Prisoner's Dilemma Games and Price Cooperation

In chapter 8 we showed that firms that use Bertrand (price) competition can figure out the long-term problem with a price war and ultimately choose not to try to undercut their competitors' prices. We called this version of the Bertrand model price cooperation (recalling that it is still noncooperative.) When we showed that result in chapter 8, we used a finance tool known as present value. We can also get this result using a prisoner's dilemma–style game.

Suppose we have two stores trying to decide whether they should cut their price or keep it the same. The profits they predict from all possible choices are shown in figure 9.2.

Both stores have a dominant strategy to cut their prices, and both stores make profits of $2 million if the game is played one time. They also can see that they would be both better off if neither of them cut prices (both would make profits of $5 million). It turns out that playing the game two or three or any finite number of times does not change this result. What we find is that the stores will always cut their price in the last period, and that makes them cut their price every period.

But suppose the game has no last period; suppose it is played repeatedly and forever. We can use a trick and our present value finance tool to see how this changes the game. The stores know that there are only two outcomes that could happen every period forever. They could both cut their prices and get $2 million every period forever or they could both not cut their prices and get $5 million every period forever. The other two choices, one store cuts and the other store does not, could never happen every period. The store that was getting $1 million (the one that did not cut) would always change its choice the next year to get at least $2 million. So both cut forever or neither cuts forever can be thought of as a Nash equilibrium—neither firm would unilaterally change—whereas the scenario in which one firm cuts and the other does not cut is not a Nash equilibrium. If we keep the interest rate and present value calculation that we did in chapter 8 the same, that lets us perceive the forever payoff matrix, as shown in figure 9.3.

STORE A

		Cut	Not Cut
STORE B	Cut	A gets $2M B gets $2M	A gets $1M B gets $10M
	Not Cut	A gets $10M B gets $1M	A gets $5M B gets $5M

Figure 9.2   Prisoner's Dilemma Applied to Question of Cutting Prices

STORE A

	Cut	Not Cut
STORE B — Cut	A gets $40M B gets $40M	A gets $1M B gets $10M
STORE B — Not Cut	A gets $10M B gets $1M	A gets $100M B gets $100M

Figure 9.3 Prisoner's Dilemma Played Forever Payoff Matrix

In this version of the game, neither player has a dominant strategy. Two outcomes are possible. Either both cut forever or neither of them cuts forever. They both know that if they try to get the $10 million in any period, it will move the game forever from neither cuts to both cut. The cost of getting the $10 million in one period is losing $80 million in present value profits!

So playing a prisoner's dilemma game forever—with no last period—moves the result to the cooperative solution. That's consistent with the result from chapter 8 that gave us price cooperation. It's also a powerful result in game theory. If players perceive no last period, they are much less likely to make choices that are self-interested.

9.6 Coordination Games and First-Mover Advantages

Some games do not have an easy path to one equilibrium outcome. Suppose there are two firms—let's call them Kellogg's and Post—that are trying to decide which of two possible new types of cereal they should introduce. Their choices are a new extra-crunchy cereal or a new extra-sweet cereal. Their market research indicates that the new cereal will succeed only if they don't both introduce the same cereal.

The payoff matrix for this game looks like what is shown in figure 9.4.

Neither company has a dominant strategy. This game instead has two Nash equilibria that are equally good for both firms. Basically, both firms are equally well-off as long as they don't pick the same new product. Either Kellogg's choosing crunchy and Post choosing sweet or Kellogg's choosing sweet and Post choosing crunchy would be an equilibrium; neither firm could unilaterally improve its outcome by changing its choice. The question to be answered in this case is how to structure the game to allow both firms to get to one of those outcomes.

We didn't make some parts of this game explicit. For example, we didn't say how or when each company would make its choice. Sometimes the game-theoretic construct

KELLOGG'S

	Crunchy	Sweet
POST Crunchy	K gets – $1M P gets – $1M	K gets $10M P gets $10M
POST Sweet	K gets $10M P gets $10M	K gets – $1M P gets – $1M

Figure 9.4   Payoff Matrix for Prisoner's Dilemma Game Involving New Products

KELLOGG'S

	Crunchy	Sweet
POST Crunchy	K gets – $1M P gets – $1M	K gets $5M P gets $15M
POST Sweet	K gets $15M P gets $5M	K gets – $1M P gets – $1M

Figure 9.5   First-Mover Advantage in Prisoner's Dilemma

allows us to find rules that would let the players reach an equilibrium. Here, if we simply let one player choose first, both players would succeed. Because the only thing that determines a good outcome is not choosing the same new product; who goes first doesn't matter. When a game has equilibria but needs a set of rules that allows the players to reach one of the equilibria, we say it is a game of pure coordination. Remember, these are all games in which the players cannot or do not cooperate, so the coordination mechanism has to be something like the timing of decisions.

Suppose the payoff matrix shows that crunchy is more profitable than sweet (see figure 9.5). Now the player that chooses first will always choose crunchy and get the best outcome, $15 million. We say this game has a first-mover advantage.

This is an important change. Focusing on the lessons that we get from a game's setup, if a game has multiple Nash equilibria but can be solved easily with some approach, such as letting anyone go first, the outcome of the game is easy to predict. If there is no simple algorithm for reaching one of the equilibria, the game is much harder to solve and the outcome is harder to predict.

Sample Exam Question 9.1

Simply allowing either player to go first doesn't work if the game has a first-mover advantage. But you could combine that timing rule with another rule if the game is played repeatedly. Explain. (*Hint:* In tennis, serving is a first-mover advantage in any game. How do the rules of tennis deal with that to allow the game to be fair to both players?)

Curiosity 9.2
Prisoner's Dilemma Games and Social Structure

The basic result from the prisoner's dilemma game is that self-interest drives us to a sub-optimal outcome. That lesson can be used to explain the existence and importance of many norms and social structures. Religions, family values, and civics classes all try to ingrain the importance of making choices that are good for those in the group, not just good for the individual. If people are raised in these systems, they will make choices that lead to better outcomes for all.

Unfortunately, as we see in prisoner's dilemma, the superior cooperative outcome critically depends on everyone (at least the vast majority of people) making the cooperative choice. To enforce that choice, our social structures often include a payoff (punishment) for making the right (wrong) choice. Religions have heaven and hell, family values talk about damaging the family's reputation, and governments have fines and other punishments for some bad choices.

Game theory and prisoner's dilemma are twentieth-century constructs that correctly explain social structures that are as old as humanity.

Sample Exam Question 9.2

Using the logic of game theory, explain why people are less inclined to clean up after their dog if they live in a large apartment complex and more inclined to clean up after their dog if they live in a single-family house where the dog does his business in the backyard. How does that result explain why pet-friendly apartment complexes usually charge a pet rent?

9.7   Commitments, Promises, and Threats

There are many game-theoretic aspects of our daily life that we learn by doing. Among them is how and when things like commitments, promises, and threats work. While we don't usually think about it, all these actions are things that we do in situations that are consistent with the setup that was outlined in section 9.2. There are two or more players,

SUNDANCE

		Confess	Not Confess
BUTCH	Confess	B gets 7 years S gets 5 years	B gets 4 years S gets 10 years
	Not Confess	B gets 12 years S gets 1 year	B gets 3 years S gets 5 years

Figure 9.6 Prisoner's Dilemma with Dominant Strategy

each making decisions that affect the outcome for everyone. We make commitments, promises, and threats in order to change the choice of other players and ultimately change the outcome.

A commitment is something we say we will do before our choice is made. An important aspect of commitment is that the player who makes the commitment is better off if the other player believes the commitment is genuine. Commitments work best when one player has a clear dominant strategy (always chooses the same thing) and the other player does not.

Suppose we tweak the prisoner's dilemma setup a bit. Butch is a hardened criminal with a long record, but this is the first time Sundance has been arrested. So Butch is going to receive a longer prison sentence than Sundance. Butch is told he'll get four years if he confesses and Sundance does not, twelve years if Sundance confesses and he does not, seven years if they both confess, and still three years on the lesser charge (see figure 9.6).

Now, Butch does not have a dominant strategy. If Sundance confesses, Butch would be better off confessing (seven is less than twelve), but if Sundance does not confess, Butch would be better off not confessing as well (three is less than four). What this means is that Butch does not have a choice that's *always* best for him. We did not change Sundance's numbers, so he still has a dominant strategy to confess. We can figure out how this game will end if Butch knows the prison terms that Sundance is being offered.

If Butch can figure out that Sundance has a dominant strategy to confess, then he simply makes the choice that's best for him when Sundance confesses. Butch would also confess and the game would end, as it did before, with both players confessing. But the path to this solution is different in one important way. Butch cannot make his choice on his own. He must base his choice on Sundance's dominant strategy.

Suppose Sundance said before they were caught (before the game was played) that he would never confess. He committed to not confessing. Since Butch's choice is based on Sundance's choice, this commitment would lead Butch to change his choice to not confess. Assuming Sundance followed through on his commitment and did not confess, they would both get sentences of three years. That commitment changed the outcome and made both players better off.

But the assumption that Sundance will follow through on his commitment is not one that should be taken lightly. Sundance could take another path. He could bluff the commitment, get Butch to confess, then not confess himself and get a sentence of only one year. Given that, and figuring that Butch can see that possibility, Sundance will have to find a way to make his commitment unchangeable if he wants to get Butch to change his choice from confessing to not confessing.

This game highlights two important components of commitments. First, the player making the commitment will be better off if the commitment ultimately makes him better off. When that is true, we say that the commitment is credible. Second, for the commitment to change the other player's choice, it has to be irreversible. There can't be a way to bluff the commitment (and make the player making the commitment better off with the bluff alone).

Promises and threats are like commitments except they are done in games where the choices are sequential rather than simultaneous. Sequential games are ones that are structured like the board games chess and checkers. Each player moves after the other player has made his move. The timing of a sequential game makes players think in steps: "If I do this, he'll do that, so I'll do the other thing. . . ."

Following this sequential process, promises and threats are usually publicly stated announcements prior to the first move. A promise or threat says to the other player, "If you do this, then I'll do that." They are your response to the other player's choice. Parents often use promises and threats to get children to make better choices. "If you don't eat your vegetables, you won't get dessert." "If you get straight A's, I'll buy you an iPhone." Like commitments, there's a credibility component to promises and threats. The player making the promise or threat must be better off if the promise or threat seems to them better off.

Promises and threats are usually used in games where neither player has a dominant strategy. In this case, there are usually many possible solutions to the game. A classic (if unpleasant) case would be when a mugger wants your money but doesn't want to hurt you. The mugger will often say something like, "If you don't yell for police, I won't hurt you." The idea is that he wants your money and he wants to get away. If you yell, he is more likely to get caught. His jollies would be higher if he got your money, didn't get caught, and got away. Assuming you'll have to give him your money either way, your jollies would be higher if you also didn't get hurt. In this case, the promise/threat makes both of you better off (all things considered) and it solves the game. You won't yell for the police.

Examples

Example 1 The hot-dog-stands-on-the-beach example has been used in political science to explain the observation that when two candidates are running for an elected office, they usually sound very similar by election time on most of the issues. The logic is that voters are equally distributed in a political sense on most issues

(we usually think of the endpoints as very conservative and very liberal, with most people falling somewhere in the middle), so winning means getting more of the middle and all of one end or the other. If that's true, most two-candidate elections should be very close.

Did the hot dog stands model work during the 2018 U.S. presidential election?

Yes and no. Hillary Clinton won the popular vote by a substantial majority over Donald Trump, so the voters did not perceive them as being similar (in the middle) on the issues. But Donald Trump won a narrow majority of the states (and thus the Electoral College), and he won many states by a very narrow margin, so if the issues that mattered were more regional than individual, then yes, the hot dog stand model worked as predicted.

Example 2   The Cold War and nuclear arms buildup that the United States and the USSR experienced for many decades in the twentieth century showed signs of reversal in the late 1980s when both sides agreed to scale back some of their missiles.

Why was this cooperation easier at that time?

Let's think of the Cold War as a version of the prisoner's dilemma game. The cooperative solution, namely, that both countries have fewer missiles, is better for both countries than the Cold War outcome, both have lots of missiles. That cooperative solution is hard to achieve because each country thinks it is better off if it has lots of missiles and the other country does not.

Cooperative solutions in prisoner's dilemma games work only if both countries adhere to them. That usually requires verification and some form of observation. By the late 1980s, spy satellites had gotten so good that each country could observe the other's activities, thus allowing verification.

Example 3   If they aren't owned by municipalities, most electricity providers are regulated because they are what we called in chapter 7 natural monopolies. An interesting game-theoretic problem occurs when cities try to regulate them. To get the price of electricity closer to the competitive price (lower than the monopoly price), the regulator needs accurate cost information. Usually, the electricity provider—the company being regulated—is the one that has that information. Assuming the electricity company wants to sell at the highest possible price, it has an incentive to tell the regulator that costs are higher than they actually are. Because of that, the regulator usually uses lower costs than the electricity provider gives it. This creates an interesting game between these two entities.

Suppose the electricity provider wants to be completely honest about costs. In the environment described above, can it?

No! If the regulator is going to assume the cost numbers it is given by the electricity provider are inflated, providing the regulator with accurate (lower) cost numbers will mean the regulated price will be too low. The regulator will lower the costs provided to it, even if those numbers are accurate.

Chapter Summary

- We developed an understanding of the circumstances in which we need game theory.
- We examined the structure of a game.
- We learned how to solve game theory problems under various circumstances.
- We saw how incorporating the game theory approach often changes the outcome and might lead to a different response by policymakers and regulators.

Exercises

(B exercises are more challenging.)

A9.1 In the famous barroom scene in the movie *A Beautiful Mind*, a young John Nash points out the problem with all his friends asking the same woman to dance. Suppose there are five men and six women, everyone wants to dance at the same time, but no woman will accept an offer to dance if she is asked second (after the man asks another woman first). What do you think John Nash told his colleagues would occur if they all asked the same woman first?

A9.2 How might a government regulation (e.g., a permit for a specific location only) solve the hot dog stand problem in a way that's no worse for the stand owners and better for customers?

A9.3 When a couple goes out on a first date, they often end up doing things that neither of them actually likes very much. Why?

A9.4 If you and another driver reach a four-way stop at the same time and perpendicular to each other and you wave the other driver to go ahead, how have you solved that game of coordination?

A9.5 To answer this question, we need to make an unfair generalization: in the United States, most Democrats are politically liberal (on the hot dog stand continuum, they are left of center) and most Republicans are politically conservative (right of center.) The winner of a general election captures more of the center and all of her side. Parties pick their candidate in primaries in which only their party's voters can vote. Why do incumbents usually win general elections?

A9.6 One player committing to a choice that could end up getting both players to their best possible outcome is a good way to help solve a game. Why does this work, given that commitments don't always work?

A9.7 A well-known coordination game is called the dropped call game. If two people are talking with each other on cell phones and the call gets dropped before they finish talking, who calls whom back? You know that if no one calls back, you don't get to talk anymore (which you both want to do), and if you both call back, you get a busy signal and thus don't get to talk. Suggest a coordination mechanism.

A9.8 How is the Cournot approach to finding an oligopoly output for each of two firms the same as a Nash equilibrium?

A9.9 Why do many waiting rooms (e.g., at a doctor's or dentist's office) try to ban the use of cell phones by those waiting for an appointment?

A9.10 Suppose you see a mugger beating up someone in the park. He approaches you next demanding money and says the familiar phrase, "If you don't scream, I won't hurt you." Would you scream?

B9.1 Religions usually have rules and structures that try to lead to cooperative outcomes. Those rules and structures punish people for making choices that are self-interested, like cheating. But cheating is often impossible to observe. How do religions fix this problem?

B9.2 When the Tax Cut and Jobs Act of 2017 was passed, no Democrat in either house of Congress voted in favor. No Democrat in either house took an active role in determining the tax law changes. Not surprisingly, the majority of people who saw their taxes increase through this bill live in heavily Democratic states, such as California and New York. If we assume members of Congress are always trying to do the best they can for their constituents, did the reluctance of Democrats to participate make sense strategically?

B9.3 An interesting if unfortunate reality that we glean from game theory is that a different cultural background or upbringing can lead to a badly imbalanced outcome in certain situations. Suppose you were raised to be generous and considerate of others at all times, and every day, while walking to the coffee shop, you meet a panhandler who cares only about himself. Some days you have only enough money in your pocket to buy your coffee. How will you solve this game?

B9.4 Along the same lines as the previous question (and harking back to question A.6), suppose you were raised to always tell the truth—you never lie—but you are in a game-theoretic situation with someone who does whatever is necessary to maximize his outcome. There's a choice that could make both of you better off than either of you would be without a commitment, but it would not be the best overall outcome for the other player. Why would commitments be harder to keep in this case?

B9.5   Commitments often require an ability to observe the choices of other players so that you know the other player's commitment isn't a self-serving bluff. Observation, or proof, is the opposite of what we usually refer to as faith. Most religions are built around faith. Why?

10 Input Markets

Apples, strawberries, and every good we've mentioned in this book need inputs, and, like those final goods, inputs must be produced and purchased. Inputs also have a market: a supply and a demand. That might seem a little strange since one of those inputs is labor, which we think of as people—and we don't comfortably think of people in terms of supply and a demand. But the input known as labor is people choosing to work, and they make that choice based on a price: wages.

We actually see market forces at work in the labor market all the time. If wages in some industries have been pushed up by high demand or by external forces such as government policy, producers will choose to employ other, cheaper inputs in a process similar to the substitution effect that we discussed in chapters 2 and 4. In every respect, inputs are produced and distributed by a market, and as such, we can make liberal use of the concepts we learned in our earlier discussion of supply and demand.

Input markets are an important application of our microeconomic tools. But we often hear about these markets as part of policy debates concerning such things as minimum wages. That gives people the impression that the government prices some inputs. Sadly, many of those government policies don't apply market principles correctly, and that leads to what people have come to call unintended consequences.

We'll talk about input markets in purely economic terms, then discuss how and when government intervention might improve outcomes. We will also talk about innovations in input markets and how innovation will change the use of and compensation to various inputs.

On completion of this chapter, you should

- understand that a market similar to the market for final goods allocates inputs,
- see how the input market determines the compensation for inputs,
- understand the forces that determine the optimal combination of inputs, and
- understand how government policies can affect input compensation and use,

---

10.1   What Are Inputs?

When we grew and picked apples in chapter 2 or strawberries in chapter 5, we used land and labor, and we talked about other factors of production, such as seeds, fertilizer, and water. These are all inputs in the production of fruit. Inputs are the resources that are necessary for the production of any good. Inputs might be tangible factors, such as machinery, steel, and electricity, or they might be skills and services, which require training, education, or experience.

Inputs are also larger, macroeconomic factors such as capital stock, the accumulated value of the country's factories and machines, and so on. The capital stock for any one company is what investors (stock- and bondholders) own. So the capital stock exists as a result of people's decision to save or invest. Infrastructure—our roads and airports and sewers—exists as a result of the government applying the economic concepts we'll discuss in chapter 11. Even labor, when we aggregate it, becomes a national issue, as we see people get and lose jobs economy-wide during the booms and busts of the business cycle.

A solid understanding of input markets is critical for the efficient operation of a business, and the aggregate of that process will determine the current and future success of the entire economy. As we'll see, government policies that are considered the purview of microeconomics, such as setting the minimum wage, ultimately have an impact on the macroeconomy.

10.2   Factor Compensation: Firm Level

To get a basic understanding of factor markets and compensation, it is important to simplify the production process first. We'll return to the production process that we used in chapter 5, picking strawberries. There we noted that many inputs were required to go from entering the strawberry industry to getting the strawberries to market: land, seeds, water, fertilizer, labor, and more. But in explaining the supply side of the market, we focused on the end of the process, picking the strawberries. Let's start there again.

Table 10.1

Workers	Total Berries Picked (qts/hr)	Increment (Marginal Product of Labor)
1	100	100
2	190	90
3	270	80
4	340	70
5	400	60
6	450	50
7	490	40
8	520	30

Think about adding labor to a fixed field of strawberries. The first worker will have a field full of strawberries to pick and, because of that, he will be the most productive worker whom we hire. That worker will never have to think about bumping into anyone else; he won't have to slow down to find strawberries on plants that someone else has already picked from. Every worker after him, though, will be less productive. The fixed field size and fixed quantity of strawberries mean that every additional worker is a little less productive than the worker before him. We show this in table 10.1.

The change in total output as we add more workers is called the *marginal product of labor*. This is an important number for employers. If you asked the owner of the strawberry farm how many laborers she would hire to pick her strawberries, she would say that she would hire any worker who paid for himself. Let's see how that works.

Suppose the wage rate that prevails in similarly skilled industries is $10 per hour (fixed) and strawberries sell for twenty cents a quart (also fixed). The farmer could sell the hourly production of the first worker for $20, which easily covers the $10 hourly wage rate. Similarly, workers two, three, four, and five cover their own hourly cost. Worker six produces an extra fifty quarts of strawberries beyond that picked by worker five, which can be sold for exactly $10, his hourly cost. Arguably, the farmer is indifferent about hiring that worker (we usually assume the worker would be hired, because why not?), but worker seven produces only forty quarts, which can be sold for $8. Worker seven does not cover his costs.

The farmer would hire workers until the value of the marginal product of labor—the price of the output times the marginal product of the last worker—just covered the wage. This rule gives employers a relatively simple way of knowing how many workers to hire: you wouldn't hire anyone that actually decreased your profits.

The assumptions we made at the outset ensure that this rule is both fair and accurate. This employer viewed the wage rate as fixed; that means this is a small employer relative to the labor market (analogous to a price-taking firm in perfect competition). The overall labor market will act the same as this individual employer and equate the wage rate to the value of the marginal product of labor, but no one employer will affect that. That means that this farm did not lower wages for everyone when it hired an extra worker.

Some people argue that making labor decisions this way means that the firm is profiting on every employee except the last one. They pay the sixth worker $10, and he generated revenue of $10. But they also pay worker number five $10, and he generated revenue of $12. And they pay worker number one $10, and he generated revenue of $20. We can see this another way. The farm will pay $60 per hour for all workers, and they will pick a total of 450 quarts. Those strawberries will sell for $90. So the firm made $30 in profits. Doesn't that mean the firm can hire more people or pay higher wages to all of its employees? Generally speaking, no.

Labor isn't the only factor of production. There are other inputs that the firm needs to pay for. This rule ensures the firm will hire every profitable worker—no more, no less. And when the rule is applied to all factors, a competitive firm dealing with competitive input markets won't make excess profits, so it won't have extra money available to hire more labor or pay higher wages.

Put differently, the firm will use this approach for each of its inputs. When it adds up the cost of all its variable inputs, it will have marginal cost. And in perfect competition, it will be producing where price equals marginal cost, or zero excess profits. If the firm is able to make profits because the industry is not perfectly competitive, the case can be made that some of the excess profits—which usually go to the owners of capital—could or should be paid to labor. Government policies such as high minimum wages are an attempt to force that transfer. As we'll see, that often backfires when optimizing firms decide to decrease the amount of labor they employ.

> **Sample Exam Question 10.1**
> Labor unions use a strategy called collective bargaining to increase wages. They get (force) all workers to join the union. Then the union says to the employer, "Either hire seven of us at $12 per hour or nobody." What's the problem with this demand?

10.3   Factor Compensation: The Market

When all employers use this approach, the combined value of the marginal product of labor becomes the demand for labor in an industry. It will be downward sloping because of the diminishing marginal product of labor. If an employer is going to hire the next, less-productive worker, it will have to decrease wages to maintain the equality between wages and the value of the marginal product of labor. The supply of labor is based on population, skills, and other similar factors. From this market model comes the market's compensation (the market-determined wage rate) and the market quantity of labor employed.

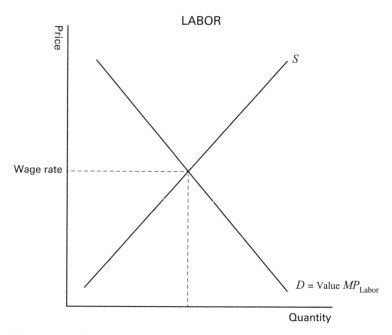

Figure 10.1 Supply of and Demand for Labor

This approach works for all inputs. The demand for the input is the aggregate value of the marginal product of that input. The supply is different for different inputs, but it is the physical quantity of the input that is available. The supply of land is more or less determined by nature for any one place. More historically interesting is the ownership of land, which in earlier times determined the distribution of wealth (or lack thereof) in many countries. This is a complicated issue, but once ownership is determined, landowners earn rents for allowing the land to be used.

The supply of capital comes from people deciding to save or invest part of their income back into the firm. Invested money is used to build things like factories, and thus capital owners own the factory and the profit it generates. In the case of capital, the compensation is sometimes stated as a rate of return rather than a dollar return. For our purposes, the return on capital (often an interest rate) is a proxy for the price of capital, even though it is not a dollar price.

The recurring story here is that all inputs are owned by someone and all compensation for the use of these inputs is thus someone's income. We often hear policymakers focus on the compensation to labor as the only compensation that goes to "people." But all input owners are people.

10.4   Minimum Wage

For many historical and cultural reasons, the "market" for labor has made people and policymakers uncomfortable. Concepts of fairness and other moral and ethical issues are often brought forth to supersede market forces. In the United States, the federally mandated minimum wage was a New Deal policy put forth during the high-unemployment years of the Great Depression. Those were extraordinary times and, arguably, not a period when input markets worked well. We'll explain some of the possible reasons for this in the next section. For now we are left with the reality that the government often takes a role in determining wages for some workers.

The minimum wage applies to everyone, but it only affects workers for whom it is a binding price floor. Like the price floors we discussed in chapter 3, the minimum wage is supposed to help the supply side of the market—here, entry-level and low-skilled workers. If neither the supply of nor the demand for labor is particularly inelastic and if the minimum wage is set above the market wage, the impact of the minimum wage is clear: some people will lose jobs because of this policy. In figure 10.2, we see that the minimum wage causes a surplus of labor because it decreases the quantity demanded of labor while increasing the quantity supplied of labor.

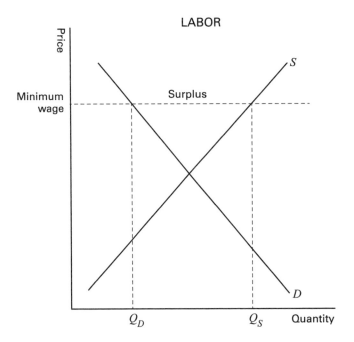

Figure 10.2   Minimum Wage Effects

Focusing on the earlier discussion of wage determination, if wages are set artificially high by the minimum wage, employers will need to decrease the number of people they employ in order to increase the marginal product of labor (assuming the output price is constant). The end result of this dynamic is that minimum wages help some people (those who keep their jobs and now make higher wages) and hurts others (those who lose their jobs).

Staying within the market model, there is one way that minimum wages would not have this problematic trade-off. Some economists argue that the demand for labor, specifically this type of labor, is inelastic. The argument has been put forth with the logic "someone has to flip the burgers, someone has to sweep the floor." The idea here is that businesses fundamentally need these lower-skilled workers to do some important but menial jobs.

If we redraw the market for labor with an inelastic demand and apply the minimum wage, we see the possibility that most people keep their jobs. There is a surplus, but only because more people want to work at this higher wage rate, and everyone now makes higher wages. While we can draw the labor market with that inelastic demand in order to get that result, the logic behind it is strained. At best (very best), this would be a short-run possibility. Companies would pay all current workers the higher minimum wage, but they would certainly decrease the number of people they employed in the long run (see figure 10.3).

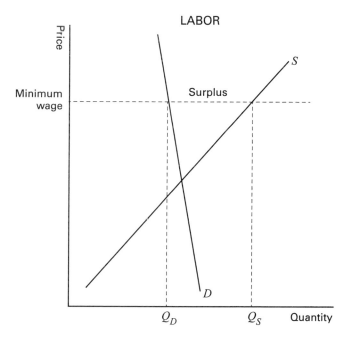

Figure 10.3 Minimum Wage with Inelastic Demand

People and politicians often support the minimum wage using arguments like "a family of four can't live on the current market wage." While that might be true, the market for labor doesn't have any way of incorporating it. At high wages, employers can't hire as many workers. That's because of the limits to productivity of labor and other factors that are out of the control of the employer.

Recalling that all inputs are owned by people, we find it interesting that only for labor is this unfairness concept invoked. One never hears that the compensation for landowners or capital owners is too low and unfair. Lest you think that's because those input owners are all "rich," remember that capital owners—stockholders—are often retirees who are not in any sense of the word rich.

> **Sample Exam Question 10.2**
> True or false, explain: Several employers have announced they will increase their starting wage to a level higher than the federal minimum wage. This means the federal minimum wage is too low.

10.5   Monopsony, Unions, and Minimum Wage Redux

The assumption that individual employers are too small to affect wages is important to an analysis of minimum wages and many other aspects of the labor market. Suppose an employer is large enough to create an impact on wages through its hiring decision. That firm would be analogous to monopolies. The employers would incorporate this impact into its hiring decision. It would ultimately hire fewer workers and pay them a lower wage than the whole competitive labor market.

The limiting case of this behavior would be a monopsony. A *monopsony* is a firm that is the only buyer of a good. The classic setting of monopsony is a mining or mill town ("company town") with one major employer. That firm cannot assume its hiring decisions have no impact on wages; indeed, it would assume the more labor it employed, the higher wages would be. A monopsony would therefore not use a fixed wage rate in making tits hiring decisions but rather an overall change in labor costs.

Suppose the demand for labor looked like this to the monopsonist:

Rather than making hiring decisions based on the wage rate, the monopsonist would look at the change in the overall cost of labor, known as the *marginal factor cost*. To get a sense of how this would change the firm's decision, if it was willing to hire five (thousand) workers at $14 per hour, knowing this would increase wages, it would choose to hire only three (thousand) workers because that level has a marginal factor cost of fourteen.

The monopsonist, knowing it was having an impact on wages, would hire fewer workers than a collection of smaller firms that did not (individually) have an impact on wages.

Table 10.2

Labor	Wage Rate ($/hr/worker)	Cost of Labor ($)	Marginal Factor Cost ($)
1	10.00	10.00	10.00
2	11.00	22.00	12.00
3	12.00	36.00	14.00
4	13.00	52.00	16.00
5	14.00	70.00	18.00
6	15.00	90.00	20.00

Note: Labor and cost of labor numbers in thousands.

Table 10.3

Labor	Wage Rate (Per Person)	Cost of Labor	Marginal Factor Cost
1	$14.00	$14.00	$14.00
2	$14.00	$28.00	$14.00
3	$14.00	$42.00	$14.00
4	$14.00	$56.00	$14.00
5	$14.00	$70.00	$14.00
6	$15.00	$90.00	$20.00

Note: Labor and cost of labor numbers in thousands.

The latter is what we think of as a competitive labor market. So monopsonies hire fewer workers and pay them less. The monopsonist is like the monopolist discussed earlier; it is aware of its impact on the market price and it acts accordingly. In this environment, a minimum wage works the same way a price ceiling does for a monopolist. If the government (or regulator) knows what the competitive or market wage would have been and sets the minimum wage at that level, the monopsonist would not be able to decrease wages by decreasing the number of workers it hires. Until the market wage is above the minimum wage, the (fixed) minimum wage is the marginal factor cost, and effectively the demand for labor as well. Because of that, the perfectly placed minimum wage would be able to increase wages and increase jobs.

Suppose the competitive labor market would have produced a wage rate of $14 per hour and five thousand jobs, but the monopsonist had reduced the number of jobs to three thousand, where the marginal factor cost was $14 but the wage rate was only $12 per hour. Imposing a minimum wage of $14 per hour (the market wage) would make our chart look like table10.3.

The monopsonist's unregulated hiring practices allowed it to make excess profits by artificially lowering wages. The perfectly placed minimum wage forces the monopsonist to hire the same number of workers and pay the same wage rate that the competitive labor market would have created.

Curiosity 10.1
Minimum Wages: How History Changed a Market Forever

As mentioned earlier, the federal minimum wage in the United States was instituted during the Great Depression. The extremely high level of unemployment that prevailed during that era (peaking at about 25 percent) was caused in part by the dislocation of low-skilled workers because of the collapse of the agriculture sector (primarily in what came to be called the Dust Bowl), which made the market for low-skilled labor uncompetitive. With so many people willing to take too few jobs, employers could push wages below the market level, similar to a monopsonist. In that environment, the government's minimum wage, set at the market wage, would be able to correct a market imbalance.

But as is the case with many regulated prices, once the government believes it determines a price, the government often oversteps and pushes that regulated price to levels that cause bad market outcomes. So, while setting a minimum wage at the market level might undo the effects of a monopsonist and increase wages without decreasing the number of jobs, setting the minimum wage above the market wage rate will decrease the number of jobs even if employers are monopsonists.

This is also the environment in which labor unions became necessary in these mining and mill towns. The cornerstone of a union is collective bargaining: the firm cannot hire workers individually; it hires everyone in the union or no one. This "all or nothing" approach works just like the minimum wage.

Unions and minimum wages both came into existence to control hiring practices that were clearly bad for labor. But both of these institutions suffer from a similar flaw. If the government sets the minimum wage too high—above the free-market, nonmonopsonist wage—fewer people will be employed. And if union wage demands are too high, they will ultimately hurt the job prospects for the union's members.

Labor activists who use economic arguments for increasing the minimum wage (some do) argue that the majority of entry-level labor employers coordinate, or collude, in the labor market to hold down wages (Google this topic and you'll find many such stories). The reality behind this assertion is difficult to determine. Historically, most minimum-wage jobs were in food service (fast food restaurants) and large retailers. More recently, warehouse jobs in distribution centers are at or near minimum wage. While nothing is impossible, it is hard to imagine Walmart, McDonald's, and Amazon.com all coordinating their entry-level wage rate on such a large scale.

10.6   Optimum Input Combination

Like the consumption goods in our market basket in chapter 4, inputs can be substituted for each other when firms produce their final goods. You can make a widget with many combinations of labor, capital, and other factors. When we looked behind the demand line in chapter 4, we were ultimately trying to find the lowest-cost way of reaching some level of happiness. Applying the same logic here, we note that producers will try to find the lowest-cost combination of inputs that can produce some level of output.

Let's see how this would work. The firm wants to produce, say, one hundred widgets per day. Widgets are made with labor and capital, both of which have production and marginal product similar to those shown in table 10.1. From any starting combination of capital and labor that produces the desired level of output, the firm can exchange some capital for some labor or vice versa and keep output constant. The trade-off would depend on each factor's marginal product. The easiest exchange would occur if the marginal products were about the same. Suppose, at the current combination of inputs, the marginal product of labor and the marginal product of capital were both ten. (We'll keep this simple and assume these marginal products are independent of each other. This is not a particularly realistic assumption, but we'll talk about how this would work if they were interconnected.) The firm would be able to trade one unit of labor for one unit of capital (or vice versa) and keep output constant. In this case, the firm would make a trade if one of the inputs was cheaper than the other.

This is the same logic we used in maximizing utility in chapter 4. And the end result of this process will look the same for producers trying to find the perfect combination of inputs. Firms will ultimately balance the marginal product of each input with the cost of each input. For example, if labor and capital both have a marginal product of ten (and these don't change much when we rearrange our input combination), and capital costs $20 per unit while labor costs $10 per unit, the firm would buy one more unit of labor, one less unit of capital. Given the marginal products, output would stay the same but the firm would save $10 ($20 − $10). This rearrangement would stop when the ratio of marginal product to input cost became the same for all inputs.

As was the case with utility maximization, there are real-world problems with this process. The units (caviar) problem is one obvious problem that recurs. In theory, we would add and subtract small amounts of each input until we reached the cost-minimizing combination. In reality, some (most) inputs don't come in small amounts. Usually we can't add a little more factory. Because of the way land is bought and sold, we usually can't add a little more land. And realistically, we don't employ "just a little more" labor. Our inputs come in notoriously big increments.

This limitations do not negate the results. Firms would still try to combine inputs in combinations where the ratio of marginal product to cost is equal. But if the "units" problem prevents precise equality, some trial and error would be required to find the next best solution. Similarly, and not unlike the case in chapter 4 in which goods were complements and their jollies were interconnected, we can see how the productivity or inputs might be interrelated; inputs can be substitutes or complements.

While a complete analysis of a complementary input relationship is beyond the scope of this book, we can get a sense of how employers would deal with this. For our farmer, a new tractor would be considered capital and its addition to the input combination would depend on the marginal product of the tractor and its (high) cost. The tractor would likely replace a lot of labor, but the labor that remained would be much more productive. That's consistent with labor and capital being substitutes.

One laborer, however, will be much more productive than he previously was: the person who gets promoted to drive the tractor. That laborer is obviously a complement to the tractor, not a substitute. Indeed, the tractor cannot drive itself (although that is changing with recent innovations!). If we assume any of the remaining laborers could drive the tractor, we can handle this problem much the same way we did condiments or pairs of shoes in chapter 4. The tractor and one laborer will be a package deal, a set that can't effectively be broken up.

10.7   Innovation

We can use this substitute/complement reality to abstract a more general result about the relationship between capital and labor, and to develop some understanding of the impact of innovation on input markets. When capital replaces labor, which has been the direction of change since the beginning of the Industrial Revolution in the late eighteenth century, labor productivity and wages both increase. Our earlier analysis tells us why. When less labor is employed (because capital is a substitute for labor), the marginal product of labor increases. But capital is also a complement to labor, so the productivity of labor increases more. Innovations in production should decrease employment in an industry and also increase wages for the remaining labor.

That we still have a lot of jobs in the overall economy is in part due to new industries (the internet and related technologies) and a move toward traditionally labor-oriented service industries. Since the 1950s there has been a dramatic increase in the number of two-worker families—families in which both spouses are employed. That means those families need to find ways to make dinner, clean the house, and cut the grass. Those services, once done by a stay-at-home spouse, are now done by a paid service provider.

This story has been the happy-ending story of innovation for many iterations. Innovations replace some jobs, but they lead to overall economic growth and new jobs. Henry Ford's assembly line led to cheaper cars, which created a need for roads and gas stations and fast food restaurants. The universally available internet gave Amazon.com a way to provide many goods at a lower price. That led to the closure of many traditional retailers and the loss of associated jobs, but it created jobs for delivery truck drivers. This process, which is sometimes called "creative destruction," has been discussed for more than 150 years (by some accounts, it springs from the writings of Karl Marx, but it is most frequently associated with the economist Joseph Schumpeter). The only part of this process that is problematic is the question of where it ultimately ends. If every job could be replaced by a robot, what would people do with their time?

Curiosity 10.2
The Future of Humanity

This process, while initially being good for some people and bad for others, has a somewhat scary endpoint. In a futuristic world, couldn't everything be produced by robots and machines that are controlled by computers, thus taking human labor out of the loop and leaving people without a paycheck? This is the stuff of science fiction movies and television shows, but the possibility is closer today than it has ever been. It is an important part of many futuristic societies (as portrayed on *Star Trek*, *The Orville*, and many other television shows) that people don't work for money anymore. When they explain their economic system, they say they are able to provide the necessities of life for everyone, thus allowing people to pursue other things, such as science and art. It's a nice idea, but in other versions of that future, such as depicted in *The Terminator* and *The Matrix* movies, machines eventually start eliminating people.

   This may seem like an odd line of discussion in a microeconomics book, but recall that we started with an analysis of the labor market and the compensation to labor, wages. Labor is us: the innovators, the rule-makers, the people who will determine the future. Economists believe that markets work well in most areas, including inputs. But, there are seven and a half billion people in the world (and growing), and it's not clear that we're moving down a path that will give us billions of jobs in the future.

Examples

Example 1   High minimum wages and in some cases labor unions have caused an interesting change in the marketplace, specifically in the retail marketplace. Many major retailers have installed self-checkout lines. It has been said that this is an inevitable change from labor to capital because of technological innovation.

How are high minimum wages and labor unions part of the story, if this is the result of innovation?
Innovations are always expensive and imperfect when they first come along. While innovations may lead to the substitution of capital for labor, we would expect this to be a slow process. If, however, the cost of labor is being increased artificially and excessively, employers will likely speed up the transfer. An unfortunate part of this story is that the transfer rarely reverses. When capital replaces labor, the jobs are likely lost forever.

Example 2   There is a well-known correlation between educational attainment and income. This is a straightforward application of factor returns being based on productivity.

Straightforward isn't always obvious. Bachelor's degrees are correlated with higher incomes even for people who do not work in the area of their college major. Why?

Going to college teaches many things: communication skills, analytical skills, and simply learning how to learn. In addition, completing college is a signal of a person's ability to undertake and complete a long-term process. All these are signals of higher productivity.

Example 3   Prior to the Great Depression in the 1930s, a large fraction (almost half) of the population of the United States worked in the agricultural sector. Much of the labor displacement occurred during a period characterized by the Dust Bowl, when overuse and severe dust storms in the North American grasslands caused a massive decline in the productivity of land. The agricultural workers of that day were largely sharecroppers, uneducated tenant farmers who paid for their existence with a share of the crops they grew. (This period is famously depicted in the movie and book *The Grapes of Wrath*.)

Given all of this history, can you now give a reason for some of the long-term unemployment problems that existed during the Great Depression?

Employment is ultimately based on labor productivity. The displaced sharecroppers had but one skill, farming, and that skill's productivity was wiped out by the Dust Bowl. Those displaced workers had no other skills, and there were literally millions of them. The labor market could not reemploy that many people until they were retrained and educated during the New Deal and, later, World War II.

Chapter Summary

- We discussed the nature of inputs and argued that inputs, like the outputs that they produce, are transacted in a market and thus have a supply and demand.
- We described the dynamic that exists for the productivity of inputs, specifically the observation of what we called diminishing marginal product.
- Input compensation was determined in an unregulated input market and found to be the price of the output times the marginal product of the input or the value of the marginal product.
- We discussed the complicated relationship between some inputs, namely, that they are both substitutes and compliments, and related that to innovation.

Exercises

(B exercises are more challenging.)

A10.1   Suppose you got your first job while you were in high school, busing tables (clearing off the used dishes) at a local restaurant. You were probably the lowest-paid employee in the restaurant. Why?

A10.2   If you continued working at that restaurant, you might have become a waiter or waitress, and in so doing, you almost certainly increased your hourly pay. Why? (*Hint:* If the new busboy calls in sick, you can still do his job, but what else have you learned how to do?)

A10.3   Driverless cars represent a technological breakthrough that is close at hand. That's exciting for everyone except, possibly, taxi drivers and delivery people. Explain.

A10.4   Explain the following statement using the concept of monopsony and assuming no government intervention: If there are many small independent firms in a town, they will probably employ more people combined than if there is one large firm.

A10.5   Smart phones have most assuredly eliminated a lot of jobs. Among them are radio disc jockeys, the people who used to work in photo development, and people who gave out maps at the AAA. In each case, explain why those jobs are disappearing.

A10.6   Use the concept of opportunity cost to explain the following: Government-mandated benefits such as employer-provided health insurance and guaranteed vacation and sick days decrease employment, all else being equal.

A10.7   There is a strong correlation between income and educational attainment in the United States. That's generally consistent with the value of marginal product approach to wage determination. Explain.

A10.8   As a follow-up to the previous question, there are big differences in pay among people who hold bachelor's degrees. Engineers typically make twice what people who majored in religious studies make. How is that discrepancy consistent with value of marginal product wage determination?

A10.9   The technological innovations of the past two decades have made people more productive. Or have they? In what ways are people less productive at work because of the internet, smart phones, and the like?

A10.10 Use the answer to the previous question to explain the following. Recent technological innovations decreased employment in many industries. Assuming diminishing marginal product of labor, that should mean higher wages for the remaining employees. But wages over the past decade have been stagnant.

B10.1   In the United States, anyone can buy shares of stock and other investments that pay the holder a share of the return on capital or land. This gives people a somewhat broader perspective about economic growth. Explain.

B10.2 Knowing what we know about education and income, let's try to improve on the market-unfriendly policy of minimum wages. Suppose the government required everyone to have a bachelor's degree but college is free and professors cannot fail anyone. Would that be an improvement?

B10.3 College degrees are overrated! A master electrician earns as much annually as most people with a college degree. Why don't more people become master electricians?

B10.4 People usually make more money if they enjoy their job, all else being equal. How does that accord with our wage determination equation?

B10.5 Tractors are now fitted with GPS technology, which allows their precise location to be determined via satellite. That innovation has increased the productivity of farmer and tractor alike. Why? Specifically, what does GPS technology allow farmers to do?

Appendix 10.1   The Graphical Approach to the Cost-Minimizing Combination of Inputs

The graphical version of the capital-labor trade-off starts with a new graph called an isoquant. An *isoquant* is every combination of inputs that's capable of producing the same level of output (if this sounds familiar, it's not unlike an indifference curve for inputs and outputs). Because our inputs have diminishing marginal product, the trade-off between inputs changes as we take away one input and replace it with another input.

As we try to replace labor with capital, the marginal product of the lost labor is bigger and the marginal product of the replacement capital is smaller; we'll need an ever-increasing amount of capital to replace our labor. That would work as we tried to replace capital with labor as well. The result of all of this is a curve showing the trade-off between capital and labor, the isoquant. The slope of the isoquant can be determined from the fact that output is constant, so:

$$d\text{Labor} \times MP_{\text{Labor}} = -d\text{Capital} \times MP_{\text{Capital}},$$

and therefore:

$$d\text{Labor}/d\text{Capital} = -MP_{\text{Capital}}/MP_{\text{Labor}}.$$

The total cost of producing any level of output is:

$$\text{Cost} = P_{\text{Labor}} \times \text{Labor} + P_{\text{Capital}} \times \text{Capital}.$$

The slope of this total cost like is:

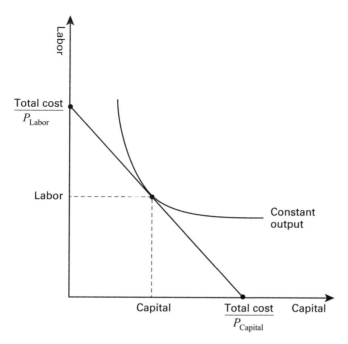

Figure 10.4   Cost-Minimizing Combination of Inputs

dLabor/dCapital $= -P_{\text{Capital}}/P_{\text{Labor}}$.

The producer will find the lowest-cost way of producing any level of input. That will happen when the cost line just touches (is tangent to) the isoquant. At that point, the slopes of the lines will be equal (see figure 10.4), and we will get the cost minimization condition:

$P_{\text{Capital}}/P_{\text{Labor}} = MP_{\text{Capital}}/MP_{\text{Labor}}$.

Rearranging that, we get the condition we described in section 10.6:

$MP_{\text{Capital}}/P_{\text{Capital}} = MP_{\text{Labor}}/P_{\text{Labor}}$.

Appendix 10.2   Monopsony with Minimum Wage

When an employer is big enough to affect the market wage, it includes that impact in its hiring decision and actively decreases the number of people it employs. By doing so, the employer will have decreased the wage it pays relative to a competitive labor market. When this has occurred, the government can increase wages and increase employment by putting a price floor, a minimum wage, on the labor market. This works because at the

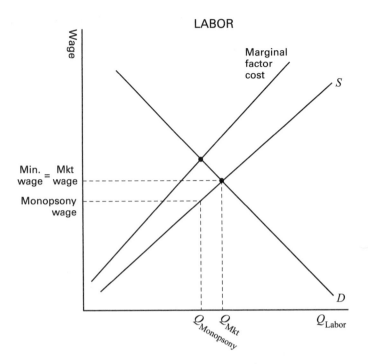

Figure 10.5   Minimum Wages with a Monopsonist

minimum wage, the employer's hiring decision will not decrease wages. That's because the marginal factor cost, which is the determinant of level of employment, will be constant at the minimum wage unless the employer wants to pay more than the minimum wage.

We can see this in figure 10.5. The marginal factor cost is a line above the supply of labor that includes the positive impact that a large employer's hiring decision has on wages. The monopsonist would align the marginal factor cost with the value of the marginal product of labor, which is the demand for labor. The monopsonist would hire fewer workers and pay them less. The minimum wage removes the employer's impact of wages at or below the minimum wage. That means the marginal factor cost is the minimum wage unless the firm pays more than that.

In this case, the minimum wage actually increases employment and wages. It's worth noting that this works only for a reasonable minimum wage; maximum employment occurs when the minimum wage is equal to the (nonmonopsonist) market wage rate. At a very high minimum wage, there could be fewer jobs than with the monopsonist!

11   Welfare and Public Economics

Many of the early economists were considered philosophers during their lifetime. They pondered such fundamental aspects of the human condition as happiness and relative value, and they defined concepts, such as logic, that attempted to describe the process that humans use in making choices and decisions. As economics was carved out of philosophy, the relationship between the well-being of the individual and the well-being of everyone in a society was an important area of discussion. Such is the nature of welfare economics.

In analyzing societies and economies, we have to look at the rules and norms that individuals operate under and ask whether those are the best rules for most people. One thing we observe when we look at the history of most societies is a need for what we call government. Analyzing government's role in the economy is the purview of public economics.

Government as we know it is an invention of society, and it was invented to have specific purposes. Economists have long been aware of the inability of the market to adequately produce and distribute some goods. In chapter 4, we connected the purchasing of a good to the jollies a good gives its consumer. The presumption in that chapter was that only the person who pays for the good gets the jollies. But some goods, by their very nature, don't work that way.

There are goods that give jollies to (or in some cases remove jollies from) more than just the original consumer. There are also goods that can be used by everyone without paying directly. In these cases, the market cannot accurately price the good. We say the market as we have previously described it is incomplete, or in some cases that the market doesn't exist.

The goods we are describing all have a social aspect to them, and over time, people have come up with social decision-makers—governments—to make decisions and choices about these goods for the group. These decision-makers could be the governments we immediately think of in our capital cities or they could be representatives we choose to make decisions for our clubs or our condominium complexes. The idea is the same in all cases: take the decisions and choices away from the individual and have others make choices with the entire group in mind.

On completion of this chapter, you should

- understand market failure,
- understand the concept of a public good and the concept of free riding,
- understand the concept of negative and positive externalities,
- see how governments can help society if these market failures exist, and
- understand the benefit principle and the ability to pay approaches to taxation.

11.1   Market Failure

When we talked about supply and demand and market price and market quantity in chapter 2, we also referred to these market measures as equilibrium price and quantity. Equilibrium implied balance or stability. In this case, it means there is balance between producers and consumers, between jollies and the cost for the last unit produced. Roughly speaking, the last unit produced cost exactly what the last consumer was willing to pay. But all of that assumes there is a one-to-one connection between the person paying and the jollies associated with the good.

Suppose a neighbor knocked on your door and said he wanted to put in a swimming pool for everyone in the neighborhood to use and he wanted everyone to pay some of the cost. He asks you to predict how often you'll use the pool and pay, say, $10 for every day of use each month. Once the pool is completed, it will be open to everyone in the neighborhood.

Knowing that your prediction and your payment have no impact on how often you will be able to use the pool, you'll always guess low. "Oh, that's a nice idea, but I doubt I'll use it more than once a month." At the end of this process, the pool builder will have raised only a fraction of what he had hoped, and the pool, if it is built, will be too small for anyone to enjoy.

When we disconnect payment, usage, and jollies, the market fails to produce an adequate quantity of the good. This type of *market failure* is what we see in the case of the neighborhood pool, an example of a public good and the subject of the next section. In other cases, goods exist with no clear owner. People can use those goods in excess because no price is attached to usage. Those goods are subject to our second type of market failure, the influence of externalities, which obscures the true cost of producing goods.

11.2 Public Goods

Markets can produce and distribute apples or strawberries reasonably well. If consumers are willing to pay the cost of producing an extra apple or strawberry, they will be able to buy it. Apples and strawberries are goods that provide jollies only to the consumer, and, if we assume these goods were acquired legally, the consumer paid for these goods and thus these jollies.

But suppose a neighborhood wants a pool or a city wants a public park or a country wants an army to defend its borders. Those are goods that people can all use at the same time (within limits). We call this unusual feature "simultaneous consumption." People can use those goods even if they do not directly pay any of the cost of their production. If you don't pay for apples or strawberries, the producer cannot provide them. Things like city parks and national defense are so big that we don't depend on any one person's payment.

We call things like neighborhood swimming pools, public parks, and national defense *public goods*—goods we can all consume simultaneously (sometimes called nonrival goods) and goods we can consume even if we pay none of their cost. Once they are produced, they are shared. We say that public goods have a *free-rider* problem. You can get the jollies from using them without paying anything.

We can see the free-rider-problem in a literal form. If you are the only student in your dorm suite with a car, you will find yourself taking your suitemates to the grocery store often. Since you are already going, they will want to go along, getting a free ride to the store. That doesn't seem like an imposition at first, but at some point the extra gas and time that you are expending—and the fact that you can't get your groceries and those of all of your new friends into your trunk—will probably begin to bother you. And too, none of these riders will feel compelled to get a car of their own or to take a bus to the store. Eventually there won't be enough transportation to the store. The free-rider problem has created a shortage.

Because of their unusual nature—they are subject to simultaneous consumption and free riding by users—the market will underproduce public goods. Too few people will voluntarily pay for them. In the worst-case scenario, no one pays for the good—everyone tries to free ride—and there is no money to pay for producing the good. One solution to this problem is to somehow combine the needs of all potential consumers into one large consumer and make the production and allocation decisions at a larger level.

This is precisely what we try to do when we elect what we call a representative government. One person is chosen to speak for thousands. This representative knows that his or her role is to choose a level of these public goods that is correct for many people simultaneously. While this approach isn't perfect, it does work better than many alternatives, and it shows that in the case of public goods, we need the government to fix this market failure.

Curiosity 11.1
Free-Riding Cities and Countries

Everyone has experienced free riding, either as the provider who had free riders or as a free rider himself. Grouping people together and forming a government that acts for the group is one solution that we often see. Even in small collectives, this approach is often taken. Condominium owners usually elect a representative board of some kind that decides on matters such as repairs to the parking lot or the pool, and then tells everyone the share of the cost they have to pay.

But public goods can also be provided by one collective for its residents but used by others. Suppose my city's residents want a lot of public parks with picnic tables, swings, and sports fields. The citizens as a group are willing to pay for the parks with higher property taxes or the like. Their assumption, as a group, is that their families will be able to use the parks on occasion. But if my city has a lot of public parks, the cities all around mine can free ride. Anyone within walking or driving distance can come to my city and use my parks if those parks are truly public, open, and unrestricted.

If the free riders are few relative to the taxpayers, this probably won't be an issue, but cities sometimes have to find ways to limit access to their residents. Not wishing to impose too many limits and make the public good less public, cities often try things like parking restrictions (resident-only parking using annual parking permits placed on a car's bumper). But free riding is part of human nature, so no perfect control exists.

Countries can free ride as well. If the United States builds a large military (including defense systems such as missiles) to protect it from invasion by the Cold War USSR, that military certainly protects Canada as well. Canada does not need as many missiles if the United States has thousands of them. If a country has socialized medicine—free health care for all comers—nearby countries can free ride by encouraging their sick citizens to cross the border when they need a doctor. Like cities with a free-rider problem, countries often find a way to limit the abuse of their public goods. The United States might ask Canada to allow it to install radar or other military assistance items in strategic Canadian locations. The free-health-care country might require proof of citizenship before those seeking care could take full advantage of that system. Even at a national level, free riding can make the provision of public goods much harder and, in some cases, much less public.

Sample Exam Question 11.1
What is and isn't a public good has always been a matter of opinion. A popular assertion in political forums is that health care is a right, not a privilege. What that assertion means is that health care is a public good that should be available to all. While this makes for good politicking, looking at the attributes of a public good, would you say health care qualifies?

11.3   Externalities

The market model assumes that all costs and benefits are incorporated in the supply and demand lines. Then, and only then, can we be sure that the market correctly prices and produces goods. In reality, there are often costs or benefits that have been left out by the market. We call these omitted costs and benefits *externalities*.

How can a cost or benefit be left out? The easiest way to see that is to look at an input that isn't owned by anyone. When we discussed the supply line in chapters 2 and 5, we said a producer has to pay for labor, land, and other inputs when producing apples or strawberries. But what if we use rain for irrigating our orchards and fields, supplemented by water we pump (without paying anyone) from the river that's adjacent to our field? We didn't pay for any of that water and we didn't have to because no one owned it. The cost of the river water we use is not included in our decision to produce apples, and because of this, we might be wasting or misusing some of it. Without that cost being included in our decision to produce, the supply line is in the wrong place; the true cost of producing our crop is higher, so the supply line is too low.

We call an omitted cost a *negative externality*. When we include that cost in the market model, we see that the correct market price is also higher (see figure 11.1).

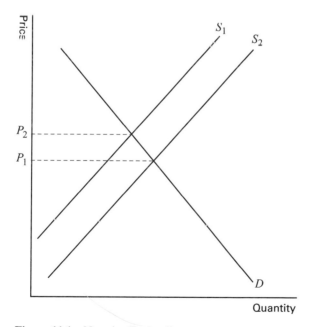

Figure 11.1   Negative Externality

Air pollution is another good example of a negative externality. An oil refinery knows that it has to pay for crude oil, labor, and most other inputs because if it doesn't pay for these goods, it can't use them. But it can pollute the air near the refinery without paying for using up the clean air because no one owns the air. The market failure in this case is that there is no market for the air that's all around us. Since there is no cost for the air, the refinery will probably use too much of it. It will pollute the air near the refinery with impunity. People living, working, or even passing close to the refinery will be negatively affected by this excess use. Anyone, any creature or plant, that relies on clean air near the refinery will be damaged. If you live near the refinery and you get sick because of the pollution, you will ultimately pay for the refinery's use of the shared air.

There are many possible solutions for these negative externalities. One would be to use our earlier invention, government. Any time a cost is left out by the market because of a market failure, the government can step in and create the missing market by charging a fee (or tax) to anyone who wants to use the air, water, or whatever input is being treated. For a large obvious negative externality, such as the consumption of air an oil refinery with huge smoke stacks belching out air pollution, the government knows what entity to tax, and it even has a sense of what to charge: the cost of the damage to those who have to breathe the air.

Let's now consider something subtler, like a noisy neighbor. You want peace and quiet in the morning so you can sleep, but your neighbor is an opera fan with a penchant for singing along. Whether or not you like *The Barber of Seville*, you don't like it at seven in the morning, and your neighbor doesn't sing well. In theory, the government could tax your neighbor and give you the proceeds, but there's no way to actually figure out how much that tax would be. In cases like this, the government claims ownership of the sound space within reasonable limits, and simply bans excessively loud music. While this isn't a perfect substitute for the missing market for noise, it does show what government regulations are trying to accomplish.

Negative externalities don't always require government intervention. In some cases the market has included the cost by changing the demand for the good. Homes located near an airport are usually less expensive because of noise pollution and traffic considerations. If a person buys such a home knowing the airport is nearby, the new homeowner can't reasonably expect the government to start taxing the airport even though there is a negative externality. In this case, timing and knowledge are important. The homebuyer did not have the negative externality thrust upon him *after* he paid for the home. The below-average home price was the compensation for the negative externality.

Not all externalities are bad. Sometimes the market that produces a product has failed to account for a benefit. This usually happens when there are benefits to the actual consumer in addition to benefits to other people in society. A good example is when someone gets vaccinated to prevent a communicable disease. If all my friends get a flu shot every year, they will have a lower probability of getting the flu, and so will I. When I interact with my friends every flu season, their not having the flu means I am less likely to catch it. Given that, I should pay some of the cost of their flu shots.

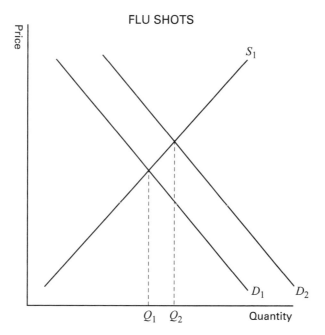

Figure 11.2 Positive Externalities for Flu Shots

Of course, I'm not the only one who shares this benefit. Everyone benefits when some people get flu shots. In the case of "missing benefits," benefits that extend beyond the purchaser of the good, government can step in and pay some of the cost of the good. The government can subsidize flu shots. A *subsidy* is the opposite of a tax in that it *lowers* the cost to consumers. By lowering the price, the government will help more people afford the flu shot, which should increase the number of flu shots being administered.

Compared to what we see in a market without government intervention, the true demand for goods with *positive externalities* is higher in a market with government intervention. For any level of consumption, there are more jollies than just those accruing to the consumers who pay for the good (see figure 11.2).

Goods with positive externalities are really underproduced and undervalued when we include all those who benefit from any level of consumption. In that sense, positive externalities and public goods are very similar, and government policy toward them is also similar: tax everyone to help pay some or all of the price of the good. While distinguishing between them will largely be left to other texts and other classes, one way to think about the difference is how much of the good's benefits go to the direct consumer. If you get a flu shot, it might mean I won't get the flu, but the *primary* beneficiary will be you.

By forcing the market to include missing costs or benefits, the government is acting on behalf of all members of society and working through the market mechanism to get closer to the correct level of output for most goods. Of course, there are many problems with this, some of which we discuss in the next section. But providing public goods and correcting externalities are functions of government that most economists agree on.

> **Sample Exam Question 11.2**
> In theory, waitpersons should be paid more to work in the smoking section of a restaurant to compensate them for the risk and potential costs of second-hand smoke. Why doesn't the government simply impose that regulation rather than banning smoking in restaurants?

11.4   A Caveat or Two

While public goods and externalities both show an important role for government in an economy, the devil is still firmly rooted in the details. Beyond issues such as determining the correct taxes and subsidies or dealing with elected representatives who get corrupted by special interests, there has always been the question of what goods are truly public goods and what externalities require government intervention to manage.

Let's consider the curious case of education. When a person becomes more educated, she garners skills and capabilities that should benefit her throughout her lifetime. But she also becomes a better member of society. She makes better choices, becomes a more informed voter, and may contribute more to society. In general, educated people improve everyone's well-being, not just their own. Education has positive externalities.[1] So, in line with the logic of vaccinations, education should be and is heavily subsidized. But making education effectively free also might make people feel it isn't very important. Some consumers might think it's just something to do, a place to hang out with friends. Even as governments pay the cost of education, it still has to show the value of consuming it.

Governments enter markets where there is a market failure, to try to "fix the problem," but they rarely maintain the efficiencies of the market. Governments try to be all things to all people, and they do not produce and distribute goods efficiently. So, while there are sound justifications for a government role in many parts of the economy, people need to control the tendency that governments have toward excess and inefficiency.

---

1. Some say education is a public good. As we discussed earlier, some goods are hard to categorize between positive externalities and public goods. Everyone consumes public goods simultaneously. On the surface, that does not seem to be true of education. The classroom setting notwithstanding, the student gets his or her education independent of others. But is the student the true consumer of education? Or is the consumer the workplace and society as a whole? This is beyond the scope of this book, but it is interesting to think about.

Curiosity 11.2
Libertarian and Related Perspectives, and the Concept of Second Best

There are many different political perspectives out there that could generate useful discussions about the appropriate scope of government in society. A politically conservative perspective that some economists espouse is called libertarian (Nobel Prize winners James Buchanan, Gary Becker, and Milton Friedman are often said to be libertarians). Roughly speaking, this perspective espouses very small, very limited government. The opinion is that the inability of government to engage in efficient market activity means government's participation in most areas of the economy does more harm than good.

Libertarians also contend that market forces together with a well-operating legal justice system can fix most of the aforementioned problems. If the oil refinery pollutes the air and does you harm, you can sue it to recover damages, and the refinery will have to include that "cost" in its production decision. That is certainly one possibility, but think about what must be true for this to work. The first few times someone is hurt by pollution, that person sues, and the company learns what the cost is and incorporates it—but only *after* someone was hurt. Furthermore, the legal system is not perfect. The oil company hires its own lawyers, and since it has more resources, it will probably hire better lawyers. In that case the oil company might win even though it is harming people.

This is an incomplete version of the story, but it is worth pondering which is worse—the inefficiencies of government when it participates in the market or the biases in the legal system. This example also highlights a belief generally held by many economists: if the market can do it, let the market do it. Market incentives usually lead to the best attainable outcomes. That means that when there is a market failure, such as an externality, the best possible outcome is to fix that failure, and then let the market work after that.

Economists have an interesting way of expressing this ranking. They say that the first best solution to a market failure is to fix the failure and then let the market produce the good. Having the government take over the market and become the producer or distributor is what economists call second best.

11.5 Income Redistribution

The market can produce many things that we all want and need, but it has also proven to produce one thing we need to be wary of: poorly distributed income and wealth (where wealth can be thought of as accumulated income). Bill Gates and Steve Jobs invented things that were very popular and thus sold millions of copies and versions. They became very wealthy even as others in society struggled to find and keep jobs. Economies that are built around competitive markets usually create this sort of imbalance.

History has muddled our view of income inequality. The primary source of wealth and income over most of history was land and natural resources. Monarchies and wealthy families often acquired and maintained ownership of these natural resources, generation after generation, making it virtually impossible for anyone else to be rich. Poorly distributed income—having a comparatively small number of very rich people—is often associated with something inherently unfair—or even worse—afoot in the economy.

So another role that the government has taken upon itself is to transfer income from high-earning people to lower-earning people. Most people in the United States have heard of programs like the ones we call "welfare" and "food stamps." There are many such programs that attempt to help lower-income people with basic necessities. Income redistribution is not a traditional public good, but among the frequently stated reasons behind it are attributes that we think of as having a public benefit. These reasons include:

1. Helping those that are less fortunate is part of the ethos of many societal groupings. Many religions espouse this activity, as do clubs, corporations, and governments. One could argue that the desire to help others in need is human nature.

2. If the income distribution becomes badly skewed, often characterized as "the rich get richer and the poor get poorer," countries tend to become less stable politically. People begin to question the fairness of the system and to suspect that the rich have done something wrong. This perspective could be called the "French Revolution" problem. The rich all inherited their wealth together with all the land—the primary source of most income—so the poor were in a literal sense at the mercy of the rich. Income distribution–driven revolutions in France, Russia, China, the Middle East and North Africa region, and other countries throughout history have made governments aware that allowing incomes to become badly distributed has the potential for social upheaval.

3. Even if fairness is not invoked, some people believe that being rich is mostly the result of luck. To some, this includes inherited wealth, having access to better schools, or simply having the good fortune to be raised in a better neighborhood. These arguments certainly resonate with many people when you read them, but they can be contrasted with other reasons for success, such as like working harder, being better at physics, or having the "good fortune" to be seven feet tall and able to play basketball.

   The apparent randomness of some people's success creates a justification for redistribution that's not unlike insurance. Taking some of the results of good luck away and giving it to those with bad luck can be seen as correcting the income distribution for risk or randomness.

4. Historically, many U.S. social programs started during the 1960s, when the United States was engaged in the Cold War. Ignoring the nuclear annihilation part of the Cold War, it was also a time when capitalism and communism were being compared and contrasted. Redistribution was one way of showing that the capitalist U.S. economy really could make everyone better off.

5. Income redistribution can also be useful in helping people better themselves. If the government helps people with basic necessities (e.g., food, clothing, housing), they should have more time to search for jobs, attend school, or otherwise improve their

prospects in the future. When we talk about long-term economic growth in chapter 12, we will discuss other, related policies that change people's lifetime income.

We could probably think of a dozen other justifications for it, but the fact is, most modern and progressive governments redistribute income and wealth across income classes. Transfers serve many purposes in society, but they also come with caveats and assumptions. In giving people anything, we're assuming there is no negative impact on their activities and attitudes. There are many people who are concerned about the mentality that's created by what are called "entitlements." What every member of society is entitled to is a difficult, dicey question.

Income redistribution is a big part of many governments. As such, we would like to say it is addressing a market failure. While some of the justifications we stated might be considered market failures (being rich means you were lucky in some way), others are purely political. We will consider income redistribution an example of government intervention in the economy that has economic as well as other rationale.

Curiosity 11.3
Social Welfare Functions and Pareto Distributions

Redistribution of income is a big part of what governments do—and with ample solid justification. One reason not on this list is that $1,000 would mean more to a poor person than to a billionaire. While this sounds right to many people, there's no way to know that it's true. The problem is, you don't know the utility function of everyone involved when you take something away from one person and give it to another. If we had a measure of jollies that we could apply to *all* people, it is entirely possible that the $1,000 might turn out to mean more to the billionaire than to the pauper.

Much of this analysis is attributed to the Italian economist Vilfredo Pareto. Pareto described allocations or distributions of goods in a simple, straightforward way. From any starting point, you can't say you've improved the group through a process of tax and transfer unless at least one person is *clearly* better off and *no one* is worse off. What that means is that the only resources you can transfer and be certain that doing so improves the group are resources that were being wasted under the original distribution.

Pareto's approach is appealing to economists who want to be careful not to say things we can't know for sure, but the pauper and the billionaire story is part of many political and emotional perspectives. Without saying it, many people are using what economists call a social welfare function, a utility measure for everyone in society added together. Pareto says you can't get a social welfare function by simply adding up everyone's utility function, but that doesn't mean there can't be such a function. We can imagine overall jollies being created by such social attributes as safe streets, clean air, fair markets, and other economy-wide attributes. This sounds right, but you can see the problem with taking this approach to government policy. What is deemed important for society as a whole, and how important it is deemed, both depend on whose version of the social welfare function you use.

11.6   Paying for Government: Taxation

Following the approach that we're taking in this chapter, we won't look deeply and hard at all forms of taxation but rather take a big-picture, conceptual look. The primary source of funding for governments at all levels—federal, state, and local—is tax revenues. It sometimes seems as though governments tax everything: most sources of revenue come from the personal income tax, consumption purchases through sales taxes, the value of your home through property taxes, and on and on. In an attempt to keep this enormous space relatively simple, we'll focus on the rationales or approaches that the government takes in choosing how to tax.

The Benefit Principle

Some taxes are associated directly with the government good or service that they fund. When the government uses this approach, it is applying the *benefit principle*: those who get the benefits of the government expenditure pay the taxes to produce them. Easy examples of this are toll roads and bridges, gasoline taxes to fund roads, and property taxes to fund schools (historically, bigger houses meant more children).

In applying the benefit principle, the government is clearly acting as a market. It is trying to find a *price substitute* for public goods. The logic here is fine, but taxes aren't as easy to change as most other prices. If the government taxes too little or too much, it might not be able to adjust these taxes very quickly. The government also doesn't have competitors in most of the areas where it produces or provides goods. That takes away the dynamic optimization process that many other businesses use to iterate to the correct price (we saw that in chapter 2, where the apple producer learned if she set her price too high, people bought other fruit instead).

For many government enterprises, benefit principle taxation isn't practical. Income redistribution, for example, explicitly taxes one group in order to compensate another. In addition to that problem, benefit principle taxes tend to be cumbersome. Toll booths on highways slow down traffic (note the move on many toll roads toward using transponders in pass-through lanes rather than human toll collectors).

The Ability to Pay Principle

The fastest and easiest way to get tax revenues is to tax the people who have the most money: tax the rich, tax large corporations, tax expensive property, or tax anything or anyone that's worth a lot. The ability to pay principle is practicality at its finest level. Raising $10 million in tax revenue is easier and faster if you tax one entity that has $100 million as opposed to 10,000 people who each are levied $10,000. Most arguments in favor of the ability to pay principle refer to fairness, but fairness is hard to invoke here. There's nothing fundamentally fair about taxing one person or a small group of people much more than others. So practicality—or, as some economists would put it, lower transaction costs—is a better justification.

U.S. income taxes are called progressive taxes because the tax rate—the fraction of your income that you pay as taxes (on the last dollar you earn)—rises as your income rises. This is an ability to pay tax. The government looks are people earning $30,000 per year and decides they can't afford to pay an average rate of more than 10 percent in income taxes. But a person earning $300,000 can afford to pay an average rate of 35 percent because he or she will still have a lot of money left. The richer person is said to have deeper pockets, so the government can reach further into them.

The problem with the ability to pay principle is that it does tend to put a much larger burden on wealthier people, corporations, and other entities, many of whom are capable of taking their money and running. Well . . . not always "run," but when you know you're paying millions of dollars in taxes, you have an incentive to hire accountants and lawyers to help you *avoid* that liability. U.S. corporations find many ways of avoiding taxes: they may relocate their headquarters to a lower-taxed country, take on debt (interest payments are tax deductible), and take full advantage of tax deductions and loopholes. These activities might seem inappropriate to some, but from a shareholder's perspective, paying more taxes than one is obliged to would not be considered good business. Taxes are, after all, just another expense.

Sample Exam Question 11.4
State and local governments often use sales taxes to finance general expenditures. Food, medicine, and some essentials are often exempted from sales tax. If sales taxes are done that way, are sales taxes more like a benefit principle tax or an ability to pay tax?

11.7   Tax Incidence Redux and Market Distortion

In chapter 3, we showed how the market model actually determines who pays the taxes that are imposed on goods. We showed that a tax on cigarettes would be borne by the

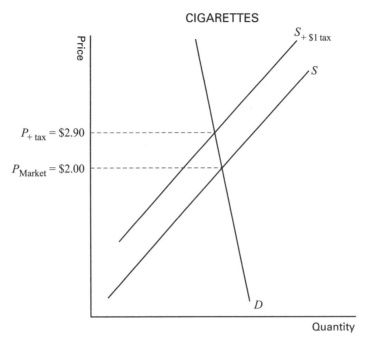

Figure 11.3   Cigarette Tax and Price Increases

consumer because the demand for cigarettes is relatively inelastic (nicotine is addictive) (see figure 11.3).

We can use that result to make another interesting point. Taxes on goods change the market price and level of output. In some cases, for instance if a negative externality exists, that is the point of the tax: to force the market to incorporate a missing cost. But many taxes are levied simply to raise revenue to finance government spending. In that case, how should the government decide what goods to tax?

One approach is to explicitly consider the change in the market that the tax causes. The decrease in quantity caused by the tax is what economists call a distortion; the lost quantity makes people worse off. One approach toward choosing which goods to tax is to minimize that distortion. If we consider now a tax of any size, a smaller change will occur if one side of the market has an inelastic line.

For simplicity, let's suppose a tax is charged to producers (so the supply line shifts up), and there is an elasticity difference between consumers and producers: demand is relatively more inelastic than supply. In this case, there will be a smaller distortion in the market with the more inelastic demand (see figure 11.4). In chapter 2, we said a good with an inelastic demand was often a necessity. So in choosing goods to tax, the government

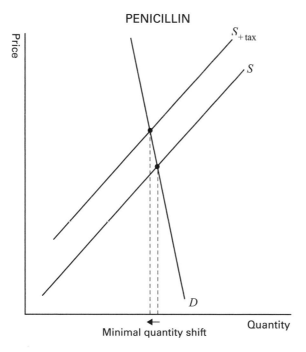

Figure 11.4   Inelastic Demand, Minimal Quantity Shift, Small Distortion

is sometimes in the uncomfortable position of trying to minimize distortions by taxing necessities.

11.8   Debt Financing

Governments, like businesses and households, can pay for their expenditures by borrowing money instead of through taxation. When governments do this in any one year, we say the government is running a deficit. The accumulated deficits from all years is called the government's debt.

Government borrowing is controversial. Conservative politicians decry government borrowing with slogans like "We're saddling future generations with the burden of repaying our debt." Of course, we're also passing along the things, the assets, that we bought with that debt. No one is being "saddled" if we use debt to finance part of an interstate highway system that will last for generations. We pass both an asset and some of the cost along to future generations, which, one could argue, is fair.

There's a logic that businesses and households use for financing expenditures that works just as well for governments: if the expenditure has long-term benefits (a factory or a new home), it makes sense to finance it in part with debt. If the benefits accrue mostly to the current generation, the government should use taxes to pay for it. There will still be controversies: some people believe social welfare programs have long-term benefits, while others think the benefits are purely short term. These different perspectives on temporal benefits do argue for a blend of debt and tax financing.

Another argument against debt financing is that it makes wasteful government spending easier. The reason is, if you don't make every generation pay for all or most government spending, one generation could borrow for something completely wasteful—say, a giant national yearlong party in which everyone took the year off—because the beneficiaries do not have to pay the cost. The only way out of that is to have people care about their children as much as they care about themselves.

11.9   Cost-Benefit Analysis

Having identified a need for governments and policies to correct market imperfections, it behooves us to ask, how do we know when we're using the best possible policy? One obvious approach is to compare the cost of the policy to the value of the benefits that it creates. Spending $50 million of taxpayer money to mitigate the impact of the traffic noise that will be created by a new freeway might make sense if the noise impacts 50,000 people, but not if the noise affects only five people. Hopefully, it would be cheaper to simply move five people away from the new roads.

Trying to analyze government policy in this way is the purpose of cost-benefit analysis: comparing the cost imposed on society by a policy to the benefits that policy creates. In theory (although not always in practice, since governments operate with many stakeholders in mind, including government employees), we would want to enact policies where the benefits exceed the costs, and in trying to solve any one problem, we would want to choose the one policy that gives the most benefits for the smallest cost. But by now we've learned that measuring costs and benefits is not an easy task.

One approach that economists use for comparing a policy's costs and benefits is related to consumer surplus (discussed in curiosity 4.4). We said that the area under the demand line and above the market price is the total value that consumers were willing to pay but didn't have to pay if the market price was determined by the intersection of supply and demand. Everyone is paying that (one) market price even though some consumers were willing to pay more than that. That's what's called consumer surplus (see figure 11.5).

We can describe a related concept, *producer surplus*, as the area above the supply line and below the market price. That's the total value of the units producers would have been willing to sell at a lower price but didn't have to once the market price was determined.

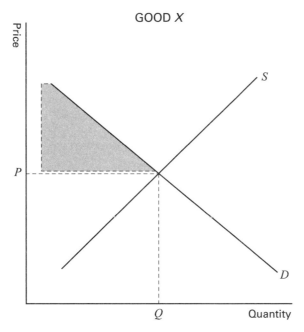

Figure 11.5   Consumer Surplus

Like consumer surplus, producer surplus exists because every unit is sold at one price rather than at the cost of producing each unit individually.

One approach to cost-benefit analysis is to look at how the consumer or producer surplus is hurt by the market failure—the lost benefits that the policy can restore—and compare that with the cost of implementing the policy fix.

Suppose the problem our government is trying to fix is that one company has monopolized the market and has restricted output and increased the price of the product above the market price. At that monopoly price, both consumer surplus and producer surplus will change: there will be two triangles of lost surplus associated with this higher price and known as deadweight loss. We can think of those two triangles as the total value to the economy of the units that the monopolist chose not to produce. For a large market with thousands or even millions of consumers, that lost value could be millions of dollars.

With this lost value in mind, policymakers try to force the monopolist to sell at the market price (a price ceiling) or to compete with other firms (through antitrust laws.) The cost of one or the other of these policies for controlling a monopoly could be large; the costs of government bureaucracy, litigation, or of finding the correct price ceiling are all nontrivial.

11.10   Cost-Benefit Analysis and Negative Externalities

History tells us that policy to correct market failures—especially negative externalities—often comes after the problems show up and, unfortunately, after the lost benefits can be calculated in terms of damage to consumers. That said, we could use the concept of deadweight loss to predict the magnitude of the problem. The deadweight loss in this case is lost benefits that come from producing too many units; recall that producers were basing production on a supply curve that did not include the costs of things like pollution. So the triangle that represents the deadweight loss is now the value of damages.

As we recall now the earlier discussion of how difficult it is to know or estimate exact supply and demand lines, this approach to estimating the damages from the impact of a negative externality might appear limited at best. But this market-based approach can tell us some important things, such as the more a producer pollutes and the more people that pollution affects, the bigger the deadweight loss will be (see figure 11.6). In this respect, the benefits of policy are similar to those of regulating a monopoly. In both cases, if the market involved has many consumers and the extent of the market failure is large, then the benefits of the policy will be correspondingly large and thus warrant even costly policy.

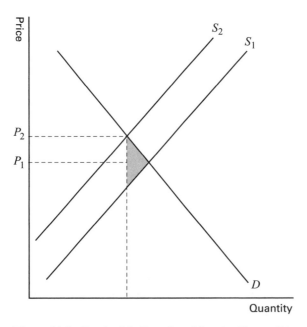

Figure 11.6   Deadweight Loss from Negative Externalities

This approach should not be construed as justification for a wasteful, excessively costly policy. Even when there are obvious and substantial benefits from policies enacted to correct things like negative externalities, many governments' historical tendency to expand into an inefficiently large bureaucracy pushes the cost of the cure beyond the benefits that could be realized. There is a market explanation for this. Governments don't have competitors that force them to be efficient. So government policy, even when called for, can have higher costs than benefits.

Examples

Example 1   "Health care" is a contentious good that some politicians have moved beyond labeling a public good, now calling it a right. Health care is a good (a collection of goods, really) in that it needs to be produced and distributed. When the government takes over this market, and when it produces and distributes health care in what's usually called socialized medicine, it assumes the responsibility for replacing the market. In this case, the government must become both the supplier (shown as the supply line) and the consumer (demand line) of the product.

On the demand side, if there is free access to all medical services (paid for through taxes on income), how would the government allocate services? Wouldn't this be an all-you-can-eat buffet?

If it works the way it does in countries that try this approach, there are lots of queues and lots of time spent waiting for medical care. So the opportunity cost of treatment is very high. And waiting for treatment for some medical problems is, in effect, a death sentence.

On the supply side, if the government is now paying all providers, will there be any change in the quality of medical care?

Probably. In many countries, being a doctor is not an especially well-paid profession. As such, it does not attract the same quality individuals as it does in the United States. Similarly, hospital care, prescription drugs, and other parts of health care would likely end up being provided at a lower level of quality.

Example 2   Transportation projects such as highways have usually been undertaken by governments in the United States and paid for with tax revenues (e.g., the tax on gasoline). Unlike other public goods, there is private alternative for funding these projects: toll roads. This approach to financing the building of roads, bridges, and other transportation projects was unpopular—but not unheard of—for much of the twentieth century, but there is renewed interest in toll roads across the country.

Why were toll roads an unpopular alternative for most of the twentieth century?
In toll roads' earlier incarnations, paying tolls changed the nature of the good: paying tolls slows you down. Whether the toll was collected intermittently along the highway or at

exits, money had to be collected, change had to be made, and other transaction costs (diverting into a pay line and waiting in line at the toll booth) made toll roads slower.

Why is there new interest?

Most toll roads these days use electronic devices, transponders, that are connected to a credit account to charge drivers without making them stop. While there is still an explicit cost of driving on a toll road, many of the transaction costs have been eliminated.

Example 3 For much of the past thirty years, France has had one of the highest marginal tax rates on millionaires in Europe. This policy has been very good for Belgium.

Why?

A quick Google search will turn up dozens of articles about the rich moving out of France because of the high taxes. Those millionaires could be moving anywhere, but an easy move would be right next door to Belgium, where French is the second most commonly used language.

Chapter Summary

- A market failure is a situation in which the market cannot correctly produce or price a good.
- Public goods are goods that many people consume simultaneously. These goods can often be used even if the consumer doesn't pay for them, and therefore they are said to have a "free-rider" problem.
- Representative governments acting on behalf of the entire society can provide and pay for these goods better than individual markets can.
- Externalities are costs or benefits that are not counted by the market. Governments can incorporate these missing costs and benefits using taxes or subsidies in the existing market.
- Broadly speaking, the government determines taxes using the benefit principle and the ability to pay principle.
- The incidence of a tax imposed on a good, determining who actually pays the tax, depends on the elasticity of supply and demand, not where the tax is charged.

Exercises

(B exercises are more challenging.)

A11.1   Offering to pay for a tank of gas every so often when you go to the store with your roommate in his car is one way to be sure he always tells you when he's going. Explain.

A11.2   Fred bought a house next to the freeway and paid 20 percent less than the purchaser of the same house a mile away. After a while, Fred got tired of the noise and hired a lawyer to sue the government to make it install a soundproof wall. Should Fred get his wall? Explain.

A11.3   Cigarette taxes are, in part, correcting a negative externality. What is that negative externality? One interesting component of cigarettes is that the problems they create (e.g., lung cancer) are realized long term or far in the future. If we imagine the government has a longer-term view than most individuals, why are cigarette taxes especially appropriate?

A11.4   California is considering an increase in its state cigarette tax by $2 per pack. That would more than triple California's cigarette tax. Based on current cigarette sales in the state, government officials say this tax could generate hundreds of millions of dollars in new revenue. Can you see any problems with this analysis? Could this actually decrease state tax revenues?

A11.5   A pundit said, "If the government finances consumption goods (such as food stamps) with debt, it is passing along a liability to the next generation but no corresponding asset. We are, therefore, making the next generation worse off." Make a case to the contrary using the idea that income redistribution prevents social unrest.

A11.6   The condominium owners in a local condominium complex are trying to figure out how to get a pool for everyone to use. Their first idea was to ask everyone to say on a scale from zero to ten how much they wanted one, knowing that they would be charged $100 times the number they chose.

   That approach ended up raising $400 from the fifty residents polled. Why? Suggest a better way to raise the money for a general-use, private pool.

A11.7   The local city council had to change the policy about music in the public park. The initial policy permitted no loud or offensive music. The revised policy removed the word "offensive." Why?

A11.8   If the most important goal of tax policy is minimizing distortion, which good should the government impose an excise tax on, water or pizza? Explain.

A11.9 If raising revenue is the focus of taxation, ability to pay is the best approach. If correcting an externality is the focus, the benefit principle is the best approach. Explain.

A11.10 If you hate needles, you love government subsidies that make flu shots more affordable for everyone. Explain.

B11.1 If national defense were handled on a state-by-state basis in the United States, there would be much less, and in all likelihood not enough, defense expenditures. Why?

B11.2 Every politician is pro-education, but not every politician supports big spending on schools. If every politician believes there is a public good or positive externality here, why the difference?

B11.3 Some states have a sophisticated pollution tax system in which companies buy pollution rights from each other (every firm is given the right to pollute a little bit, but heavy polluters can buy more rights from another firm that isn't a heavy polluter). If it works well, this system allows more firms to remain in the local economy while the community still gets clean air, compared to a situation in which polluting beyond some level is banned outright. Explain.

B11.4 Income inequality is a popular topic in the United States and other wealthy countries but statistically, the worst income inequality in the world is in very poor countries in Africa and Central America. Can you figure out why?

B11.5 "Using government debt to pay for the interstate highway system in the 1950s made sense. Using debt to fund research to cure cancer makes sense. But using current government debt to pay for current exorbitant government retiree benefits makes no sense." Explain.

12 International Economics

Students are often surprised to discover that international economics is a topic in a microeconomics book. The headlines in this area usually concern trade deficits or exchange rates, and these are traditionally macroeconomic issues. But international economics is fundamentally about trade and the gains from trade, and those concepts are decidedly microeconomic. To see this straightforwardly, let's recall the discussion of utility in chapter 4: consumers in every country have the opportunity to increase their overall jollies if they have the option to consume goods that can't be produced domestically. That's the basic concept behind what's called *the gains from trade*.

The basic tenets of gains from trade are one aspect of economics about which most economists agree. Starting with a simple model in which people are endowed with different amounts of goods, we show that trading becomes the avenue through which we can undo an imbalance in allocation of goods between countries. The gains from trade can be extended when goods are produced with inputs that are differentially distributed across countries. In this case, we will show that the world is better off when we trade; in the simplest production model, trade increases the output of all goods.

Another general agreement among economists is that the gains realized from trade are not equally distributed within a country. When an economy opens up to trade, there are always winners and losers. We'll argue that, in most cases, there are sufficient gains to allow everyone within a trading economy to be better off. And we will show all of these things by applying the concepts that we discussed earlier in this book.

On completion of this chapter, you should

- understand the nature of gains from trade,
- see how trade can increase the level of output of all countries, and
- understand why not every citizen in every country benefits from international trade.

12.1   Gains from Trade

Why does the United States trade with other countries? The United States is the largest, most diverse economy in the world. But being large and diverse does not mean that the United States can produce all goods equally well. Some goods are located underground (titanium) or on plants (coffee) that do not naturally occur in the United States. Because we want to consume these goods, we need to trade with other countries to get them.

Resources are not equally and evenly distributed across all countries, but most people want to consume a very similar assortment of goods. Coffee is one of the most widely consumed beverages in the world, but coffee can be successfully grown in only about ten countries. That most people like coffee but only a few people can produce it is one of the easiest examples of gains to be made from trade.

Let's create a situation that leads to gains from trade. Consider a simpler world where there are only two (equal-sized) countries, US and THEM, and two goods, apples and oranges. In this simple world, the citizens of each country get a daily endowment of fruit (the fruit falls from trees that need no tending, so no one has to work in these countries initially). Everyone in US gets a daily endowment of ten apples and two oranges and everyone in THEM gets two apples and ten oranges. US was endowed by nature with more apple trees and THEM was endowed with more orange trees.

The citizens of each country are alike in all ways. Importantly, they both have what we'll call balanced preferences for fruit: they would like to eat an equal number of apples and oranges each day. Unfortunately, their endowment does not allow that. If we allowed people to buy and sell each fruit within each country, we would expect apples to be cheap and oranges to be expensive in US. Correspondingly, oranges would be cheap and apples expensive in THEM. To explain the difference in fruit prices within each country, let's consider the comparative markets for each fruit in each country.

The demand for each fruit is the same (balanced) in each country and what we might think of as average. Supplies are not. Apples are plentiful in US and oranges are scarce. Oranges are plentiful in THEM and apples are scarce. That means apples are (comparatively) cheap in US and oranges are (comparatively) cheap in THEM. These prices are a manifestation of unfulfilled desires. The citizens of US want more oranges than they were endowed with by nature and citizens of THEM want more apples.

If we recall the concept of marginal utility from chapter 4, this distribution of goods means that when the people of US eat their endowment, they get very few incremental jollies from the last few apples. They would get more incremental jollies from eating a few more oranges, but they have no way to make that change. The citizens of THEM are in a similar if reciprocal situation. They are forced by nature to eat more oranges than they strictly speaking would prefer; they would get more incremental jollies from eating a few more apples. Nature has endowed these countries with a supply of fruit that is not aligned with their preferences.

International trade can fix that. If these countries are close to each other (so we don't need to worry about transportation costs), their citizens will likely see the price differences and begin buying the cheaper good in one country and selling it in the other. That means US will export apples and THEM will export oranges. The citizens of US will happily trade their copious apples and the small incremental jollies associated with eating them for some scarce oranges. As in the shopping story in chapter 4, this will increase the overall jollies of everyone in US. The citizens of THEM will similarly increase their happiness by trading oranges that give them few incremental jollies for less plentiful apples, which give them more.

Remember, the citizens of both countries have balanced preferences. Interpreting that as getting maximum jollies from consuming an equal number of apples and oranges each day, they will have to trade with each other if they are to maximize their utility. If trade is free of transportation costs, the citizens of both countries will consume six apples and six oranges.

The basic tenet of trade theory is really the simple concept of gains from trade. Trade allows people in all countries to consume combinations of goods that do not exist in their country. "Allows" is the key word. No country has to trade; trade simply gives the trading country's citizens an opportunity. Trade lets people consume previously unattainable combinations of goods. A graphical rendition of this example can be found in appendix 12.1.

> **Sample Exam Question 12.1**
> If your country has a relatively big endowment of oil compared to the rest of the world, but your citizens like oil more than any other good, will they export or import oil?

12.2   More Potential Gains and the Downside: Production

Reallocating an existing supply of goods is the easiest way to see how everyone might benefit from trade. But there are no free lunches, and that includes apples and oranges. If

US has comparatively more apples and fewer oranges than THEM, it is almost certainly because it is comparatively easier to grow apples in US. Let's rework our simple example in a world where both fruits have to be grown in both countries.

Suppose US is located north of THEM. The cooler northern climate in US is more conducive to growing apples but not very good for oranges. The warmer southern climate in THEM is great for growing oranges but not very good for apples. Productivity is the difference between the countries that allows both countries to consume a balanced amount of each good—but at a high price.

In US, the climate allows apples to be grown comparatively easily. To grow oranges takes more effort (keeping the trees warm), and thus more of the population must work to produce US's desired oranges. The reverse is true in THEM. A lot of people work in the apple orchards combating the detrimental effects of the naturally warmer weather.

Suppose there are one hundred people in each country. The productivity of each citizen of US is twelve apples per day and four oranges per day. To get an equal amount of both (still the desired combination), there must be twenty-five people working in the apple industry producing three hundred apples per day and seventy-five people in the orange industry producing three hundred oranges. Every day, people trade internally and end up consuming three apples and three oranges. That's equal, but very inefficient. Because their climate isn't good for growing oranges, US has to employ a lot of people in the orange industry.

The climate difference in THEM means that country will have the exact opposite productivities. Oranges can be produced at a rate of twelve per day by each citizen of THEM and apples produced at a rate of four per day. To achieve (the same) balanced consumption, seventy-five citizens of THEM will produce apples each day and twenty-five people will produce oranges. As in US, each person in THEM will end up consuming three apples and three oranges (see figure 12.1).

If internal trade works like a farmers market, apples will be comparatively cheap in US and oranges will be comparatively cheap in THEM. The productivity difference will mean it is cheaper to produce apples in US and cheaper to produce oranges in THEM. When these countries meet, the price difference will lead people from both countries to buy apples in US and buy oranges in THEM. In this simple world, US will produce all of this simple world's apples and THEM will produce this world's oranges. Given the productivities, that would lead to twelve hundred apples being produced in US and twelve hundred oranges being produced in THEM (see figure 12.2). Each country would trade half of its output for the fruit it no longer produces, but everyone can now consume six apples and six oranges per day (see figure 12.2, where it is assumed each country exports half its production). Specializing in what you're good at and trading with others means that we have more of both goods, so the world is better off.

This is a powerful, compelling argument in support of trade. But this example also gives us a first taste of how international trade is not always seen as a good thing. Even though there are more apples and oranges in the world and all the citizens of both countries are

	Oranges	Apples
US	4/day x 75 workers = 300	12/day x 25 workers = 300
THEM	12/day x 25 workers = 300	4/day x 75 workers = 300

Figure 12.1   Production and Consumption Pre-Trade

	Oranges	Apples
US	0	12/day x 100 workers = 1200
THEM	12/day x 100 workers = 1200	0

Figure 12.2   Production Post-Trade

	Oranges	Apples
US	600	600
THEM	600	600

Figure 12.3   Consumption Post-Trade

better off—consuming more—both countries got there by closing an industry. US ultimately went out of the orange business and THEM stopped growing apples. In this simple exposition, all of the workers (who are also all of the citizens) in the closed industry simply moved into the other, more productive industry. But no one likes losing a job. Having to learn how to work in a new industry, and possibly having to move to a new part of the country, is trying. The people who work in the less-productive industry are paying for the economic progress.

And in a more realistic world where jobs require skills, location, and other costly attributes, we can't say for sure that everyone ends up working in the most productive industry in each country. Indeed, we know from observation that when an industry is put out of business through trade, some of its former employees cannot be relocated and end up unemployed for many years.

Curiosity 12.1
Ricardo's Trade Theory, Comparative Advantage, and Specialization

Our apples-and-oranges trade model is a rough version of the trade model and trade prediction of the nineteenth-century British economist, David Ricardo. Ricardo showed that trade will increase world production because each country will specialize in what it is comparatively better at producing. His model had an interesting feature. He showed that trade gains could exist even if one country was better (more productive) in both industries because there would always be one good every country was comparatively better at producing.

The comparative productivity story is interesting. Suppose it takes a worker one hour to pick a basket of apples in US and two hours to pick a basket of oranges. Suppose it takes two and a half hours to pick a basket of apples or oranges in THEM. Workers are more productive in both industries in US. We say the workers in US have an absolute advantage in both industries. But workers in US are *comparatively* better at picking apples. It takes them half the time to pick apples compared to oranges. Or, put differently, every basket of oranges that workers pick in US costs two baskets of apples (two hours could be used to pick one basket of oranges or two baskets of apples).

Thinking of the cost of one good in terms of the other allows us to say that oranges are comparatively cheaper to produce in THEM. We say THEM has a *comparative advantage* in producing oranges. Since it takes the same amount of time—two and a half hours—to produce a basket of either fruit, workers in THEM should pick the oranges for the two countries and workers in US should pick the apples. When market forces allocate labor across each country that way, the two countries will have the maximum amount of fruit. (Strictly speaking, both countries would completely specialize in their best industry if they were about the same size and the productivity differences were not too big.)

Comparative advantage is a useful mentality in many other places. If everyone in the organization or on the team has to do something, they each should be tasked with doing the thing they are comparatively best at. Jane might be better at cooking, waiting tables, and cleaning dishes than anyone else who works at her restaurant, but she cannot do every job. So she should specialize in the one job she is comparatively best at doing. If George can carry the biggest tray of dinner plates but can't cook and is allergic to the dishwashing liquid and Edward is a so-so cook, always drops the tray on the way to the table, but is a great dishwasher, Jane should cook, George wait tables, and Edward wash, even though Jane is better at all three jobs.

Sample Exam Question 12.2
Ricardo's comparative advantage assumes everyone has to do something, so you do what you're comparatively best at doing. In the restaurant example, is it possible that one person is so bad at everything that everyone else is better off if that person does nothing?

12.3   Interference with Free Trade

Trade with production is more compelling in that there is more of everything available to the world. But this increase in output comes at a cost. In every country, some people will experience a transactions cost: the cost of transition. Some people will have to change jobs in order to get this increase in world output. And those people will likely resist this costly change even if they are told it means more production (and potentially higher wages overall).

In addition, countries often become concerned about the decline, and in many cases demise, of one of their industries. If the industry being forced to reduce because of trade is something viewed as vital to the county's existence (e.g., the rice industry in Japan or the steel industry in the United States), political forces often trump economic ones and protections against the effects of international trade are often imposed.

The easiest way to protect an industry from trade is simply to not trade, to close your borders to trade and go it alone. That would certainly protect jobs and industries, but at an enormous cost to citizens. The ability to consume goods that cannot be produced in your country (e.g., coffee) depends on trade. Going it alone means forgoing a lot of goods.

That potential loss is extended when we talk in more detail about production. We saw in chapter 10 that innovation can be the key to increasing productivity. Innovation, like most things in economics, needs to be stoked. Knowing there are better firms out there makes your firm work harder and strive to be state-of-the art. That economic pressure happens even if the superior firm is in another country. Closing your borders to trade virtually ensures that all your industries will fall behind.

Another, less draconian way to protect domestic industries is to impose a tariff. A *tariff* is a tax, often per unit, like a sales tax, imposed on goods produced in another country and imported. The logic behind a tariff is that your (inferior) domestic industry can't produce its good as inexpensively as the (superior) foreign firm. That shows up as lower prices on goods produced in the foreign country. Assuming consumers always buy the cheaper good, the domestic industry (again, the less productive firm in this case) will lose customers and sometimes go out of business.

Suppose the difference in price between the foreign and domestically produced version is 20 percent. The domestic government, wishing to save the local industry from demise, could impose a 20 percent tariff on the imported good, allowing the domestic firm to compete and survive. If this works the way it is supposed to, the people working in the domestic industry can keep their jobs. That sounds like a good thing, but there's a cost. The domestic industry can now be 20 percent less efficient (using these numbers) in the long run and it would not need to innovate in order to survive.

Of course, there are lots of other possible reasons for trade patterns. Foreign countries might allow their producers to use what we in the United States consider illegal production practices (e.g., child labor, water and air pollution). That would make their goods cheaper,

Curiosity 12.1
Protectionism and Game Theory

We can apply the game theory approach that we developed in chapter 9 to the problem of protectionism. Suppose there are two countries, US and THEM, and they can either have free trade or impose tariffs and other protectionist measures. Free trade is best for both countries; protectionism is good for either country only if the other country doesn't protect as well. Like the classic prisoner's dilemma game, if both countries are too self-interested, they both protect and both countries are worse off. We see from the illustration that if THEM chooses free trade, US would prefer to protect (eight is bigger than five) and if THEM chooses protect, US would again prefer protect (two is bigger than one). US has a dominant strategy to protect. The same holds for THEM. IF US chooses free trade, THEM prefers protect, and if US chooses protect, THEM prefers protect. US and THEM both have a dominant strategy to protect, and the game should end up with both players growing by 2 percent and both seeing they could have gotten 5 percent. Knowing this, countries try to make commitments and similar agreements that (theoretically) lead to freer trade and a better outcome for everyone.

		US	
		Free	Protect
THEM	Free	US grows by 5% THEM grows by 5%	US grows by 8% THEM grows by 1%
	Protect	US grows by 1% US grows by 8%	US grows by 2% US grows by 2%

but not because their businesses are more productive. It is also possible that a country's government subsidizes an industry in order to promote exports. While the rationale behind that is complicated, it means that trade does not necessarily lead to more of all goods. It also means that it is possible that one country is losing jobs or industries to another for reasons other than competitive advantage. Economists sometimes say that a country should not impose tariffs to undo the effect of a foreign subsidy because that constitutes two bad policies, or, as the cliché goes, two wrongs don't make a right. It is, however, common practice as of this writing.

12.4   Implications and Predictions of Trade

Several famous propositions and theories come directly from microeconomic concepts. We've seen that the gains from trade come from the natural distribution of productive resources. Natural resources are not evenly distributed, so every good can be produced more easily—and more affordably—in countries that are endowed with resources that are used in the production of that good. Coffee grows best in one particular type of soil and at one particular altitude; that makes Colombia, Kenya, and Brazil the best places to grow coffee.

That same logic can be applied to other productive resources. We often divide inputs other than natural resources into categories, such as land, labor, and capital. This schema is obviously oversimplified, but it will allow us to predict trade patterns. Just as a certain soil and altitude are best suited for growing coffee, some goods can be produced most affordably using a lot of labor, or a lot of capital, or a lot of land. Trade theorists call those goods labor intensive, capital intensive, and land intensive. To be precise, these intensities are all relative. That is, we assume all goods need all three inputs, but each good needs one of these inputs relatively more.

The best example is agricultural grains, for example wheat and corn. To produce these agricultural goods affordably you need (relatively) lots of land. Computers, on the other hand, need lots of capital (factories and equipment). Consider two countries with about the same population, Russia and Japan. Comparatively, Russia has (a lot) more land and Japan has more capital. If these countries trade with each other, we would predict that Russia will export grains and Japan will export computers. This result springs naturally from the results in chapter 10 on input markets.

A related, ominous result of unfettered trade is that inputs around the world should ultimately earn the same return in every country. The easiest way to see why that's true is that unfettered free trade means the world has no borders and no countries from an economic perspective. So, factor returns (wages, rents, return on capital, etc.) will be determined by the relative world supply of each factor. When countries with very large populations (China, India) begin trading with the rest of the world, that effectively increases the supply of labor and, everything else the same, lowers the return on labor (wages) in all other countries.

12.5   Multinationals, Sweatshops, and Trade's Bad Reputation

There is no doubt that international trade is what we today call a disruptor. Job loss, factory closings, and community upheaval can be accurately blamed on the relocations that our models predict. Lower-cost consumer goods and worldwide economic growth are more positive outcomes from the internationalization of the world's economies.

But if there are goods and bads from this process, there are also misattributions. International trade has been blamed for sweatshops, child labor abuses, and even political oppression. Although these things are largely outside the realm of basic microeconomics, we can discuss them with the tools that we've developed in this book.

In many cases, the abuses blamed on international trade are, in fact, problems that already exist within countries and come to light or are exacerbated by trade. Child labor, for example, is not something that is demanded by a multinational company when it relocates to a country. In the poorest countries in the world, most members of a family need to work in order to subsist. Put differently, children were working already. A country needs to reach a level of per capita income before it has the ability to eliminate things like child labor. International trade helps countries do that, but it doesn't happen overnight.

It is a challenge to policymakers to find ways to deal with economics and politics simultaneously. If a country's land is owned entirely by the ruling family and its primary export is an agricultural good that is grown on that land, most of the gains from trade will go to the land-owning family. The people who live in the country and work for the family will see little of the gains from trade. But what's the answer to this conundrum? Not trading with that country certainly doesn't help the workers either.

The point of this discussion is an important one as we conclude this book. Economics can explain many things. It can show people and policymakers the best way to produce and distribute goods. It can show how markets can operate fairly or be manipulated to operate for the benefit of the few. But economic outcomes are always determined within the structure that is provided by our societies and political systems. Economics did not invent oppression or slavery or gender bias. It can explain outcomes within systems that allow those things, but economics, in general, finds that the best outcomes occur in the most open, fair, and unbiased societies.

Examples

Example 1   A headline reads "Bolivians Discover the Downside of International Trade." The story was about quinoa, a trendy grain called the food of the gods. Bolivia is one of the world's largest producers and exporters of quinoa. But now that the bulk of the annual crop is being exported to the rest of the world, local quinoa prices have risen to the point that many Bolivians can no longer afford this food staple.

While one remains sympathetic to the change in diet that Bolivians have had to undertake, what's the upside of this story?
Because quinoa is being sold to the world at a much higher price than it used to sell for locally (pre-trade), Bolivians can afford to buy many other goods that were previously unattainable. Suppose we price all world goods in dollars. Pre-trade quinoa sold for, say, fifty cents per pound and a quinoa farmer could sell a thousand pounds of quinoa per month for $500. That would allow the farmer to have a subsistence living at best. When Bolivia opened the quinoa market to trade, that same farmer could sell his quinoa for $3 a pound and make $3,000 per month. While this higher income allows quinoa farmers to

buy more of all goods, the substitution effect will likely incline them away from consuming as much quinoa as they did pre-trade.

Example 2   President Trump tends to focus on what are called bilateral trade balances, or the difference between exports and imports between any two countries. If imports exceed exports, a country is running a trade deficit. Some people believe that a persistent trade deficit between the United States and a trading partner is evidence of unfair trade practices on the part of the trading partner—they must be tariffing our goods and hurting the market for our exports.

Give a simpler (and completely fair) explanation for a persistent, bilateral trade deficit.
If trade patterns are determined by differences in productive resources across countries, we would not (necessarily) expect a trade balance between any two countries. Suppose all countries use dollars. Saudi Arabia exports oil to the United States and imports corn from Mexico. The United States exports computers to Mexico and imports oil from Saudi Arabia. Every pair of countries has a bilateral trade imbalance (either deficit or surplus), but every dollar that left the United States to buy oil from Saudi Arabia came back when Mexico bought computers from the United States.

Example 3   Manufacturing jobs have been leaving the United States for decades, but the pace of departure increased when China and India and their two billion-plus populations opened their economies to international trade. The U.S. jobs that were insulated from this departure were service jobs. After all, you can't import a haircut or a drain cleaning from China or India.

While that is still true to a large extent, what other major shift in the economy did cause service jobs to leave as well?
The internet. While you can't import a haircut, you can import accounting services, call center services, and other services that can be transmitted on the World Wide Web.

Chapter Summary

- Gains from trade encompass the basic idea that you can increase your happiness if you have the opportunity to consume things that your country cannot provide.

- These gains from trade can be extended to an increase in world output of all goods if there are differences in productivity across industries and countries.

- The reality, however, is that gains from trade are not guaranteed for all citizens of all countries, which may provide political justification for trade protection.

- The reality behind some of the stories that have given trade a bad reputation in recent years lies in existing social structures and conditions, not in trade per se.

Exercises

(B exercises are more challenging.)

A12.1   If you live in the United States and you like real Champagne (Google "Champagne" to see what is meant by real Champagne), then you are a fan of international trade. Explain.

A12.2   Probably the most common complaint about free trade is that when we trade, the United States loses jobs to "cheap foreign labor." Based on the trade models we have discussed, do we?

A12.3   Following up on that answer, doesn't something similar usually happen when a company moves from California to Texas or from Michigan to South Carolina?

A12.4   Gains from trade are nothing more than an application of chapter 4's utility theory combined with the natural differences that exist between the counties of the world. Explain.

A12.5   Trade theory works in many places. With both teams looking like potential playoff teams this year, the Redbirds just traded a pitcher to the Bluebirds in exchange for a home-run hitter. What would you guess the pre-trade "endowment" of each type of those players was on each team?

A12.6   One of the critical determinants of trade patterns is transportation costs. Canada and Mexico are the second- and third-largest trading partners of the United States because of proximity. In an unusual twist, the invention of the World Wide Web created an opportunity for importing service goods (accounting, computer coding, and many similar services) from places like India. How is this related to the transportation cost factor?

A12.7   Imposing a tariff to protect a domestic industry from job losses caused by trade is, in effect, "protecting" a country from many of the gains from trade. Explain.

A12.8   If countries around the world did not trade, some currently wealthy countries such as Saudi Arabia and Kuwait would become among the world's poorest countries. Explain.

A12.9   Trade patterns and the gains from trade should be based on the distribution of productive resources around the world. This should work for things like tourism, too. Countries with potentially popular tourist attractions should be able to benefit from that "endowment." Political instability is, therefore, problematic for countries in the Middle East (e.g., Egypt.) Explain.

A12.10   One unfortunate historical alternative to the gains from trade is the "gains" from invasion. If the country next door has lots of something your country needs, it might be cheaper to invade that country and take it. How is that similar to increasing your jollies by stealing goods, as we discussed in chapter 4?

B12.1   Economic growth in the United States and in every other country is associated with specialized skills. The nineteenth-century, jack-of-all trades, self-sufficient farmer has given way to the master's-degree-in-computer-sciences programmer for Google. That increases a country's output and makes everyone better off if, and only if, a form of free trade exists within the county. Explain.

B12.2   The president has made a point of renegotiating most of the trade agreements that the United States entered into in the past two decades. His political base is working-class voters who want jobs to be brought back to the United States from China, India, and other such countries. Considering the factors that determine trade patterns, would you expect that to be likely?

B12.3   Let's put comparative advantage to work when you play sports. You have five friends on your league basketball team. Everyone has to play tonight (you have no bench players.) One teammate, Jay, has been playing with you for many years and works hard, but he's twelve years older than anyone else on either team. Jay is of average height and, because of his age, a lot slower than the fastest players on the other team. Jay has to guard (defend) someone. Would you tell him to guard one of the other team's fast players or one of their tall players?

B12.4   Subsidizing an industry so it can be an exporter of some good sounds ominous, but it presents a long-term problem for the subsidizing country. Suppose the government of Iceland decides the country should produce and export coffee, a warm-weather crop. To that end, the government uses tax money to build a large number of greenhouses allowing coffee to be grown there. What's the long-run problem?

B12.5   The opening of China to capitalist economics was considered a win for the United States and other countries that disagreed with the tenets of communism. That might have been a public relations win, but it was not a win for many workers in the United States. Explain.

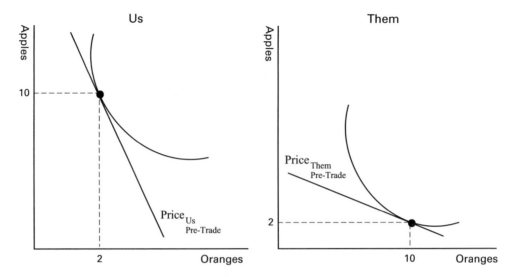

Figure 12.4 Pre-Trade Endowment, Consumption, and Prices

Appendix 12.1   The Graphical Approach to Gains from Trade with Endowments of Goods

In section 12.1 we had two countries, US and THEM, and two goods, oranges and apples. We said that the citizens of US had a daily endowment of ten apples and two oranges and the citizens of THEM had a daily endowment of two apples and ten oranges. We also said the citizens of both countries had the same preferences, and these preferences favored a balanced consumption of apples and oranges. We show the pre-trade situation in each country in figure 12.4.

The slope of the line in each country represents the price of the good on the horizontal axis, oranges. In US, this line is steep: it has a comparatively big slope, meaning oranges are expensive in US. That makes sense. The demand (preferences) for both goods is equal, but US has a relatively small supply of oranges. THEM has a flat price line with a comparatively smaller slope. Oranges are comparatively cheaper in THEM because again, demand is the same for both fruits, but the supply of oranges is comparatively big.

When these two countries trade, US can buy cheap oranges from THEM, lowering the price of oranges in US and flattening the price line that citizens of US see. Drawing this flatter price line through the endowment (which is income in each country), we see that everyone in US can increase their utility with trade. They can sell some of their plentiful apples for scarce oranges and achieve their desired balanced consumption. In THEM, the

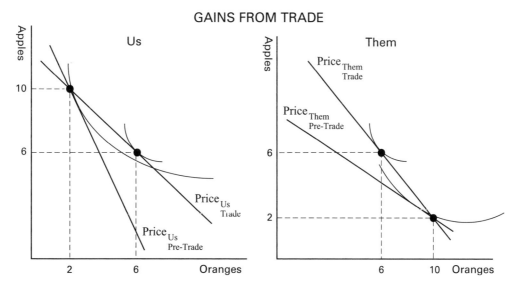

Figure 12.5   After-Trade Prices, Consumption, and Higher Utility

price of oranges will rise with trade as they sell some of their plentiful oranges in US. The price line after trade is steeper, and again, everyone in THEM increases their utility by getting a more balanced consumption combination (see figure 12.5).

These simple gains from trade show the easiest rationale for trade. Trade allows countries to undo the imbalance in the natural distribution of goods. As such, and assuming people everywhere want to consume a more balanced combination of goods, trade makes everyone better off in this simple world.

Ironically, we don't need a more complicated version of the model to show how these gains from trade could be problematic. Suppose things in US are slightly different. Half the citizens of US have orange trees and the other half have apple trees. The apple tree owners are endowed with twenty apples each day but no oranges. The orange tree owners have four oranges each day but no apples. Every day, these fruit tree owners meet in a farmers market. Notice the average endowment is the same—ten apples and two oranges (add up the endowment for one apple tree owner and one orange tree owner and divide by two). They still have the same, balanced preferences, so when they meet at the market, apple tree owners will sell ten of their apples for two oranges; that's the closest everyone in US can get to balanced consumption. The price of each orange is five apples. Oranges are expensive in terms of apples because apples are comparatively plentiful in US.

If US opens its economy to trade and finds a trading partner (like THEM) with a high price of apples and a low price of oranges (prices are relative prices, one good in terms of the other, so the price of one good is the reciprocal of the other), it will find gains from trade, which we can see from the average endowment point or the post-farmers-market point. But those gains are now unevenly distributed. Apple tree owners in US will sell their fruit to the new trading partner for a higher price—more oranges. Since trade will lower the price of oranges, orange tree owners in US are actually worse off than they were when they traded only with domestic apple tree owners.

Appendix A: Answers to Sample Exam Questions

2.1 From the customer's perspective, the "price" of a good is the opportunity cost, which includes the time and effort needed to purchase the good. Going to the department store at the mall has a higher opportunity cost than shopping on Amazon.com. This assumes you don't need the good right away, since Amazon still takes a day or two to deliver things to you.

2.2 Good weather increases the supply line—shifts it to the right—but does not cause a shift in demand. The supply line moves along the demand line, causing an increase in quantity demanded but not an increase in demand.

2.3 Unlike apples, you can't increase the production of Rembrandt paintings in the long run. Rembrandt has been dead for 350 years.

3.1 Other than the cost of enforcing the policy, rent control is inexpensive. Building or subsidizing the building of new apartments is expensive. If voters don't understand or believe in market forces, they might think rent control will solve the problem, and they reward—re-elect—politicians who support this cheaper alternative.

3.2 The difference would be in the ultimate price of cigarettes. The quota would effectively raise the price of cigarettes because it decreases the quantity supplied without decreasing demand. The negative advertisements decrease demand—shift the line to the left—which would decrease the market price.

4.1 Advertisement isn't as effective as sampling for some attributes (e.g., how something tastes). Giving away samples sounds expensive, but advertising is also expensive, and in the final analysis, the firm has to decide which approach is the more cost-effective way to inform consumers about its product's attributes.

4.2 Assuming this is something like collecting state quarters, your coin collection can be liquidated—spent—any time you find a better use for the money.

4.3 Yes! Without a reason not to, people would steal because consuming more increases your utility.

5.1   At $2 per pound, your fifty pounds will sell for $100, which is exactly your fixed costs and thus sounds like an acceptable offer, but how will you pay for picking the tomatoes? Assuming there's any cost for picking—even the cost of your own time—you'll need that variable cost to be less than $100; otherwise your loss— which starts with your $100 fixed costs—will get bigger.

5.2   Short-term losses occur when the business can't cover fixed and variable costs in any given year. Large fixed costs, such as factories and machinery, make manufacturing firms especially vulnerable to declining prices. If, for example, both firms had to shut down for year due to a decline in their prices, the service firm's largely variable costs could be entirely avoided. The manufacturing firm's fixed costs could not.

6.1   In the real world, you'll probably have some customers who are willing to pay the extra fifty cents, but others will hear about lower prices and go to another stand. You will probably lose enough customers to convince yourself that you aren't actually making more money at the higher price.

6.2   Opening and operating a business takes time. Even if you aren't working, your time is worth something. The opportunity cost of the business owner's time (among other things) has to be compensated with some of the accounting profits of the business.

7.1   Once he announces the new pricing policy, he will lose some sales in the hour before the last hour as people wait for the half-price donuts. Suppose he sells twenty fewer full-price donuts in the time before the last hour and ends up selling them at half price. He has lost $20 worth of full-price sales and is now selling forty donuts at fifty cents for a total of $20. He's no better off!

7.2   No. Demand for eight-track tapes has fallen so much over the years that you can't sell them at a price that is higher than average cost. In effect, the demand line is now completely below the average cost line.

7.3   Suppose the regulated price is set at the intersection of supply and demand, and that regulated price cannot be adjusted quickly. If demand for the good increases—shifts to the right—and the price cannot, there will be a shortage. The electric company will have to shut off power at times.

8.1   Rent, don't buy. Expand flexibly. Taking advantage of the good times isn't a mistake, but the firm has to do this in way that doesn't permanently increase fixed costs.

8.2   No. The gas station on the northeast corner will be paying higher rent or, if the station owns the land, the station on the northeast corner had to pay more for that land.

8.3   At the prices we determined, $Q_{Firm1} = 94$, $Q_{Firm2} = 56$.

Profit$_{firm1}$ = $(P_{firm1} - AC)Q_{Firm1}$ = $(51.31 - 20) \times 94 = 2{,}943$.

If we tried a lower price for firm 1, such as $P_{Firm1} = 50$, we would get $P_{Firm2} = 47.5$.

And $Q_{Firm1} = 97.5$, making Profit$_{Firm1}$ = $(50 - 20) \times 97.5 = 2{,}925 < 2{,}943$.

9.1   Play the game repeatedly and alternate who goes first.

9.2   In an apartment complex, the pet owner is likely to assume someone else (perhaps the people paid to take care of the grounds) will clean up after pets do their business, so the pet owner will not clean up. If the pet owner lives in a house alone, there is no one else to clean up, so the pet owner has to. Of course, there's always the neighbor's front yard. . . .

10.1 Collective bargaining takes away wage determination based on the last or marginal worker. The all-or-nothing aspect makes the employer look at total, not marginal product. For seven workers, total output would be 490 quarts per hour, which would sell for $490 \times \$0.2/\text{qt} = \$98/\text{hr}$. The seven workers, based on the union's demand, will earn $7 \times \$12/\text{hr} = \$84/\text{hr}$, so the employer could conceptually meet the union's demand.

The problem comes when you consider paying all other inputs (land, capital, etc.). If the unionized workers get their demand, labor will earn $84 of the $98 total revenue leaving $14 per hour for all other inputs. If workers are paid based on marginal productivity, the firm will hire six workers and pay all of them $10 per hour They will pick 450 quarts per hour, which will sell for $90. The workers get paid $60 of the $90, leaving $30 for other inputs. So collective bargaining's ability to increase the pay of union members comes down to the legitimate cost of all other inputs. If the firm can survive paying $14 per hour to all of its labor, then the union has succeeded. If the firm cannot survive, the company closes and all the jobs and wages are lost.

10.2 False. The federal minimum wage is for all entry-level, unskilled labor anywhere in the United States. Individual employers have their own entry-level requirements. If a firm requires more skills of all its workers, it will have to pay more for those workers than the federal minimum wage.

11.1 Some aspects of health care are a clearly a public good. Controlling contagious disease is a good example of something that provides benefits to more than the initial consumer. Other things, such as an individual getting a knee replacement, is a private good, just like my eating a slice of pizza. There's a tendency to say things like "everyone is better off when people are healthier" and that health care is therefore a public good. But it can't be as simple as that. Everyone is better off if everyone lives in a castle on the beach, too. A public good is a good that, by its nature, cannot exclude people once it is provided. Clearly, a hospital or a doctor's office can require payment before use. So most of health care is a private good: perhaps an important private good, but still a private good.

11.2 It's too hard to figure out the risks and corresponding payments. In addition, it's tedious to collect the payments from each smoker, especially if the payments are per cigarette. Sometimes it's just too hard to fix a market failure.

11.3 Policies like this take away incentives for people to move themselves out of the lower rungs of the income distribution. Paying people for being poor might—and this is in no sense a well-accepted certainty—keep people poor.

11.4 Ability to pay. That approach exempts basic necessities that everyone—rich and poor—has to buy and focuses the sales tax much more on luxury goods.

12.1 In the simplest trade example with endowments, we allow only endowments to differ. We assume preferences are the same (and balanced). But the same logic for gains from trade work if you allow a country to have a stronger preference for a good. That means it gets more jollies from that good. So an oil-rich country can increase its jollies by importing oil if it really likes oil a lot. The United States is such a country.

12.2 In the Ricardian world, there's always something you can do that's better than nothing. It's a matter of not having the time to do many things at the same time. So Jane can do all of the jobs better than anyone else, but time she spends carrying dishes she can't spend cooking. It isn't usually part of the Ricardian setup, but you could have someone who is so incompetent that that person actually lowers the productivity of others. If that's true, the others might be more productive with that person not working.

Appendix B: Answers to Even-Numbered Exercises

A2.2   This would cause a decrease in the supply of gasoline. A decrease in supply would be a shift to the left of the supply line. The supply line would move along the demand line to the left, and prices would rise.

A2.4   Good weather for farm goods means an increase in supply, or a shift of the supply line to the right. The supply line would move along the demand line to the right, and prices would fall.

A2.6   There were two shifts associated with this problem. Demand decreased—shifted left—and supply decreased—also shifted left. If the shifts were about the same, the market price would not change.

A2.8   The increased number of rooms would be an increase in supply a shift to the right—which would have caused room prices to fall. But the new attractions increased the demand for rooms—a shift to the right—and since room prices rose, the demand shift must have been bigger than the supply shift.

A2.10 Increase. Using the nonspecific good "health care," the Affordable Care Act increased the demand by giving many more people health insurance. That would shift the demand for health care to the right. With no supply shift, the price of health care would rise. *Note:* This price is best thought of as an opportunity cost. Among other things, the time spent searching for a doctor and waiting for appointments increased.

B2.2   Knowing the directions of the shifts, you could use the ultimate price change to determine the relative magnitude. Supply decreased; that would have caused prices to rise. Demand also decreased; that would have caused prices to fall. Once you observe how the market price changed, you could determine which shift had the bigger impact.

B2.4   A few days before Christmas everything is short run, and thus both the supply and demand lines are steep (inelastic). Intuitively, shoppers have less time to search for the best price and gift recipients are less likely to be flexible about what they want.

A3.2   The only way to decrease price and increase quantity is to increase supply—shift the supply line to the right. Imposing a price ceiling in order to lower price causes the quantity supplied to decrease. And a production quota at a quantity higher than the market quantity won't work unless it is subsidized, which *is* a supply shift to the right.

A3.4   Price ceilings invariably lead to shortages, meaning people have to spend much more time searching for a good whose dollar price has been artificially lowered. The opportunity cost of the good—the combined dollar cost and value of time—is the relevant price from the consumer's perspective.

A3.6   Price supports—a price floor—set the legal price above the market price, meaning consumers have to pay more for the good. Buying up the resulting surplus will require the government to raise taxes, a cost that is also borne by consumers (assuming they are also taxpayers).

A3.8   A minimum wage above the market wage causes a surplus: quantity supplied exceeds quantity demanded. Open borders would likely cause more people to relocate to the high-minimum-wage country in the long run (assuming people do not find out until they have moved that there aren't jobs available at that high minimum wage). The high minimum wage together with the flatter long-run supply line means the surplus gets bigger in the long run.

A3.10   The supply of Picasso paintings is inelastic because he is dead; he can't paint any more paintings, regardless of the price. We said that the incidence of a tax would fall on the more inelastic side of the market. There are other artists for consumers interested in Picasso's style, so demand is not likely to be inelastic. So an excise tax on Picasso painting will ultimately be borne by the supply side—the sellers of his paintings.

B3.2   The Affordable Care Act and the aging of the baby boomers have both caused the demand for prescription drugs to increase—shift to the right. A price ceiling below the new, higher market price would lead to shortages. Assuming the drugs are important for the health of consumers, shortages will make them worse off, even if the dollar price they pay is lower.

B3.4   Like any other price ceiling, a price ceiling on the price paid to doctors will cause a shortage. In the short run, those who have gone to medical school might continue practicing medicine, choosing only to decrease the amount of time they spend with each patient. In the long run, fewer people will go to medical school, perhaps because they can see that the compensation they will receive (at the price ceiling) will not allow them to pay their student loans. The supply of doctors is more elastic in the long run and the shortage gets bigger.

A4.2   You can get jollies by association. Thinking you're drinking the same beer as your favorite movie star can make you enjoy the beer more. But the movie star saying that drinking the beer will make you a movie star is a liar. You can't maximize your utility if people lie to you about the jollies that a product will give you.

A4.4   The logic, like it or not, is that the government is better at knowing what's bad for you. The concern is that simply informing people of dangers would not always stop them from using a product. Though we don't wish to take sides on this, cigarette smoking would appear to support the "government is better at making some decisions for you" approach.

A4.6   If every good that you buy costs $1, utility maximization is a relatively simple matter of comparing the marginal utility of (the last unit of) every good in the store.

A4.8   With no dollar price for another unit of food consumed, people have a tendency to consume everything at the buffet until the marginal utility of the last unit is approximately zero. The price that we often ignore is the price you pay when you eat so much you feel sick. The popular expression "your eyes are bigger than your stomach" suits this situation well.

A4.10   Diminishing marginal utility can be applied over time as long as you remember that a jolly in the future isn't as good as a jolly today. If you're thinking about everything you consume—all goods—they too should display diminishing marginal utility. So if you have spendable income today of $100,000 and you know you'll have no income next year, you will figure out that the marginal utility of spending some of that income next year is greater than the marginal utility of spending it this year, even knowing a jolly next year is worth less. You will spend a little more than half your income this year and save the rest for next year.

B4.2   The opportunity cost is much lower. You don't have to drive, park, stand in line, sit next to strangers, or even wear clothes! Popcorn is cheaper, and you can pause the movie whenever you want to. Big-screen TVs aren't the same as a movie screen, but they are getting closer.

B4.4   For any new product, unfamiliar jollies are harder for people to justify buying. The "units" problem—the product size forces you to give up many other goods—makes it harder to buy any good. So new products in general, and new products in a space where consumers already know how to maximize their utility, should be sold in smaller sizes and at lower prices until consumers learn about their attributes.

A5.2   We said that the fundamental reason for increasing variable costs and thus increasing marginal costs is diminishing marginal product of labor and other variable inputs. While that concept is a good generalization, the way a company might see rising variable costs is something more straightforward, such as overtime pay. To get existing workers to work beyond some level (such as forty hours per week), you have to pay them a higher wage per hour. Combine that with possibly needing more workers as you expand, and you have a higher marginal cost.

A5.4   In the short run, having already paid fixed costs, Joan will sell any meal that at least covers the cost of the meal. She will produce where $P = MC$ even if $P < AC$. But her hope is that demand for her meals will rise, increasing the price of each meal and allowing her to cover both marginal and average costs.

A5.6   Starting a business in your parent's garage or basement probably means low or possibly no fixed costs (depending on your parents' generosity). A business can survive much longer if it doesn't have to worry about paying back fixed costs.

A5.8   You almost certainly won't have any customers at three in the morning, but staying open means you will have new, variable costs. You are generating losses that you can avoid.

A5.10 The cost of adding an additional student to an online class is minimal. They watch the same streaming video lecture that everyone else is already watching from their home. The school doesn't need a building or parking lot or public restroom or any of the fixed costs of schooling associated with students in a classroom. Of course, the quality of the experience is different as well.

B5.2   About zero. If variable and thus marginal costs are close to zero, our pricing rule would say you can sell every unit at about zero. Unfortunately, that means you'll never make enough to pay the fixed costs. These goods require a different pricing strategy.

B5.4   How businesses buy goods in the real world makes the attribution of variable versus fixed costs harder. Because the egg inventory (a dozen eggs) has already been purchased, the eggs would appear to be a fixed cost. But inputs that are kept in inventory are there for immediate use, so they are more like a variable cost.

A6.2   Don't buy the bigger house. Profits happen, but they never last more than one growing season. You won't be able to make the higher house payment after this year.

A6.4   If fixed costs stay constant, the only thing that pushes prices back to the breakeven point is the entry of new firms. If fixed and therefore average costs are rising as well, it will require fewer firms to enter the market in order to eliminate excess profits.

A6.6 No one exited because the bad news was temporary. Everyone knew that the story was false, and believed—correctly, as it turned out—that demand would return to its pre-bad-news level by the following year.

A6.8 Good and bad news comes randomly, meaning excess profits and losses occur randomly. The key to surviving bad years—years when your firm is experiencing short-term losses—is to have something to live on when those years occur. If you save some or all of your short-term profits in the good years, you'll have that available to get you through the bad years.

A6.10 Demand fell so much that prices fell below average variable costs. In that case, the firm's best strategy is to shut down completely.

B6.2 You will have thwarted entry, but you will not have saved your profits. Now, instead of your profits being eliminated by new firms increasing the supply and lowering prices, your profits have been eliminated by the cost of the land you bought to prevent entry.

B6.4 The assumption of same technology usually works like this in the real world. You discover something, such as the plastic idea, that does lower your costs and make you profits for a year or two but all the other strawberry farmers can see it, and they all begin to do it. Market supply ultimately increases, market prices fall, and profits are eliminated in the long run.

A7.2 That point isn't on the demand line for cable TV. Even if they were a monopoly, there were substitutes for cable TV, such as using an antenna. In addition, the income effect would say that most people simply wouldn't have enough money to pay $5,000 per month.

A7.4 No, sorry. With the advent of smart phones that can record movies, there is no demand for camcorders. You can't sell a camcorder at any price that's higher than average cost.

A7.6 If the monopoly was the result of a merger of previously competitive firms, there would be market data on costs and price/quantity trade-offs. The regulator would have a better idea where the competitive market price and quantity were in this case.

A7.8 The customers at these different retailers must be completely separated from the alternatives. That is, people who are buying from the vending machine can't simply walk across the street to the grocery store or dollar store to buy Kit Kats. In the worst-case scenario for the makers of Kit Kats, when they start selling them for $1 at the Dollar Store, no one buys them at the grocery store or vending machine anymore.

A7.10   If demand is inelastic, a small decrease in output leads to a big increase in price. All else the same, it's easier for a monopolist facing an inelastic demand to get to a price that exceeds average cost.

B7.2   No. Amazon is now a competitor to all traditional retailers, so there is no combination of traditional retailers that will have pricing power relative to Amazon's.

B7.4   Assuming the same thing was true for the monopolist that was true for perfectly competitive firms, they would still be breaking even (making a fair return) at $10 for five thousand units, so they could continue to produce. Knowing this level of output was where the monopoly maximized profits, and not at minimum average cost, the firm could actually increase output at a fixed price of $10 and end up making a small profit. Oddly, the $10 price is less of a problem than the "produce five thousand units."

A8.2   The landowner got the profits. Either your rent is higher or you paid more for the land when you bought it.

A8.4   If either firm produced all of the remaining one-third of the market, the price would fall to the competitive level, eliminating profits for that firm (actually, for both firms). There are other quantity competition models that give different results. In what's called Stackelberg competition, one firm realizes that the other firm is always producing half the remaining share of the market, so that knowledgeable firm produces a bigger share of the market and the naïve firm produces a smaller share. This lowers the price and industry profits relative to the original Cournot model but the knowledgeable firm gets a bigger share of the profits.

A8.6   They would capture a bit more market share, but they would also decrease their profits on all of their existing customers. All told, they don't get enough new customers to be worth the profits they would lose on their existing customers.

A8.8   The original competitors differentiated so much that they all abandoned the middle. The new generic firm entered this market and was able to capture this middle market.

A8.10   More likely. Price cooperation is more likely if it's easier to change prices because every store knows that its price change will bring forth an immediate response. If it takes time to respond to a price change, you are more likely to keep your prices low, knowing any competitor could capture your market share for a substantial amount of time by undercutting your price.

B8.2   No. The turnover of that restaurant indicates that excess profits no longer exist in the local restaurant industry. Your lucrative job is almost certainly going to pay you better than your break-even restaurant will.

B8.4   Profitable oligopoly strategies are often tied to certain aspects of the market. Brand reputation and tying up retail space worked for decades, but online retailers have no shelf space, and modern information sources (e.g., online reviews) make brand reputation much less important. All the brand-based consumer product companies are struggling in this new environment and they have likely seen the end of their high profits.

A9.2   By being forced to stay at the one-third-mile and two-thirds-mile spots (e.g., by being issued permits that don't let them move), both stands would still get half the customers, but customers on average will walk a shorter distance to get a hot dog.

A9.4   Your wave is a promise not to go, allowing both of you to get through the intersection without incident.

A9.6   The key is that both can reach their best possible outcome. If the commitment allows that, then no one will be better off by bluffing.

A9.8   According to the Cournot model discussed in chapter 8, each firm observes the other's output, assumes that output is fixed (each firm concedes the other firm's existing market share), then maximizes profits in its own share of the market. So each firm is doing the best it can, given what the other firm is doing. That is a Nash equilibrium.

A9.10   You'd certainly be more likely to scream since you have evidence that the mugger is inclined to hurt you. You should ask yourself if you heard the other victim scream. If you did not, you might assume the mugger is going to hurt you either way, so you should scream.

B9.2   In the short run, no, assuming they knew the bill was going to pass. At least not if there was a decent chance they could have mitigated the impact on their constituents by taking an active role. Of course, there might be other reasons for nonparticipation having to do with politics or longer-run considerations.

B9.4   The other player isn't like you. You never lie, so if you make a commitment, you will keep it. If the other player knows that, he could use that against you. Furthermore, a commitment from the other player is more likely to be a bluff (a lie).

A10.2   You increased your skills over time, and in so doing, you increased your marginal product of labor. Using the hint, you can still do the busboy's job, but you can do more than that as well.

A10.4   If there are many small employers, they do not individually have the ability to increase wages. Each firm takes the wage as given or fixed and hires workers until the wage equals the value of the marginal product of labor. The single large employer, the monopsonist, knows that its hiring practices increase the wage rate, so it hires fewer workers and pays lower wages.

A10.6   Opportunity cost teaches us to include all the costs of doing something, not just the official price. To the employer, the opportunity cost of hiring an employee is everything the employer would ultimately have to pay the employee. More than just the hourly wage, the cost of the employee includes the costs of all the benefits that the employer is required to provide and paying for time off. It is that all-in cost of labor that has to be compared to the value of the marginal product of labor. That comparison will mean the firm hires less labor overall.

A10.8   A person with a bachelor's degree is perceived as being more productive than a person with a high school diploma or less. But within the bachelor's degree group, a person with an engineering degree has more marketable skills than a person with a degree in religious studies. This is best seen when you think about the value part of the value of the marginal product of labor. Even if both graduates are good at what they do, the thing the engineer is producing sells for more.

A10.10   There are fewer workers, so the marginal product of labor is higher, but those same technological innovations have given workers new ways to work less at work! Facebook and Candy Crush decrease the marginal product of labor.

B10.2   This "policy" misses the point of education. This is giving everyone a degree, not providing everyone with skills and education. So this would not work. In fact, it would hurt the signal connected to having a bachelor's degree. The policy would make that signal useless.

B10.4   Productivity comes from many things—skills, experience, and even attitude. Liking your job usually makes you do it better. So this observation is consistent with the general notion that income is correlated with productivity.

A11.2   The freeway noise is indeed a negative externality from Fred's perspective. The question is, did he already get paid for it? The lower cost of his house suggests that he did. It is also important to remember that Fred bought the house knowing that the freeway was there. Timing matters in determining the remedies for externalities.

A11.4   The enormous increase will certainly cause a decrease in legal cigarette sales even if the demand for cigarettes is inelastic. If we recall that any decrease in cigarette sales will decrease the revenue the state is getting from its existing cigarette tax, we see it is possible that the new tax will actually decrease overall cigarette tax revenues.

A11.6   Everyone wanted to free ride. Everyone wanted the other condo members to pay for the pool so they could use it without paying. But when everyone took this approach, no one volunteered to pay, and there wasn't enough money to build the pool. A better approach is to elect a small number of representatives to speak for the group and give them the authority to build the pool if they see fit, and to charge everyone an equal fraction of the cost.

A11.8   Water. Water is a necessity for human life and has no substitutes. The demand for water is inelastic, so an excise tax on water would lead to a small change in quantity—a small distortion.

A11.10   Flu shots have positive externalities because you only get the flu from someone else who has it. If most of the population gets a flu shot, you don't have to. You are, more or less, protected by other people getting flu shots.

B11.2   Education isn't the same as spending on schools. Education includes student and family participation, as well as cultural and socioeconomic factors. Having well-paid teachers and nice schools is part of a much larger, much more complicated problem. It would be easy for a politician to say he helped foster education because he voted for every school-funding bill that came along. Representative governments don't serve their purpose when they blindly fund things.

B11.4   In very poor countries, what wealth there is comes from natural resources such as land, minerals, and forests. Historically, much of the land in these countries has been owned by a small number of people and families. The "fairest" income distributions tend to be in countries where everyone has equal access to the means of production.

A12.2   Yes. But we lose the jobs we are comparatively worse at doing, and in the trade models, we replace them with jobs we are comparatively better at doing. While this should work, it doesn't happen overnight, and those people who lose jobs tend to be disenchanted with the results of free trade.

A12.4   We get jollies from consuming, and we try to balance jollies per dollar spent on the last unit of every good. Because nature made it easier and cheaper to grow or produce goods in one country as opposed to another, we can maximize our utility best by buying goods from countries that are able to produce them at a lower price.

A12.6   Anything digital can be sent over the internet (more or less for free). So with universal access and availability of the internet, data-based services can be handled in the country with the lowest cost of production. With a large, highly skilled, low-cost population, India has attracted many of the data-based jobs, which can now move at close to zero transportation costs around the world.

A12.8   Saudi Arabia and Kuwait have a huge endowment of oil but not much else. If they couldn't trade and had to live on their endowment, they would have a problem. You can't eat oil.

A12.10   Actually, it is exactly the same as stealing to increase jollies! Gains from trade assumes markets, property rights, and such things. Stealing is problematic in many ways, but to keep the answer economic, you can only steal something once or twice and then it isn't produced anymore.

B12.2   No. Population differences will fundamentally determine where jobs end up. China and India both have over one billion people, compared to the U.S. population of about 325 million. Jobs that left for China and India won't come back, but other jobs should replace them.

B12.4   The cost of the subsidy would be enormous. Ultimately, Iceland would lose money on every pound of coffee it grew forever, and eventually Iceland would go broke subsidizing the coffee industry.

Glossary

Average cost   Total cost divided by total quantity.

Average variable cost   Total variable cost divided by total quantity.

Bertrand competition   Competition in which each firm assumes other firms' prices are constant, allowing each firm to choose a price that maximizes its profits.

Cardinal   Describes a ranking system that specifically indicates how many things are at different positions in the ranking, such as number of jollies at different level of consumption.

Collusion   Two or more firms cooperating to determine the market price and output.

Comparative advantage   The thing you are comparatively or relatively better at doing. Even if another person or country is better than you in all things, there is always something—some area or product—in which you are closest to them in ability. That's the area or product where you have a comparative advantage. If everyone is required to do one thing, you should do the one thing in which you have a comparative advantage.

Complements   Goods that are used together or at the same time. *Compare* Substitutes.

Consumer surplus   The excess value that is created when the market sells all units at one price.

Cournot competition   Competition in which each firm assumes other firms' output is constant, allowing each firm to choose an output that maximizes profits.

Demand   The relationship between price and quantity demanded by consumers.

Diminishing marginal utility   The concept that happiness or utility rises at a decreasing rate.

Dominant strategy   In game theory, a choice in a game wherein the player making that choice cannot make himself better off regardless of what other players have chosen.

Economies of scale   The decrease in average cost that many firms experience as they increase the output of the goods they are currently producing.

Economies of scope   The decrease in average cost that firms may experience when they increase the variety of related goods they produce.

Elasticity   A measure, the percentage change in quantity divided by the percentage change in price.

Excess profit   Profit beyond the level necessary to compensate business owners for the risk and effort involved in running the business. It is profit beyond what is necessary to keep owners from leaving the industry.

Externality   A cost or benefit that is not considered by either side of the market when the equilibrium quantity is determined.

Fixed costs   Costs that do not change as the firm increases its production. Examples are the costs of a factory or machinery.

Free rider, Free riding   Person who uses a good without paying for it; the act of doing so.

Income effect   The change in consumption of any good associated with any increase in income.

Indifference curve   All combinations of goods that give the same total utility.

Inferior good   A good that one consumes less of as one's income increases.

Isoquant   Every combination of inputs that will produce the same quantity of output.

Marginal cost   The change in total cost when total output changes.

Marginal factor cost   The change in total input cost as a firm changes how much of an input it uses. A large employer, for example, would increase market wages as it increases employment, so its marginal factor cost for labor is higher than the wage rate.

Marginal product of labor   The output produced by the last laborer.

Marginal rate of substitution   The ratio of the marginal utilities of any two goods at any one consumption point.

Marginal revenue   The extra revenue that a firm gets from selling an additional unit. For small, competitive firms that do not have an ability to affect the market price, marginal revenue is the market price. For large firms such as monopolies, marginal revenue is less than the market price because increases in their output ultimately lower the market price.

Marginal utility   The change in utility (happiness) we get from consuming an additional unit of a good at one point in time.

Market failure   A situation in which the market cannot correctly price or produce a good.

Market price   The price we observe in the marketplace.

Monopolistic competition   An industry structure with many small firms each of which produces a somewhat differentiated good (the goods produced are not perfect substitutes.

Monopoly   A single firm that has the ability to affect the market price; also known as a price setter. Other firms are not able to enter the market. A monopoly must consider its market power when it chooses its level of output.

Monopsony   An input market in which there is only one customer with market power, or the ability to affect the input's price.

Nash equilibrium   In game theory, a choice in a game wherein the player making that choice cannot make him- or herself better off given what other players have chosen.

Natural monopoly   An industry that features very high fixed (startup) costs and thus has falling average cost for all of the existing market. In such an industry, only one firm can survive.

Negative externality   An uncounted cost; a cost that's not considered by producers when they decide how much to produce.

Normal good   A good that consumers want more of when their income increases.

Oligopoly   An industry with a few large producers.

Opportunity cost   Everything that a person gives up when making a purchase. Opportunity cost relates the price of a good to all the other things that could have been purchased with that money.

Ordinal   Describes a ranking system that indicates only the position things have in the ranking.

Perfect competition   The industry structure in which there are many small firms each producing the same good and none has the ability to affect the market price. Such firms are known as price takers. In addition, all firms use the same technology in production, and it is easy for firms to enter and exit the market.

Positive externality   A benefit that is not included in the purchase price of something.

Present value   The value today of anything that arrives in the future.

Price ceiling   A mandated price, set by a government regulator, that is below the market price.

Price cooperation   An oligopoly model for competition in which firms determine that their price cuts will be met by price cuts by their competitors, leading all firms in the industry to maintain higher, more profitable prices.

Price discrimination   A circumstance in which a firm is able to sell a particular good to different consumers at different prices. For example, adults' and children's movie tickets are priced differently.

Price floor   A mandated price, set by a government regulator, that is above the market price.

Price setter   *See* Monopoly

Price taker   *See* Perfect competition

Producer surplus   The area above the supply curve up to the market price. It denotes how much the firm makes on every unit except the last unit sold.

Profit   In economics, this usually means accounting profit, or the simple difference between revenues and costs, not including the cost of ownership.

Public good   A good that everyone can consume simultaneously once it is produced (a nonrival good); a good that can be consumed even if the consumer pays none of the cost of production.

Quota   A government-mandated minimum quantity that producers must produce.

Shortage   In the market model, a situation in which the quantity demanded exceeds the quantity supplied.

Subsidy   A payment by the government to producers to help cover the cost of production.

Substitute, substitution effect   Goods that can be used by consumers interchangeably to satisfy a desire or need. When consumers switch from one good whose price increased to another whose price did not, we say they are displaying the substitution effect.

Supply   The relationship between the price of a good and the quantity supplied by producers.

Surplus   In the market model, a situation in which the quantity supplied exceeds the quantity demanded.

Tariff   A tax imposed on an imported good to raise the price of that good in the domestic market, thereby giving the domestic version of the good a greater ability to compete with the imported good.

Tax incidence   An economic determination of which side of the market, producer or consumer, bears the burden of a tax charged on a specific good.

Utility   In general, happiness. In economics, a way of explaining consumer choice based on counting or ranking levels of happiness.

Variable costs   Costs that increase as the firm increases its production. Examples include the costs of utilities, raw materials, and basic labor.

Index